Kids Take the Stage

Kids

Take the Stage

Helping Young People
Discover the Creative Outlet
of Theater

REVISED EDITION

by Lenka Peterson & Dan O'Connor

Foreword by Paul Newman

Preface by Dr. Robert Coles

We dedicate this book to the loving memory of our brother, Dr. Peter Isacson,
his wife, Ruth, and our friends and colleagues Erla Schnable and Doris Fugazy.

Senior Editor: Mark Glubke
Project Editor: Gary Sunshine
Cover Design: Margo Mooney
Interior Design: Michelle Thompson
Production Manager: Joseph Illidge

First published in 2006 by Back Stage Books,
an imprint of Watson-Guptill Publications,
a division of VNU Business Media, Inc.
770 Broadway, New York, NY 10003
www.wgpub.com.com

Library of Congress Control Number: 2006921385

ISBN-10: 0-8230-7746-2
ISBN-13: 978-0-8230-7746-5

Manufactured in the United States of America

First printing 2006

1 2 3 4 5 6 7 8 9 / 14 13 12 11 10 09 08 07 06

Contents

Acknowledgments

WE ARE ESPECIALLY grateful to our children—Kevin, Brian, Darren, Glynnis, and Sean—and their spouses. We could not and would not have written this book without them.

Our deep thanks go to our first editor, Dale Ramsey; Mark Glubke our second edition acquisitions editor; Gary Sunshine, our second project editor; our agent, Carolyn French, of the Fifi Oscard Agency; James and Kathel Brennan; Clair Burnett; Richard Carter, Dr. Robert Coles; Semina de Laurentis; Roy Finamore; Mary Flynn; Rosemary and Georgiann Foley; Doris Fugazy; David Hains; Michael Junko; Pam Luchesi; Jean Luburg; Ara Marx; Paul Newman; Lin Northrup; Kent Paul; Bob Quaranta; Maureen Reilly; Peggy Richards; Adele Russell, John Schnable; Diane Shalet; Mari Share; Michael Snyder; Mandy and Bobbi Thompson, Marla Truini; Greg Tully; Toni Vairo; Clair Walcovy; Tom Woodruff; Barbara Finamore Young; and Cathy Reilly Zapson. To these and all the energetic, enthusiastic members of the Holy Family Dramatics Club, the Westchester Young Actors' Theatre, The Young Angels Theatre Company, and the Hill and Plains BookPALS, we extend our gratitude for their help, ideas, stories, and inspiration.

The wisdom of many of our teachers informs the pages of this book: Harold Clurman, David Craig, Etienne DeCroux, Elizabeth Howell, Charles Kakatsakis, Elia Kazan, Walter Kerr, Jack Lee, Robert Lewis, David Man, Joanna Merlin, George Morrison, Arthur Penn, Marty Ritt, Lee Strasberg, and Robert Williams. All of us in theater are indebted to them.

LENKA PETERSON & DAN O'CONNOR
Roxbury, Connecticut, February 2006

Foreword

THIS IS A TRULY worthwhile book. It's clear, usable, often funny, passionate, and even sensible. And it's got some great and specific games, particularly in-relaxation and trust exercises. I've asked the authors if I could hang on to their manuscript in case I go teaching. It's a reminder of a lot of the stuff we all had to learn when we were starting our careers.

I've known Dan and Lenka for decades. I've watched a number of the TV news documentaries Dan produced for NBC. And I've watched Lenka's work as an actress. We've even worked on scenes together, in the early days of the Actors Studio. But more important, I've watched their teenage theater group work. When I left I told them that what this country needs is about thirty thousand more groups like theirs. The kids were respectful, committed, and highly energetic.

The first time I was there some years ago, one of them put me on the spot: "Mr. Newman, how do you feel about all this explicit sex in movies?" I put on my best cool attitude and answered, "Well, I think when you take the mystery out of sex, it's a bad scene."

However, I think that when you take the mystery, and the fear, out of helping youngsters put on their own shows and teaching them to act better in those shows, it's a good scene. A very good scene.

My uncle Joseph S. Newman, a poet and businessman, wrote in his book *It Could Be Verse*:

> *Man is but born, eats, procreates, and dies.*
> *This sequence of events alike applies*
> *To horses, herring, crocodiles, and flies.*

Maybe, but most of us want to leave something of value behind, especially for the young.

Admittedly, as an actor I don't relish being upstaged by some kid. But as a human being, a parent, and a grandparent, I know how important it is for all of us to do whatever we can to make life better for kids. This book goes a long way to helping us do that. And, like me, you'll want to hang on to the book, too.

PAUL NEWMAN

Actor Paul Newman is the founder and president of the Hole in the Wall Gang Camp, in northeastern Connecticut, a nonprofit summer camp for children with life-threatening diseases. Youngsters from seven to fifteen years of age attend each year, free of charge, from around the nation and the world.

Preface

CHILDREN NEED TO learn their regular school lessons, of course, but they also need nourishment for their imaginative life. Again and again in classrooms I see boys and girls struggling not only with their "letters and numbers," the challenges posed by grammar and arithmetic, but struggling also to figure out what this life means, and how it ought to be lived. That latter struggle is moral in nature, and those of us who work with children will surely want to respond to it—think of how we might help young people ponder the rights and wrongs of this world. From the dawn of history such reflection has taken place on the stage—the first moral philosophers and psychologists, after all, were playwrights: Aeschylus, Sophocles, Euripedes. I well remember, in that regard, hearing Anna Freud, the first child psychologist, speak of her father's relationship to those playwrights and, by implication, the theater in general: "He thought that his own ideas were a restatement of what had been discovered long ago, in ancient Greece. He thought the theater was a place where people could learn truths otherwise not stated or acknowledged."

In fact, the theater was originally a place of meditation, of contemplation, a public gathering for entertainment, yes, but for introspection, for a shared consideration of the nature of human experience. The history of worship—how and where it takes place—connects with the history of the theater, and for obvious reasons: When we assemble to hear others talk and sing, we are moved to thought, to wonder, to awe, to a kind of inwardness that is, actually, the very essence of who and what we are—the creature of language and awareness who asks questions about life's meaning and purpose.

No wonder, then, Freud bowed to the Greek theater—and to Shakespeare and Ibsen, both of whom he mentioned in his writings. No wonder, too, our children love to hear stories, the more the better—and love to see those stories enacted in movies, on television. No wonder, also, children become so taken with dramatic productions in which they take part, or which they watch. So doing, they are living witnesses to living theater—to enactments of this life's various hurdles and dilemmas, its possibilities and its obstacles. When "kids take the stage," or are seen doing so by their classmates, life itself is being evoked, rendered, turned into an occasion for heightened awareness. In no time we are enabled to think of others, put ourselves in their shoes, wonder how we'd do were we they—courtesy of actors and actresses who are, really, our moral and psychological companions, teachers. When "kids take the stage," we are all taken somewhere important—on a journey of personal, social, ethical discovery; and so we have reason to be grateful for this book, for its offer to guide us on that journey, an important one, indeed.

ROBERT COLES

Dr. Robert Coles, the eminent child psychiatrist, is James Agee Professor of Social Ethics at Harvard University. He is the author of more than fifty books and coeditor of Double Take, *a quarterly of essays, stories, poems, and photographs.*

Prologue

Who, me?
Direct a show with kids?

HOW MANY TIMES has this response been accompanied by an icy pang of panic in the heart of an overburdened teacher, camp counselor, or community-minded PTA or church member? And how many times have anxious parents or grandparents wished they could direct a show with kids because they are well aware that our children need that kind of experience? They know the kind of joyous bonding and creative thrill that can result in a group of young people putting on a show together.

And how many times does some spunky person brave the unknown, get together a script or pageant, assign parts, read the script aloud with the kids, move them around into a line, semicircle, or stage picture with arbitrary groupings, and then help them memorize and recite the lines? And after all this effort, how many times, on the day of the performance, does he or she wonder why all the kids stand there rigidly waiting their turns to speak and flapping their arms awkwardly to emphasize the lines? Why is it somehow embarrassing and disappointing? Why isn't there more life in the acting?

A frequent conclusion is, "Well, they're just kids." But it's not because they are "just kids," and it's not because the enterprising adult is inexperienced, either.

Adults who take on the challenge of helping kids take the stage only need some guidelines. They need a simple, natural system for opening up their innate talents, and that's what this book is designed to provide.

A good number of years ago, when we were raising our children and pursuing our respective careers—Lenka as an actress in theater, films, and television, Dan as a producer of documentaries and special programs for NBC News—we began a drama program in our children's school. It offered an alternative to the one constructive extracurricular activity then available, Little League softball. We had both taught theater and directed shows, Lenka at various schools, regional theaters, and the Metropolitan Opera Studio, Dan at two universities. We formed a Dramatics Club for the elementary and middle grades that was active for six years. This later developed into the Westchester Young Actors Theatre, primarily for older teens, which continued for another six years. Even later we founded the Young Angels Theatre Company, an offshoot of the Seven Angels Theatre in Waterbury, Connecticut, made up of young people from about eleven- to eighteen-years-old. In the Hill and Plain School in New Milford, Connecticut, we also founded a chapter of BookPALS, a branch of the Screen Actors Guild Foundation, in which professional actors read to lower grade students to increase literacy. Out of this grew the "Lunch Bunch," a theater group of third graders. We believed there was a need then for this kind of activity, and, clearly, there is a greater need today. As a result of our experiences with the children and our primary professional careers, we decided to write this book.

Now we offer this second edition because we wanted to include what we've been learning over the nine years since our first edition was published. They were years filled with leading and observing scores of youngsters of all ages, in a host of meetings, sessions, rehearsals, National Theater Conference demonstrations, and community theater conventions. Years of creating more shows, theater games, and acting exercises, and learning more about which are the easiest, most effective, and productive to use.

This edition of *Kids Take the Stage* contains three parts. The first describes the needs of the director and the needs of the child. It examines the nature of acting and presents our basic approach to evoking good acting in young people. In this edition we have changed some of the emphasis to look at the nature of feelings and their importance in impelling actions and behavior.

Part II describes how to use our approach to choose, create, direct, and produce shows—an annual production with a cast of a hundred children, or just a few skits every month prepared for other children and parents to watch.

Part III takes an extended look at how to adapt these principles to teens, including developing shows with them and suggesting more difficult games and exercises. At the behest of friends who are going into teaching, we've added a new chapter addressing ways to use acting techniques in the classroom—theater games we have found to help children put what they are learning into their bodies, so they'll really enjoy and remember what they are learning more easily. This chapter aims to help teachers enrich their lesson plans as they teach the required standards.

Throughout the book we provide you with additional exercises, games, production schedules, prop lists, two sample scenes, a holiday sample script, and examples of steps in developing a script with third graders. In the Leader's Guide, on page 205, you'll find a suggested agenda and outlines for ten workshop sessions to follow in order if you choose. They contain even more theater exercises, games, and improvs. Think of it as a safety net. On page 240 you'll find, for quick reference, a large list of games, more exercises and ideas you can grab for your "cheat sheets" to keep beside you to use when you need them in your meetings. We hope these fresh insights will help you in your joyful and rewarding efforts to help kids take the stage.

Kids Take the Stage is for teachers, student-teachers, homeschoolers, parents, camp counselors, religious leaders, grandparents, recreation monitors, or your neighbor down the street. You may even be a professional theater person casting or directing children. Or you may have no theater experience at all but just want to have fun with the kids. You may want to teach them history or literature or help them with a new language. You may be involved primarily in helping young people establish self-esteem or some necessary social skills through theater participation. Or you may have taken on the important responsibility of filling their time in a safe place after school or during a long summer as an alternative to their wandering the streets or joining gangs. Never has such an undertaking been more necessary, as the national PTA has put out a report, "Doors Open After School," urging parental involvement in after-school activities, because "one million kids have no place to go when school ends." In a *New York Times* op-ed piece, Bob Herbert deplored the possibility of spending money for a sports coliseum on Manhattan's West Side when "After-school programs, which are literally life lines for many youngsters, have to be shut down because they are not 'affordable'."

If you are a retiree, the morale boost is not only for the recipients of your efforts. It is also for you. In his final op-ed column in the *New York Times*, William Safire discussed the importance of retraining and fresh stimulation upon retirement. "We can quit a job," he wrote, "but we quit fresh involvement at our mental peril."

Richard Canalori, who recently retired as principal of the Oxford Elementary School in Connecticut, directed classroom and school plays annually. He said these productions helped define his career. "I saw the love children had for acting, the real learning that was taking place, the confidence children gained in themselves, the parent support, and the teamwork necessary to complete a production. It was what was really important for true learning, active involvement and passion." He holds that "for real learning to take place children must be actively involved."

These pages are full of suggested activities and techniques. Presented in a way that will be useful even for those who have no experience in the field, these activities are here to illustrate our approach, and can help you and your group to organize your own improvs and games. Use them as they are if you like, but keep in mind that they are suggestions: their primary purpose is to prod your imagination by sketching limits and possible combinations. The nature of your work with the kids will depend on the backgrounds, information, and goals you all share and understand.

So, no matter what your limitations in time, space, and experience—find your young actors, start up the group, and DO THE SHOW. DO IT. DO IT. DO IT. Enjoy it as we did. We believe from our own experience that this book will be a valuable guide.

Children who go unheeded
are children who are going to turn
on the world that neglected them.

DR. ROBERT COLES

Inattention to children by our society poses a greater threat to our safety, har-
mony, and productivity than any external enemy.

MARIAN WRIGHT EDELMAN,
Founder, Children's Defense Fund

Part I
All Kids Can Act

Easy Universal
Principles of Acting
(or How to Act and
How to Act Even Better)

Chapter One
Getting Started

THE TEN-YEAR-OLD screamed out in panic to his buddies up ahead. His leg had been twisted when they fell off the raft, and he couldn't keep up with them in their struggle toward the refuge of the big rock. The undertow was so fierce that it made the rock seem nine miles, rather than nine feet, away. The other two boys managed, somehow, as they were treading water, to hook him onto their shoulders, keeping his bobbing head above the waves until they reached safety. They all scrambled over the barnacles and onto the top of the rock, panting heavily and spitting out salty water. Weakly, they shook hands in congratulations and fell back to open their drenched bodies to the welcome sun.

The stage lights went off and the house lights came up. The two hundred other members of the Dramatics Club applauded, whistled, and stamped their feet. The three young actors got up, grinning and pounding one another's backs as they pushed aside the chairs and table that had been the raft and the rock. Then the usual hands began waving, and children were pleading to do just one more "skitch" before darkness ended the meeting.

We weakened and gave some girls five minutes to do their skit. The scene was the King's breakfast room. The arrogant King was reading his newspaper, and the Queen was mourning the fact that he never talked to her. Just then the Fairy Godmother flitted in, wearing a pink net skirt from the costume box and the buckled galoshes her mother made her wear to school. She surveyed the scene, waved her magic wand, and announced confidently that all the King really needed was a "shot in the butt."

That was in early February in New Rochelle, New York, quite a few years ago. A year earlier, those same "raft survivors" had threatened to push another student through an open window in a third-floor classroom. It wasn't a skit. At that time, the only after-school activity, Little League, though beneficial, involved about thirty boys, and no girls, out of nine hundred students.

Jimmy, an overweight fourth grader who couldn't participate in Little League because of fallen arches, was often chased around the playground by jeering sixth graders. And the "fairy godmother" walked home from school alone, as she did every afternoon, unable to break through her paralyzing shyness. She had no friends, and no one to help her make friends.

Dear Gramma and Grampa,

Mrs. Hoffman started a dramatics club a couple of weeks ago and I did an exercise in it today. A theater game called "Poor Soul." I actually did it! One person goes up and sits on a bench and waits for a bus. Another person comes on and does something that is s-o-o-o-o annoying that the "Poor Soul" just has to leave. Then that person waits for the bus and another guy comes on.

Well, I waited on the side for my turn. My insides were jumping and buzzing, but in an excited way. I finally got this idea. I'd be a complaining old man, with a big bag of stuff—yeah.

So, I grabbed two handfuls of stuff from the prop box, wrapped it up in a big scarf and tied the ends to make a sack. When my turn came I flopped down on the bench with my sack and thought to myself, "Okay, now mumble," but I opened my mouth and there were no words. So I just groaned and grumbled and that's when I knew what my character was. All sorts of sounds came out. And guess what? The kids started laughing. They got what I was doing. They were watching me and they were having fun.

And then I pulled each thing out of the sack and put them on the kid who was sitting next to me. And I kept piling on hats, scarves, a robe, a pair of goggles. That's when the words came out, because it reminded me of Aunt Puddy—"It's *cold,* you should *dress warmer*." The kids in the club were laughing so loud and the other guy finally stood up, threw off all my stuff and stomped off the stage.

I sat back down and a big smile just came over my face. Then it was my turn to be the "Poor Soul." It was a lot of fun, and you know what? It felt so easy. I was worried about making up a character and all of a sudden there it was. And when I sat down, after the exercise, I thought, "Did I do that? *Wow.*" Hope you'll come and see our big show in the spring. Can't wait to see you again.

Love,
Jamie

A THEATER AND A SYSTEM

Parents and teachers were worried about the increasing violence and vandalism by some of the students. So we formed a Dramatics Club the following September. We distributed six hundred flyers to all students between third and eighth grade.

We eliminated kids in kindergarten through second grade who, we felt, were just too young, might require constant supervision, and were not yet able to read easily. Also, holding them after school could cause real problems for some parents. We expected perhaps twenty-five or thirty students to show up. Three hundred came.

After absorbing the stark reality of this response, we divided them into junior and senior groups, met twice a week after school, and started doing a show every spring, using as many members as we could in each show, usually about 150. Together we created a basic, logical system of developing acting skills, which they used easily in their shows.

By May, three years later, we were in production with our third show, and Jimmy was still being chased around the playground, but this time it was by sixth graders trying to get his autograph. He was playing Buffalo Bill.

We didn't form the club so that some kids could show off and be "stars." Nor was our only goal to stop vandalism and violence or to prevent eighth graders from picking on seventh graders, though we hoped for those dividends. We started it because by providing a safe and constructive outlet, we wanted them to know that we, the grown-ups, cared. Fortunately, other parents felt the same way and volunteered to help. In the six years that we produced these shows, hundreds of children had a marvelous time together. They exercised their imaginations, concentrated hard, disciplined themselves, and totally forgot about the differences between them.

Eleven mothers formed a staff, giving us a producer, choreographer, music director, wardrobe manager, secretary, prop person, two makeup artists, plus many loyal assistants. All were nonprofessional people, except for Florence May, the choreographer, who had been a Rockette.

There was the "set gatherer," who brought in things like a huge cardboard carton that, when properly unfolded and painted, might become the Wizard's secret control panel in Oz. About fifteen years after we did *The Wizard of Oz*, our first show with the Dramatics Club, Clair Reilly Walcovy, a loyal friend and collaborator during all those shows, was approached by a young fellow at a supermarket. "Hi, Mrs. Reilly!" he exclaimed. She looked blank. "Don't you remember me? I was a flying monkey!"

Glynnis O'Connor, our daughter, now a professional actress, said:

> It really means a great deal to the children. Every time I see a children's production, I cry. It reminds me of the time when we were kids and doing that. It meant so much to us. And we'll never have that time again.

Those were years and shows filled with excitement, growth, bonding, and new confidence. They were also filled with hard work, missed cues, and blown spotlights. It was live theater, after all. But the youngsters learned how to make audiences laugh, and above all, they learned to laugh at themselves. They found an environment in which they could express their deepest feelings and discover they were not alone.

There was no magic. Any committed individual or group of adults can do it. We had a ball doing it. And so will you.

WHAT YOU DON'T NEED AND DO NEED

First, because you are reading this book, we trust you already have the most necessary elements—compassion, an enthusiasm for ideas, and a desire to make life better for at least a few children. Understanding the children's needs, having positive instead of negative feelings about them, along with the expectation of success, will lead to success. Humor, zest, a tender honesty, and the ability to generate energy will keep you well connected with your young actors.

1. *You don't need a lot of money and equipment. You do need the young people and a safe, relatively private place to meet.* You can do a show with cardboard sets, sunlight, and a little space. It's the performers that matter. Of course, if you have access to any kind of recording device—a movie camera, video recorder, a tape recorder—or a real stage—these can be helpful. A light projector, if available, can be used for background projections. Microphones and loudspeakers, of course, would always help.

2. *You don't need a theater background or a lot of research. You do need a system.* In this book, we propose a system you can use to help children develop as actors—an organized set of principles. We give you a way to set up the problems and tasks and to function as the eyes and ears of the audience. (This happens when you begin to direct the show, which we'll examine in detail in Chapters 4 through 8.)

When I was a child, our eighth-grade teacher, who knew nothing about theater or acting, created a monthly class called "Auditorium." Her system was simply to separate the children into small groups to make up skits. They then went to the auditorium to do them for one another. They loved it so much they continued to play "Auditorium" at one another's homes after school.

The point is, anyone whose heart is in the right place can do at least that much for the kids. If you already have some knowledge of the theater or if you're a theater professional using this book for your work with children, that's fine. If not, this book provides enough information for those without that experience to feel secure.

3. *You don't need the feeling you're not creative. You do need to spell out the goals and listen to the kids.* We're all creative. That's the energy that runs our world. In this case, the kids will provide most of the creativity. Einstein said, "Imagination is more important than knowledge."

Listen to the imagination mothers use to get their toddlers to do what they want them to do. "O.K., little bear cub" a mother might say to the child playing under the table. "Daddy bear came back from the hunt. Why don't you climb up onto your seat on the branch here and gobble it all up?" Or "O.K., baby seal. Let's put your fur back on or you'll get cold out of the water. That's right, now on to the little right side fin."

Mary Catherine Bateson, in her book, *Peripheral Visions*, said, "When you are able to attend to something new or to see the familiar in a new way, this is a creative act." And Lee Strasberg, the famed director and teacher, always told the Actors

Studio members that creating is combining something you know with something you imagine.

Of course, no one can create something out of nothing. But we can create something simply by combining two or more existing elements in a new way—brushstrokes and canvas, musical notes and instruments—transforming them into something else. Solving problems is creative. The trick is to organize the problems, ideas, goals, and visions. Then spell them out to the kids and try to discover together what new combinations will work. For instance, what might happen if you put together onstage two adventurous kids, a "dark cave," a dim flashlight, and some weird sounds? Simply guide your young actors, give them a path, and they'll move into it.

Actually, the only thing that stops ideas from flowing is the fear that they won't be good enough. Put that away! Process is ALL.

4. *You don't need to be judgmental. You do need to be supportive.* Terminology is important. As you probably know, comparative words or phrases don't work. Avoid comparisons of one child's work to another's. Use encouraging terms:

> Good!   Great!   Well done!   Right on!

Barbara Finamore Young, who went from acting in the sixth grade to graduating *cum laude* from Harvard Law School, and on to becoming Senior Attorney for the Natural Resources Defense Council, writes:

> I was understudy for the leading lady, who was sick for one rehearsal, and I had to go on for her. I was scared to death. I knew all the lines, but when I came to the song I kept opening my mouth and nothing came out. I tried but finally I just said the words, weakly. Later, the director came to me and said, "That was fine, Barbara! Thank you for helping us." If she hadn't said that, I think I would have crawled home and never come back to the Dramatics Club again.

Recently an actress was rehearsing a small part in a scene with Jude Law during the filming of *All the King's Men*. He was playing "'Jack," and she was overacting, pushing the antagonism her character had toward Jack. The director, Steven Zaillion, as he dismissed the cast to go to makeup while the cameras were setting up, said very quietly to her, "I think we may not be quite so disapproving of Jack." You can see why actors love Mr. Zaillion and are eager to work with him.

5. *You don't need impatience. You do need patient understanding with the children.* As Bill Cosby's son, Ennis Cosby, said when he was studying for his master's degree in

education at Columbia University, "I feel that learning is a slow process, and patience is a very crucial quality to have as a teacher."

Richard Carter, the cofounder and artistic director of the highly successful Community Shakespeare Company in Lopez Island, Washington, for many years has written and directed plays for actors in grades three to twelve. The CSC could be a Best Practices Model of an example of sustainable community education. He emphasized that doing theater with kids creates a marvelous sense of community, and that it really requires repetition and patience.

All of us, but especially kids, have a natural drive to learn. Kids reach out with great energy to the world around them. This is the time to catch them before their senses become numbed or sluggish or before something happens to turn them off with fear or anxiety. Therefore, we have to be patient, to ease their progress. Jamil, for example, was the most unhappy boy in the group before we began working on the musical *Oliver!* with a cast of third to eighth graders. He had a minor physical problem that he thought was shameful, and he hated the world. We cast him as the villain, Fagin, a part that stretched his courage and imaginative instincts to the limits. Eventually he realized that the intensity he gave to the role was good. As the director, Arthur Penn, used to put it, he made his scenes "work like meat and potatoes." The first time it happened, and Jamil felt the positive response of his peers, three girls cheered, "Hey, look, Jamil is smiling!"

6. *You don't need to know how to issue commands. You need the ability to listen **with respect** to the children.* Our kids knew we would always listen to them. One day as we were rehearsing a difficult scene, a fourth grader leaped up in excitement: "Mrs. O'Connor, Mrs. O'Connor, I have the most impossible idea!" When they know you will listen and use all their best and most practical suggestions, they will all learn, to their great surprise, that their ideas are not only welcome and good, but that sometimes they are great.

You can show respect also by using language that helps them find their own answers and solve their problems. You can pepper your directions with suggestions rather than cold commands.

What if...?   Let's try...   How about...?

Tell them we all want to work toward what makes the story clear and interesting to the audience. It's remarkable how quickly children pick up terms and attitudes.

7. *You don't need to quit your job to find the time. You do need one to two hours of your time a week for starters.* One PTA mom held all her rehearsals in the morning before regular school started. One teenager held meetings with third and fourth graders during their lunch periods once a week. But with a show, if you're doing a large production you will need much more, along with the will to do it. But you might settle for a half-hour

show in the backyard, or a twenty-minute video or DVD at the end of the spring or summer…or for a special holiday. Whatever you can do will be worth it.

WHAT THE CHILDREN NEED

We have already pointed out the importance of showing the children respect. Treat them as your coworkers, avoid talking down to them, and give them a safe environment full of mutual trust—a place where they can take risks, with no fear of derision or alienation.

The two primary needs of the children are *challenge* and *support*. Children need the opportunity to come up with answers nobody has yet. They love to feel that they have "wonderful ideas." They want the opportunity to work for solutions *with* you, rather than simply coming around to your position. If you know the answer to the question you ask, or if you have already decided on the solution to the problem you put on the table, they will suspect they are being tested rather than stimulated, and the motivation to solve a problem or create a solution will vanish.

In school, students must be frequently tested: What is a verb? What is 23.5 percent of 1,164? Doing a show together requires a different kind of challenge. And they find the solutions with the adult director who has given them support. The "big idea" student-teachers are finding in the approach of the Bank Street College of Education in New York City is to teach by giving children problems and letting them find not only the answers but the best ways to arrive at the answers. And your young cast members need to search themselves for the behavior of their characters that best tells the story of the show.

Bob Quaranta, who took to the stage as a sixth grader, is now a producer of industrial shows. He recalls:

> We never felt that it was just the director's show. We felt that it was ours: We did it. In *South Pacific*, there were twenty-one sailors singing "Nothing Like a Dame," and we wanted a boffo ending to the number. We were looking for some kind of formation—and suddenly: "Oh, we got it! We can do it! Watch this!"

Except for those wearing sneakers, the kids all removed their shoes, and within a half hour had organized themselves into three pyramids, timing the formations with the music and all tumbling down at the end of the big "ride-out" on the last musical phrase.

Our Young Angels Theatre Company did an adaptation of Shirley Jackson's *The Lottery*, a Depression-era story about a lottery held each year by the villagers of a small town to determine which person will be stoned to death. The young actors decided they needed to make a more positive statement by writing a second act, which brought that same town up to the present time with their descendents celebrating the end of that horrible practice. You can read more about this project in Chapter 9.

Children also need a way to be with their friends, other than in school. Theater gives them a constructive way to gain respect and acceptance by their peers.

They need goals that are achievable, but not too easy. Goals that make a person feel "in the flow."

Of course, children also need a reasonable degree of discipline. They will follow rules better if they participate in making them. (One fifth-grader solved the noise problem in our meetings by suggesting that every member be separated from another by an empty chair.) And they'll respect club officers and group leaders more if they participate in electing them.

During final rehearsals with large casts, when the kids' adrenalin is flowing all over the place, we often needed other parents just to circulate and quiet the kids. But discipline becomes less of a problem the more interested and involved the kids are. So keep challenging them. Keep as many involved simultaneously as you can. Keep it moving!

It also helps with discipline if you avoid calling in more people for rehearsals than you are going to use. It's good to provide a separate play and/or homework space for those who are there when they are not needed in the scene being rehearsed. After-school snacks before the warm-ups help restore energy. You don't want crankiness or lethargy to get in the way of progress.

We asked Kathel Brennan, a friend who often directed musicals for her son's high school in New Jersey, how she maintained discipline. She said, "I kept them all close to me when I gave them notes on their work. And we did a lot of hugging."

Keep your young actors focused on learning and on doing a good show together, not on showing off and winning praise. You want to ensure that everyone is equally important. There are no "stars." Stress what they are *giving* the audience—pleasure and increased understanding—not what they're *getting* from the audience.

INITIAL STEPS

If you are a high school student, a principal, a counselor, church-school leader, interning or a part-time teacher, or a regular teacher in a public or private school, chances are you already have space and a means of communication. But if you are a student fulfilling a community service requirement, a camp counselor, parent, grandparent, homeschooler, organization leader, or simply a compassionate and concerned citizen, even if you work professionally in the theater you may have to enlist help from other sources. Before you begin it's always wise to ensure cooperation from those in charge of the space. Diplomacy can be everything.

Where you meet depends on which groups you want to involve. If you can get the principal of a local school, a church or synagogue, the Police Athletic League, a senior center, a regional theater, or some other community organization to give you the space, great! Enrolling members may involve making a few phone calls; having messages sent by way of the Internet, school intercoms; or fliers at churches, schools, and community centers; and postings on local store bulletin boards. A news story in the neighborhood paper or local TV station is always helpful. If time and circumstances don't permit any of these, recruit others through the few children you have already contacted. They will usually bring in their friends and relatives.

Liability Insurance

You should check on liability insurance for the space where you are working. If you can use space in a school, church, regional theater, or municipal building, you are probably covered. But it's wise to check that the insurance applies to after or before school hours.

If you are rehearsing in other spaces, even a public park, you should confirm the liability coverage for your rehearsals and performances. If you bring children into your own home to work on scenes, check your home insurance policy. If there is any question about any of this, seek the advice of your insurance agent.

FIRST MEETINGS

Once your group has gathered together and you are facing those three, thirty, or three hundred children, explain the purpose of the project and give them a quick rundown on your plans for the meetings. Talk a little about what acting is and assure them that you are confident that they are all pretty good at it already. Then promise them, if you can, that by a certain time (Thanksgiving, Christmas, Hanukkah, Kwanza, Presidents' Day, or a date for a fund-raiser) you'll be putting on a show of some kind.

Tell them that what they do in the meetings will improve their skills. Meetings are like warm-ups and practice before a big game.

It's also a good idea at this point to choose a name and start thinking about a logo for future T-shirts, caps, and so on to give the children a sense of group identity and belonging.

In ordering the meetings we have always found it fruitful to begin with a short business meeting: rules, elections, announcements, prayer, or whatever fits your particular circumstances. After that's done, guide the whole group through some loosening, relaxation, sensory exercises, and warm-up games that are described at the end of this chapter and all the ensuing chapters. Then do improvs and skits. You will find lists of usable ideas for these at the ends of chapters and in the Addenda.

Order and Discipline

Cam Smith, in her book *A Teacher's Report*, said that before order can arrive there will be chaos. And if you're willing to wait through the chaos for the kids to organize themselves, they always do, and they do it better and quicker and will stick to it if you let them do it. It's excellent advice, but keep a whistle handy.

James Brennan, director and star of many Broadway shows, has given us much good advice over the years. When he was starring on Broadway in *Me and My Girl*, he and two other members of the cast, Marianne Plunkett and Jane Summerhays, taught a dramatics class to seventh graders in a nearby inner city school. They proved the value of discipline and practice very neatly in the first two sessions. As Brennan explained:

> At the end of the first session, give them some homework. They'll groan. Tell them that for one week they are to brush their teeth every day with the other hand. It stuns them. That's all you should say about it until the week is up, when they are wondering what this was all about. It will probably generate a fifteen or twenty minute discussion. Many will say they got better at it the more they did it with the other hand. If they can teach themselves that, then they know they can learn other skills.

Maintain a fast-moving and flexible agenda. Keep things going at a good pace. As you know, tedium leads children into the dark world of non-discipline, disorder, and chaos. Still, there will always be those few who are disruptive. Announce that they will elect officers and decide on a few rules at the next meeting. At P.S. 128 in New York City, the Stage Pals group decided on five rules, which they wrote out on a big board. They chose one member to read them out loud at the beginning of each meeting. The first rule was that whenever the leader clapped in a certain rhythm, everybody had to stand still, close their lips, and listen. The kids made up a few of their own, like arriving on time, not disrupting, and picking up their own trash.

The only rules you should insist upon arbitrarily are these:

1. *No violence.* No one is allowed to hurt anyone, no matter what the scene requires. In Part II on directing the show, we discuss how to "fake" any violence the script requires.

2. *Voice projection.* Whoever is talking must be heard by everyone. If something is said too quietly, stop and ask the person to repeat it until everyone hears it, and don't allow a friend to say it instead. Speaking loudly enough to be heard and *listening actively* are theater skills they're all going to have to learn.

One afternoon while an actress was volunteering at an inner city youth center, directing a Christmas play, some friends of the cast had wandered in and were creating a lot of disturbance. The youngsters were either alternately showing off rudely to one another or yelling "Quiet down!!!" Finally she put her foot down. "Now listen, you guys, courtesy, respect, and kindness are the tools of civilization. Everyone needs them. And everyone can afford to give them. If you don't know how to give them, you're an idiot. And if you refuse to give them, no one will want to teach you, no one will want to be with you, no one will want to hire you. And you'll be stuck!" The rudeness stopped.

The faster you can learn all their names the easier it will be for you, of course. Name tags are helpful. Starting each day with a game that uses their names helps. Acting is mostly a matter of making choices. And since there are so many different ways to do and say things depending on the circumstances and/or the intentions, we use the term "as if" often. A good way to help learn names is to ask each player in turn to say "Hello," using the name of the person next to him with a different "as if," such as "as if he's a movie star" or "as if you have a big secret to tell him" or "as if you're wondering why his hair turned green suddenly," etc. Then you can play "name games" in a circle having different youngsters volunteer one at a time to try to name everyone in the circle. As a warm-up in some of the next meetings or rehearsals, ask each person to throw a ball to different members as they are named.

When you're in rehearsal and you've established a separate play space for those who aren't needed in the scene being rehearsed, it's a good idea to assign a leader for each group to keep track of when they are needed.

With these procedures and rules established, use some of the following theater activities to turn the kids on and generate excitement about the prospects ahead. The meanings of the terms *exercise*, *improvisation* (or *improv*), and *game* are so close that they are almost interchangeable. But to avoid confusion, let us say that an *exercise* is something done repeatedly to improve a skill. An *improv* is usually a short scene done by two or more people who don't know, when they begin, how it will end. A *game*, on the other hand, is an enjoyable sort of test, challenge, contest, or a competitive event that is fun for all.

Viola Spolin was the developer of the whole "theater games" concept, which has been used with great success for years throughout the world. At the end of each chapter, you'll find an additional set of activities extending the concepts introduced in the chapter preceding them—a sort of "user's guide" to exercises, improvisations, and games—that we, too, have found successful in introducing children to theater.

RELAXATION FIRST

Relaxation in acting—the ability to relax onstage or in front of a camera—can release an actor's creative energy just as plugging a cord into an outlet releases electric energy into an appliance. An exercise we've used often (also described in Session 3 of the Leader's Guide) was to ask everybody to stand, stretch up high, then tighten each part of their bodies one at a time from their toes up to their scalps and their upstretched fingers. Tell them to hold it tight, tight, tight, and then to begin relaxing each part in the reverse sequence, all the way back to the toes. Then they should shake themselves loosely and wobble.

You can get silly with them and ask them to "let their teeth fall out" or "their hair slide down to their toes"—whatever they have fun doing. Then everyone should take some deep, easy breaths and just "stay loose" for a few seconds. Then they should straighten up.

An easy follow-up is to have everybody walk around the room, writing their names with different parts of their bodies: chins, elbows, backs, feet. This lets them move around and offers the opportunity for the leader to learn their names quickly. As every teacher knows, this can give you high marks with the kids.

Peggy Richards, a wonderful teacher, had our "lunch bunch" students walk around stretching themselves out to be as big and broad as possible and then to make themselves as tiny as possible. The kids loved it.

Susan Stroman, the well-loved director and choreographer, started rehearsals of the Broadway musical, *Crazy for You*, by having everyone in the cast stand in a circle, arms stretched out in front of them, flexing their fingers in rhythm while singing "I've Got Rhythm." By the end of several verses tension was gone…or "way gone," as one of the singers said.

WARMUP EXERCISES AND GAMES

Relays with Imaginary Objects

This is a popular warm-up game that was one of the first games we did after starting our club. A good way to start a session, it is fully described in Session 2 of the Leader's Guide.

First, explain to your group that doing shows requires the use of many different imaginary elements, and this will be one of the first things they'll be practicing. Ask some kids to play catch, first with a ball, and then without one, or to have a tug-of-war with a rope, and then without the rope. Let the children create similar actions.

Second, have the children form two lines of five or six each. One line faces the other about ten to fifteen feet apart and each line extends from downstage (the front edge of the stage) to upstage (the back wall of the stage)—or the equivalent in the space you have, if it is not a stage.

Each child, in turn, carries an imaginary object to the child in the opposite line, who then carries it back across the stage.

Mirror Game

Described in Session 2 of the Leader's Guide, this is another very accessible game. In your first meeting, and maybe several subsequent ones, it's a good idea to start with one or two easy games like this for the whole group.

The children go up on the stage and form pairs. Then each pair decides secretly which one will be a leader and which one the mirror, or follower. The idea is for them to face each other as the leader moves arms, legs, and head very, very slowly and clearly enough so that the other can mirror everything the leader does exactly as he or she is doing it. After you call out "Stop!" ask the audience to guess which one in each pair was the leader.

An extension of this game is for you to call out "Switch!" during the exercise, meaning that the other child then becomes the leader. Continue asking them to switch more and more frequently until finally they're all moving together without even remembering who is the leader at any given moment. It's fun and helps develop the kind of concentration required in a show. Eventually a whole group can follow one leader.

This game is also helpful to professional actors, who aid their concentration by mentally (not actually physically) mirroring all the movements of the actors they're listening to or speaking to in a scene.

In the Broadway musical *Crazy for You,* the late director, Mike Ockrent, based an entire hilarious drunk scene in Act II on this game. Performed flawlessly by the two leading actors, it included a complete Gershwin number that lasted at least ten minutes.

Finish the Story
Send two or three children to the playing area and give them a situation to begin acting out, such as:

> You're sneaking into an old, dark, empty house that you heard was haunted. One wants to run away, the others insist on going in.

> You see a rattlesnake in your path and Rick wants to run, but Rosa says to hold very still.

> You are two aerialists in a circus waiting high up on the tight-rope when a third one gets a panic attack and can't go up.

> While you are racing home, one falls and badly hurts a leg, rendering walking impossible.

> You're painting a fence together. One gets paint on the other.

Once they get started, ask the group watching the improvs, "Now what happens?" Call on the one waving his or her hand the most wildly to suggest what happens next. The ones in the playing area then follow this idea until you ask the audience again and call on the next excited hand-waver. This can go on for several minutes. The kids usually love doing it.

A Variety of Approaches
It's important to emphasize to the children that there are many ways to do things,

not just a right and a wrong way. Etienne DeCroux, the French master of pantomime who taught Marcel Marceau and Jean-Louis Barrault, said that when he was still a poor student, he and his roommate spent their evenings endlessly finding ways to put on an imaginary pair of socks or drink an imaginary glass of water. The idea, then, is to think of a variety of ways and decide which ones work best to tell the story, reveal the plot, define a character, add to the audience's belief, or get a laugh from the audience.

An excellent approach to that goal is the exercise, Many Ways to Open a Door, which is described in Session 2 of the Leader's Guide. Or Peggy Richards's game Many Ways to Sit in a Chair. Follow that up with the As If exercise in Session 4, demonstrating that there are a variety of ways to say things, too. It uses one sentence with only a few words in a wide variety of meanings. It also works well when others in the group supply the Who, What, Why, Where, and When, about which the sentence is spoken. (These are the five Ws, which we'll discuss thoroughly in Chapter 2.)

There are two more popular warm-up games to mention here: Freeze! (Leader's Guide, Session 6) and The Machine (Session 4). Working with teenagers, we extended The Machine game into a full-length show; the description of that show can be found in Chapter 9.

SKITS

In the second half of each meeting, we often formed small groups in every hallway, nook, and corner we could find. The kids planned their skits, or "skitches," as the younger children called them, and after a half hour or so we all regrouped to do the skits for one another.

Often we suggested a list of subjects for skits at the end of a meeting, such as respect, parents, racism, loyalty, the classroom, homelessness, government, malls, Halloween, courage, and the like. They could think about them for the next meeting and create a skit based on one or two of them. Or we gave different groups a card with a few sentences on it and asked them to bring in a skit using those sentences. We kept a big box of props and costumes (usually donated to us after parents had cleaned out their attics) to be used in these short scenes. Necee Regis, a former Dramatics Club member who is now an established artist in Boston and Miami, recalls that box:

> The props were magic. Maybe they looked like props while they were still in the box, but take a ruler and put a sparkler at the end and you become a queen. Put on a black robe and you become a villain.

The kids had no serious difficulty creating the skits and did not require constant adult supervision. As our daughter, Glynnis O'Connor, said:

> We'd go off alone into the hallways and do it ourselves. We didn't

want to leave or go running around the school. We thought, "What's the point? We're doing our skit." I remember just waiting and wanting and hoping we'd have enough time so that we could all get on. There was always an excited, healthy sense of pressure.

As you help kids take the stage, you'll be teaching them many valuable lessons. One of these, developing trust, will be covered in Chapter 3. As authors, we hope that as you use this book you'll come to trust not only our ideas but also your own ability to use, with ease and pleasure, the system we've developed over the past decades. We will examine the process in the next chapter and give you the techniques throughout the book for making that process work.

Additional Exercises, Improvs, and Games

RELAXATION EXERCISES

1. Focus relaxation efforts onto specific areas of the body: the temples, the area between the eyes, the jaw, the neck, the muscles between the neck and shoulders, the lower back, the knees. Or try to relax just the little finger.

2. Imagine in detail a very quiet, restful place and situation.

3. Imagine the feeling of resting after climbing eight flights of stairs.

4. Imagine lying in a field looking at the stars.

5. The yoga series of postures, "Salute to the Sun," is a wonderful exercise to do with your group if you know it.

6. James Brennan often used the following exercise, which may take longer to describe than to do:
Instruct all the kids to lie on the floor on their backs with a book or small pillow under the head. They should first relax the feet, then the ankles, calves, knees, and thigh muscles. Tell them, "Now everything from your waist down should be totally relaxed." Go on to the rest of the body—the last thing to relax is the jaw muscle, where most facial tension is felt. This process can take up to ten minutes.
Tell them now to imagine they are lying on a disc-like object, where they can feel gravity holding them to the floor—just gravity. Tell them, "The disc begins to rise slowly into the air. Then it tilts slightly and rotates slowly, but you don't slide off." Mention any movement that won't rush them through the exercise. "The disc falls but just before hitting the ground it slows and softly touches down."
Be as creative as you want, making sure they do the movements slowly and remember the feelings as they go. That's a key to "sense memory." You might say,

"The earth is now somewhere else in the galaxy. It becomes smaller and eventually the whole universe is inside an electron orbiting inside your bodies." At the end of their voyage tell them to tense their bodies on the count of three and open their eyes if they were closed.

Sometimes we turned on the bright lights on the third count because, often, there was at least one person who had fallen asleep (only asleep, not hypnotized).

James Brennan told us, "These exercises may also help them to relax before an algebra test or, later on, the SATs, as well as for performances and auditions."

WARM-UP EXERCISES AND GAMES

1. Have the group divide into pairs. Tell them to engage in a soundless conversation, just reading each other's lips. Everyone can do this at the same time. They could be:

Best friends	Secret friends
Worried parents	Sister and brother
Enemies	Teacher and student
Winner and loser	Friends sharing great news

2. Ask one of the children to relate a short story or incident, using all the senses, trying to make it real to herself as she tells it. Then have another student act out the story as the first one retells it.

3. The Chord exercise is useful for ensemble work. All the youngsters stand in a circle or lie on the floor with heads toward the center like a hub of a wheel. On cue, all begin to hum a note of their own choice. All then strive to reach the same note, giving up their own note or holding to induce others to choose theirs. The volume modulates or swells, and discussion follows about who was loudest or who was or wasn't listening.

4. A variant of this is Finding the Chord. One person begins with one note and others fall in to form a musical chord together. Don't select the beginner. Just allow each person to pay attention to all the others and let it happen spontaneously as someone decides to begin and the others bring in their own notes that harmonize with the rest.

5. Walking and Mirroring is an exercise in which an actor chooses a certain kind of "walk." Another imitates and then begins to "mirror" the leader, and eventually they both try to walk simultaneously without changing anything. They begin slowly through imitation and eventually become the other person. They connect; they intersect. This is how acting is put together. Walking and Mirroring can also be done with picking up books, trying out chairs, going up to bat—almost any kind of movement.

6. With the whole group standing in a circle one person says "One," another from anywhere in the circle says "Two," and so on as far as the group can go. The catch is that if more than one person says the next number, the whole group must start again with "One." Going around the circle in order is not allowed. The calling out of numbers must be random. Very often they never get farther than "Three." But one Young Angels Theatre group, who had been doing this exercise every week, got as far as "Thirty-five."

Chapter Two
The Basic System

STAGE AND FILM DIRECTOR Daniel Mann, musing over a cup of coffee after an Actors Studio session some years ago, said that acting is really very simple when you think about it. Everyone in the world is always doing something at every moment. That's what acting really *is—doing*. Just choose the right actions and really do them.

Acting comes naturally to children. All kids "play pretend." Typically, as they learn and grow, they say things like:

"Let's play that I'm lost in the woods and you're my father and you can't find me."

"You're a sea monster carrying me off to your cave."

We all did those things when we were kids.

Mothers do it with infants. "Pretend like your bed is a nice soft pile of grass and you're a baby bunny who is hopping into the grass to hide."

The internationally known director/writer Robert Wilson said "All true theater people I know have a little child hidden inside them."

In this chapter, we'll look at some fundamentals that have served us well for many years in nurturing youngsters' innate acting abilities. Our approach is intended to help you find the best questions to ask, which will then, we hope, set your imaginations dancing.

TEN ELEMENTS OF ACTING

Let's start with the ten basic elements of acting. First, there are five questions:

Who?   What?   Why?   Where?   When?

And there are the five senses:

Sight   Hearing   Smell   Taste   Touch

We'll be exploring each element separately in detail, but first we'll demonstrate here the logical way to use them together. Because, in reality, they are inseparable.

The guiding principle of this approach is simply this: A play or a musical or an opera is fundamentally a *story*. It may be simple or complex. It may be scary, funny, or moving. As with any good story, it should have a beginning, a middle, and an end. It is made up of answers to what we call the five Ws:

Who are they?

What are they doing?

Why are they doing that?

Where are they?

When is it?

Audiences learn some of the story, the answers to the five questions, when they hear the lines of dialogue, the sounds, and music; and when they see the sets, lighting, and costumes. But they also learn a large number of the answers from the way the actors behave as the characters in the show, from the way they say what they say and do what they do. Actors' behavior is extremely important to the story. That is what really tells the story, or at least helps us to believe it. A sign on the wall at the Neighborhood Playhouse, the well-known acting school in New York City, quotes Sanford Meisner, the director and teacher:

An ounce of behavior is worth a pound of words.

Anything a person thinks, knows, says, or does is a result in some measure of things that the person has seen, heard, smelled, tasted, or touched. All our behavior is a result of these five kinds of sensory stimuli, either from the past or from what we experience in the present.

In the same way, the actors' behavior onstage is the result of the sensory information in the story. Of course, most of the time the sensory experiences are not real. So the actors must re-create those sensory stimuli in their imaginations, and then allow themselves to respond to them in as truthful a way as possible. Actors' behavior is the sum total of their responses to the sensory events of the story.

First, when preparing to put on a play, the actors and the director read the script to determine the who, what, why, where, and when of the story. They then choose the imaginary factors in the story, such as the wretched orphanage conditions in *Oliver Twist*. These stimulate the actors' *sensory responses*: the orphans' feelings of help-lessness, hunger, cold, and weakness. These, in turn, produce the actors' *physical behavior*: shivering, hanging their heads, scraping the porridge bowls clean, dragging their feet, and so on.

All these elements help to make the story clear and assist the audience in identi-fying with the characters. Therefore—and it bears repeating—actors must create in their minds the imaginary sensory stimuli to which they can respond physically and emotionally onstage or in front of a camera.

Acting, at its core, is make-believe and play-pretend. After all, that's neither a real prince on the stage, nor a real castle he's in. The moonlight isn't really from the moon, and the noisy crowd offstage is just a tape recording. But actors must behave as if all that were true. They must make these things real to themselves so that they will automatically respond truthfully to them. That is a basic ingredient of the actor's craft that you want to teach the children.

If a police officer onstage is supposed to be alone in a dark corridor at midnight hunting an armed thief, and if the actor playing the cop walks around carelessly as if he were out on a sun-filled golf course, he doesn't communicate the story. The actor loses the audience.

In a nutshell, here is what actors do to find their characters' thoughts and needs:

1. Determine the facts—that is, the answers to the five Ws—in each part of the story.

2. Link to each fact the sensory elements that pertain to them.

3. Make these elements "real" to themselves in their imaginations.

4. Respond to the sensory elements as they believe the characters would.

They must also relax completely, because this kind of creative thinking is impossible under tension.

The more the actors believe in what the characters are feeling, sensing, wanting, and thinking, the more the audience will believe the actors and enjoy the story. You can help young people act well by asking them to follow the same process. For example, the following table from Shakespeare's *Romeo and Juliet* and Dickens's *A Christmas Carol* correlates answers to the *Who, What, Why, Where*, and *When* questions with sensory elements and the behavior the actor might find to tell a story.

WHO	SENSE	BEHAVIOR
Juliet: *young, lovely*	breathless	stops to catch breath
	rapid heart beating	claps hands to breast
	sees bright colors	face, eyes wide and alert
	feels light, agile limbs	move easily and quickly
	straight, flexible back	stands erect, stretches, arcs
Scrooge: *old, mean*	muscles and bones ache	moves slowly and carefully
	sight is dim and unsure	squints, leans forward
	back bent	can't straighten up

WHAT	SENSE	BEHAVIOR
Juliet:	heart fluttering	body presses forward
To be with Romeo	every sense alive	eyes search avidly
	pleasurable ache in chest	tries to calm self
Scrooge:	cold, tight throat	gathers body into tight ball
To fend off ghosts	fright	hides under covers
	shaking muscles	grabs for weapon

WHY	SENSE	BEHAVIOR
Juliet:	body aching to touch him	stretch toward him
Loves Romeo		hug self, twirl, gaze
		watch, listen avidly
Scrooge:		
Feels guilty and unloved	mouth dry	purse lips, swallow
Feels world is hostile	throat tight	hold neck

WHERE	SENSE	BEHAVIOR
Juliet:	bright moonlight	looks up
Her balcony		whispers to moon
	fresh, sweet air	breathes deeply, shakes head
Scrooge:	musty, dark chilly	scrunches up, closes eyes
His bed		

WHEN	SENSE	BEHAVIOR
Juliet:	quiet, dark,	moves secretively, quietly
1:00 A.M.	full petticoat, shawl	reveals more than proper
1594	need to be obedient	checks to see not discovered
	fears parental rage	enlists nurse's help, pleads
Scrooge:	street noises, dark	tenses up, sits up
Midnight	feel of nightcap	pulls cap down over ears
1843	distant singing, bells	covers ears
Christmas Eve	sees, hears ghost	tries to hide under covers
	smell of fireplace smoke	coughs, shudders

And so on. The more accurate and specific the choices, the more interesting and informative the actor's behavior and, therefore, the more involving the story becomes.

For instance, if an older girl were playing Juliet trying to deal with her grief at Romeo's death, she could well use the description by Erich Lindemann, chief of psychiatry at Massachusetts General Hospital, after interviewing family members of those who died in the 1942 Coconut Grove fire. He described how the grief-stricken relatives felt their throats tighten, their breathing become difficult, an emptiness fill their abdomen, a loss of physical strength, and an intense sense of distress. Studying a description like that will yield better results than an effort to pretend to cry or squeeze out tears.

In your exercises with kids you can create many combinations. For example:

> Choose a Who and ask the young actors to add What, Why, Where , and When.

> Suggest a Where, and add sight, hearing, smell, taste, and touch.

> Work on a sense, such as extreme heat, and use it with different Ws. Who, for example: a cook by a stove in a hot kitchen in July, or a champion tennis player approaching the court for the final round at Wimbledon.

> Supply the Ws, but suggest that the players have lost the sense of hearing or seeing.

(A small caveat: When your group is setting up the Ws for the actors onstage, suggest that they start with a Where. Otherwise you may find, as we did once, that the group will put the characters into nearly impossible locations to play, like a football star and a fairy queen on Mars.)

Acting without using the whole body is analogous to playing the piano with one finger. Suppose you are working with a group of young actors and you ask them to imagine that the floor is covered with a swarm of biting fire ants that are beginning to crawl over their shoes and up their legs. They will almost certainly respond physically to that image, and you may be surprised at the intensity of that response. You can then point out to them that their responses to imaginary sensations would tell an audience what the actors want the audience to know and believe—in this case, that the place is infested with ants that are biting the characters and making them miserable.

Think hard about the taste of a lemon, as if you were trying to find words to describe it. Don't you find your lips puckering and your tongue pressing against the back of your front teeth? Imagine a spotlight shining in your eyes. Don't you close your eyes and look away?

The more the actor believes the imaginary sensory elements and acts accordingly, the more the audience will believe and enjoy the story and the characters. The more specific and inventive the actors, the better the show works.

If three or four children pretend that their noses are running and their fingers and toes are getting numb, if they pantomime packing wet snow into a snowball, if they break off an imaginary icicle and try to "taste" it, then their friends will know the Where and the When.

THE IMPORTANCE OF IMPROVS

Aside from constant work on exercises to help them relax, concentrate, and develop strong voices and nimble bodies, professional actors do essentially the same thing children do when they play. To learn about the characters and sensory elements of the story, they do improvisations, which we discussed briefly in Chapter 1. A sense of improvisation is integral to the spontaneity of acting.

An Ancient Acting Technique

The use of improvisation is as old as acting itself. Saint Francis of Assisi, in the twelfth century, is said to have taught Bible stories to illiterate people by doing improvised enactments of them. A theatrical form of improv probably began in the fifteenth century with *Commedia dell'arte* in Italy, and its derivative, the Punch and Judy shows in England. In modern times, the famed Russian director of the Moscow Art Theater, Constantin Stanislavski, explored improvisation as a rehearsal technique. Even the artist Pablo Picasso and his wife used improvs to prepare themselves for clients interested in buying his paintings.

Professional actors doing improvs often act out short scenes, creating the words and actions as they go, without knowing the ending and without any script. The director will give them only certain answers to the five Ws, such as where they are, what they're trying to do and one or more obstacles that must be surmounted to achieve their objectives. Making it up as they go along, actors discover how the characters might behave in those circumstances.

In the course of their training, actors move on to written monologues, single scenes, or full scripts, first searching for all the answers to the five Ws. Then they imagine, or recall from their own experience, sensory elements present in those answers and try to make them real to themselves. With those in mind, they read and reread the script aloud. When they're ready, or when the director tells them they're ready, they get up on their feet and act. They move around, look at and listen to one another, and, of course, listen to the director and follow any directions.

All good actors try, search, and try again to discover the behavior that is both specific and universally truthful for particular situations. They continue to do that until all of it comes together, until they believe and the audience believes. Finally everyone together shares an experience that leads to growth, increased understanding, catharsis, and pleasure.

Actors don't really "live the part"; they just relax and concentrate on the five Ws and the five senses and then respond to them onstage with each other. It takes almost a lifetime of work to become a truly fine actor, and by emphasizing what makes an actor believable and skilled, we're not suggesting that you train children for an acting profession. But by introducing children to a simplified version of the same process used by professionals, you can do skits and shows with kids that make acting exciting and rewarding for everyone. In their performances the young actors will fully use their whole bodies, their voices, and their imaginations, not just stand stiffly, parroting lines at one another, trying to hide their hands in their pockets, wishing they were somewhere else.

After a good grounding in this process, the kids make the transition to full-length shows naturally and smoothly. If it is not always easy, it is always exciting. The young actors have a better idea of what to look for in a script, how to write or help write one, and how to find the behavior that serves the story and makes it real, interesting, and fun to do. Moreover, children of many different ages and abilities become accustomed to being together, working on scenes, games, and exercises. Then, work on the full-length plays follows naturally.

Now let's explore the ten elements of acting in more detail. First, we'll look at two of the actor's primary tools—sensory awareness and imagination—as they relate to the five senses. We'll see how to develop them to tell a story. Then we'll examine fully the important five Ws that make up the story and combine them with the sensory elements.

Act the Setting

Early in the rehearsals of the Strindberg 1887 classic, *The Father*, for the Berkshire Theatre Festival, the young Swedish director, Anders Cato, said to his cast, "This play depends a lot on the atmosphere of the place and the time. Only **you** can give us that." So he asked his cast to assemble on the stage, sitting, standing, or walking around the set. Then he asked them to close their eyes and imagine the sounds of the place...the doors opening and closing, keys turning in locks, work noises in the downstairs kitchen, clocks ticking, horses outside, boots stomping off snow as people entered downstairs. Then he asked them to feel spots in the room that were warmer than others , to see where the light was bright or dim, to note pine smells, wood smoke, cooking. This affected the behavior of all the actors and made the whole play much more believable throughout the run.

THE FIVE SENSES

Too often we'll see an actor carrying a "heavy" suitcase in his left hand. But we know it's really empty, because the actor leans to his left instead of leaning to the opposite side to give himself a counterweight, which helps his body to support the suitcase. That actor needs to become a more observant student of the five senses.

We can't overstress the value of sensory work. Helen Keller, deaf and blind from the age of two, once said to a friend who complained that she didn't see much on a walk in the woods, "You must use your eyes as if tomorrow you will be struck blind." Her admonition applies to all the senses—sight, hearing, smell, taste, and touch.

A baritone in our church choir was blinded when he was twenty-three years old. He's eighty now, and says he can often tell, when he's inside the church, which choir member has arrived by the sound of the car stopping.

In childhood, the five senses are constantly and passionately at work. If the children know you are truly interested in them and care about their thoughts and feelings, they love to talk about and explore the gifts their senses bring them. So be sure to introduce work on the senses with love, respect, and enthusiasm. Ask the children questions, reminding them again that, in this regard, there are no wrong answers. You're all just finding out about one another's individual perceptions together. Make sure everyone is relaxed, and take your time.

Sight: Ask them to observe their hands and talk about everything they can possibly see in them—colors and differences in color, freckles, and fingernails (long, short, a little dirty, jagged?). Where are the lines? Which are deep and which tiny? Any hints of blue? Any scratches or scars? They don't have to verbalize any of the answers, just look for them. Then ask the children to close their eyes and "see" their hands in their minds just as they did with their eyes open.

Hearing: Have everyone stand silently in a circle, eyes closed, as they try to hear a siren or a small sound that is hard to identify. The most fun is to ask them to imagine music they love, to try to really hear it and do whatever they like in response to it. Having their eyes closed helps them to feel free with this. Just take care no one falls off the stage!

Smell: The sense of smell is very evocative. It can bring to mind strong memories: the smell of greasepaint (for an old actor), the smell of a hated medicine, or the welcome smell of chlorine in the pool at the YMCA.

Explore good smells with your group: the salt air of the ocean beach, burning leaves in autumn, freshly baked doughnuts, newly mown grass. (Legend has it that Sheriff Pat Garrett caught Billy the Kid by frying bacon over an open fire; he knew Billy hadn't eaten for a long time and the smell lured him out of hiding.)

Bad smells often elicit all kinds of giddiness or grossness from kids. But that may be okay, too.

Taste: Next, ask them to tell you their favorite taste. Choose one and ask the whole group to try to imagine that taste. Pretend they are tasting it right then and there. They can close their eyes, if they choose. And you can all talk about it when you're doing it.

Is the food bitter, salty, sweet, buttery, really sour? Does it feel cold, warm, juicy, sticky, slippery, chewy? How does it feel going down into your throat? Does it give you the desire for more, or do you hate it? These latter sensations might be more closely related to the sense of touch than to taste, but it's easier, especially with children, to evoke how something tastes by including something of how it feels.

Touch: Ask them to feel various objects in the room: their clothes, pencils, an orange, the wall. Identify the texture, temperature, firmness, thickness of each object. Try to imagine how different atmospheres might make their bodies feel: a hot and humid swamp; a high, dry desert; a freezing meat locker; a rain-soaked mountain pass.

Then begin exploring the ways that the sense of touch can lead to understanding emotions. For example, what sensations do their bodies feel when they're angry or excited, scared or overjoyed? If they are really afraid of something, do they have a dry mouth, wet palms, pain in the stomach? Find out about what feelings they love, such as being warm and cozy or surrounded by water. Whether it is scratching an itch, finally getting out a sneeze, jumping, running hard, or sitting down after running hard, children love to talk about their feelings. Ask them what those feelings make them want to do.

Using their senses to look for answers is what you want the children to do all the time. In subsequent meetings—or in the first one, if you think they are ready for it—explore the senses this way. Ask them for their most repulsive taste. Explore sounds that they love or hate or they think are scary or exciting. If they mention music and start to dance or respond physically, encourage it.

Once they are familiar with exploring each sense as fully as possible, combine the senses by passing an object from one to the other and calling out "Sight," "Smell," "Touch," and so on. Have the person holding the object then describe one element of it that he or she perceives through the particular sense you have named. You can try passing around a pencil, for instance. Call out, "Touch." The child answers, "hard" or "pointed." Next, call out "Smell." The answer is "woody." How do you hear a pencil? It can be tapped, or used to write and erase; it will make a scratching sound. We don't want the kids licking things, so ask them to *imagine* how it might taste: dry, salty, dusty, stale?

Sometimes we passed fruit around to smell and feel, and then concentrated on those sensations. Any object will do: a hat, scarf, bell, sealed candy bar, book. Just try to explore it with all five senses.

Transforming Objects, an activity using objects in different ways, is a popular exercise described in Session 1 of the Leader's Guide.

Sensing Imaginary Objects

Inevitably, some kids will soon be itching to get up onstage or in front of the group and do something. Ask for volunteers to line up and stand behind a table or two. Suggest that they hold an imaginary object in their hands: a kitten, a toothbrush, cooked noodles, a caterpillar, burning paper, an ice cube. Or that they dip their hands into imaginary substances. They can choose for themselves or ask the class to suggest a substance.

Sometimes it's better to write out imaginary substances to be drawn from a hat. Tell them this time that the exercise is for them, not for us, so they should not talk about what they are touching, but to try to re-create it from the feeling in their hands.

One small caveat: You can begin doing these exercises as guessing games—that's fun and easy. But acting is not playing charades or winning games. Explain to your young actors that they don't have to *demonstrate* how the substance feels. Assure them they don't have to indicate (that is, *show us*) with their faces or even with their bodies what the substance is. Just concentrate on the feeling and then do whatever comes naturally. The audience will then become engaged and ready to believe in the characters as real people, really thinking and really living on the stage.

As they are trying to feel the imaginary object, ask them questions to answer silently to themselves:

> What does it feel like?
>
> Where do you feel it? In the heel of the hand, or the joints or tips of fingers?
>
> Does it affect the arms, back, chest, neck?
>
> What does it make you want to do?

When, or if, the object moves, the child can try to re-create the feel of the movement. But don't spend a long time on it. Let everyone take turns.

One of the first exercises Lee Strasberg gave the Actors Studio members was to try to sense an imaginary cup of coffee as completely as possible. Your students will probably want to try it, even though it's a relatively difficult exercise. After doing this several times, depending on their maturity, you may find the students themselves supplying the questions. Sooner or later it might dissolve into silliness, and that's the time to move on to something else.

At a later meeting, after you've all done one or two good relaxation exercises, ask one child to describe an experience of an injury or illness. It expands kids' awareness of the sense of touch to recall the sensory details of a sprain, cut, or bruise, a very high temperature, an upset stomach, toothache, or even an operation. Ask the rest of the group to imagine it in their own bodies as he or she tells it.

This can move into more detailed work on emotional experiences and the physical sensations, primarily of touch, that accompany them. For instance, ask a girl to think of a time when she was angry, really furious. She need not tell the group what made her so mad. Just ask her to describe how her body felt. Maybe her heart started to pound, her breath got short, her throat felt tight or hot, her fists clenched, and her shoulder, back, and arm muscles felt like exploding into some destructive action, while the small of her back tensed.

Ask others individually to explore with the group the muscular pain and exhaustion of hard effort, the dry mouth and weak knees of fear, the relaxation and relief of success, the extra clarity of vision when a crisis is at hand. Here, again, ask all the children to imagine it in their bodies as they hear the description. Be prepared for an occasional bizarre response from the kids. That doesn't lessen the value of the exercise.

You can also suggest that each night before they go to sleep they think about how something tastes, feels, or smells. Constant sensory awareness is a habit that is part and parcel of an actor's tool kit. More important, it can be part and parcel of the joy of living.

Help them to see for themselves by giving a pair of young actors a short bit of dialogue such as:

A: Come on, let's go!
B: No, not yet!
A: Yes. It's time. Let's get going.
B: I don't want to. Go on yourself.

Now, have them do it several times: First, as if it's at a very noisy party. Second, as if it's in a church funeral, and they're freezing cold. Third, as if it's in a haunted house. Fourth, as if they're lying on a sunny beach. And fifth, as if they're stealing money from a store after it's closed. Have them imagine the senses in each place, then act the little scene. They will see for themselves what a difference working with the senses can make.

It takes real strength for any actor, no matter how skilled or experienced, to concentrate on a sensory choice without letting the mind wander to how he or she will be judged as an actor. When the children begin concentrating seriously, automatically, and with relish, you, they, and audiences will learn what good actors they can really be. They can create a real story and make you believe it and feel it. It's natural. But they must be secure in the knowledge that no one is going to belittle or laugh at them. Then you just point them in the right direction.

After an introductory period of working on the senses, it's time to look at the next five, and all-important, elements of acting.

THE FIVE Ws

Before examining the five W elements of a story one by one, one question should be answered: Why do we not include "How?" in our list of essential questions for learning the facts in a story? The reason is that "How?" too often deteriorates from "How am I going to accomplish this?" into "How well am I doing?" or "How much does the audience like me?" which in turn often leads to self-conscious, phony acting, or fear. Again, acting is *doing*, not evaluating. In fact, you'll see that the answers to How are often included in the answers to What. A good actor wants to engage the audience's belief, **not** its admiration!

The five questions often cross over, interlock, overlap, or depend on one another, but we'll examine each one separately for ease and clarity. It's a good idea for your group to work on them individually before starting to accumulate or combine them.

A game that makes an effective transition from the senses into the five Ws is one we call Who Am I—Where Am I? After the relaxation exercises, when everyone is sitting or lying down, ask them to close their eyes, and listen as you describe a specific five-W choice in sensory detail. Tell them only whether it is a Who, What, Why, Where, or When, and ask them to call out what you are describing as soon as they recognize it. If they guess it very quickly, have them continue suggesting specifics if they can.

Here are several examples, starting with some Whos. It's easy and fun to create your own, and once the kids get the idea, encourage them to take turns describing specific sensory details of other Ws for the group to identify.

Who am I? "My back is very sore, especially when I straighten up. My head is sweaty from the hot sun. My hands are stiff inside dirty gloves. I smell of freshly cut grass and fertilizer. I feel great pressure on the knees. I am thirsty."
Answer: A gardener.

Who am I? "I heave a big sigh of relief. My body is relaxing. I hear waves of applause. Bright lights are on me, my face is beaming. I see rows and rows of people looking at me. My feet hurt from high heels. My throat is a bit dry. I am bending up and down in bows."
Answer: A performer.

Who am I? "My legs are really sore from standing all day. Numbers, numbers are racing through my brain. My fingers feel the keys of the register in my right hand. My left hand is packing and pushing. I have a painted smile on my face. I mindlessly mutter a routine "Have a nice day." I hear background music repeating and repeating."
Answer: A clerk in a checkout counter.

What am I doing and Why? "I feel the heavy dresser against my back as I help my father shove it against the door. I hear people hollering outside. I see a mob on the front lawn. I hear the shade rip as I pull it down. I feel the pain as I cut my finger on a rusty door bolt. My heart is pounding as my parents and I climb up to the roof to escape."
Answer: Trying to protect the family from a lynch mob.

What am I doing and Why? "I feel full of energy and purpose. I love being united with the others who are sharing this effort. My throat is hoarse from shouting and chanting. My hands hurt a bit from the sign I'm carrying. But I'm full of hope, outrage, and a sense of righteousness. I want to be observed. I want others to see and hear us."
Answer: A political demonstrator, intent on changing an unfair law.

Where am I? "There are tiny wildflowers everywhere—all colors. White peaks in the distance. The river below looks like a thin blue string. Pine needles are soft underfoot. Rocks feel firm. I hear the wind through the trees, and the thin air smells fresh and clear.
Answer: High on a mountain.

When is it? "I feel sticky stuff in the corners of my eyes. My muscles are not ready to move. The sun is low on the horizon. I hear movement in the house and smell the coffee perking. My mouth tastes stale."

Answer: Early in the morning when just waking up.

It's a good idea to do these exercises, blending the senses and the Ws, near the beginning of as many sessions as feasible.

A Key to Creativity

Actress Glynnis O'Connor, a former member of our Dramatics Club, recalls:

It was always fun—but not only fun; it was stimulating and exciting, because the possibilities were almost endless. With the disciplines of the Who, What, Why, Where, and When questions, it was boundless. They created an open-ended environment. The five Ws were a very good route to use. I remember they encouraged us not simply to rely on imitating what others had done on TV or in the movies, but to use our own ideas.

Who

Choosing Who has many possibilities. When we were doing *The Sound of Music* with our group we added a few schoolroom scenes because we didn't have enough parts for the large number of children who tried out. The young cast deluged us with lists of the kinds of students and teachers we could create:

Kids who don't know the answers but always wave their hands

Teachers who bang the desks with rulers

Boys who keep using all your stuff

Girls who try to be goody-goody teachers' pets

Mrs. Hydrogen Bomb

Teachers who stare at you

We were pleased that these young people naturally described the characters with active verbs, instead of adjectives. We'll discuss the importance of that later.

The first Who choice the students usually make about the character they want to play is often related to occupation: athlete, teacher, cop, astronaut, farmer, opera singer, beggar. Very young children often want to play animals. Good. Suggest that they think about the speed and quality of the animal's movements…jerky or smooth? Which are the heaviest parts of their body? Which parts are stable and which flexible? Are they loving or fierce?

Animal Nature

In an early rehearsal of the Metropolitan Opera Studio's production of *Gianni Schicchi*, the director, Moni Yakim, asked the singers each to choose an animal similar to their characters and walk around the set, using furniture and props and following his directions. The mezzo playing Zita, the family's leader, strutted like a peacock. The baritone playing Gianni darted, stopped, circled, and eyed the others like a fox. Sometimes he was a panther and other times a monkey...all at once. The soprano playing La Ciesca was a flirtatious, sensuous kitten; the tenor who was Marco was a slow moving, dim-witted cow, and the bass played Buoso like an opossum playing dead.

Or they'll go for different ages: old lady, little kid, cool teenager. Suggesting personalities to go with them will make the acting easier. They're pretty clear about what a shy or a bossy or a silly or an excitable or a secretive person tries to do. Costumes and props, if available, will often identify to some extent who the characters are: a policeman, a clergyman, a nurse. Lines of dialogue will sometimes tell the audience who the person is, but the actors can suggest a great deal with their own imaginations. You may find yourself astonished and amused by their ideas.

Barbara Finamore recounted:

> We rewrote the story of Leif Ericson discovering America. We had it discovered by his wife, Fig Leif, instead. We were about ten at the time. We carefully wrote the skit so that it ended with all the people who had discovered America meeting the Indians and having a big dinner, which was pizza—that way we could order pizza and eat it onstage. We discovered the New World, and because the curtain was velvet and we were discovering the curtain, we called it Velvetland.

If there are no Viking explorers or their wives in the room, jog the children's imaginations by asking where the character comes from:

A farm	A crowded one-room apartment
A South Sea island	Outer space

Ask about the body type:

A jock	An elf
A beauty queen	A skinny bundle of nerves

The status of the character:

A gang leader	A king
A prisoner	A famous orator
An outsider	A famous movie star

The kind of physical behavior exhibited, nervous habits, personality traits—the character's basic rhythms:

Slow and liquid	Fast and driving	Jumpy and jerky

It's much easier for children to know how to move and do physical behavior if you suggest characteristics that will allow specific bodily movements, such as:

Talks so fast he has to breathe in big gulps
Has nervous habits: pulls on ear, scratches head
Squints
Continually moves to a rhythm
Rubs hands, cracks knuckles, fiddles with clothes
Moves with short, quick movements
Moves as if she weighs a ton
Stretches and seems to walk on air

We developed a new exercise called Physical Attitude that's almost a shortcut to characterization. This works very well even with seven- or eight-year-olds. Ask them to say, "Jack, be nimble, Jack be quick. Jack jump over the candlestick" or any short nursery rhyme they all know. As each child gets up to say it, ask him or her to "say it as if you're **this** kind of person…": Then take a strong physical attitude yourself, such as shaking your finger at a naughty kid, or backing away shyly, or slapping your thighs with your hands and laughing, or pacing like a sports coach, or shaking your fist angrily, or holding your hands in prayer. Each child will pick it up. Honestly, it usually works like a charm.

Often, kids will want to pretend to be famous television or movie celebrities or cartoon characters. That's okay, but if you can get them going with well-known historical or literary characters, current newsworthy people, or just people they know, so much the better. Of course you certainly will discourage using physical impairments as characteristics that would risk being turned to ridicule.

In the earliest exercises, it's best to use only names, gibberish, letters of the alphabet, or even la-la-la, instead of dialogue. Otherwise, kids tend to make up words instead of physical behavior to tell the story. They resort to just saying it rather than acting it.

After some discussion you can begin to explore the Who question with a few easy exercises. Send three or four people to the playing area to do some physical activity, each one as a different Who. They can do the exercise one at a time, but if they're self-conscious, let them do it together. Supply a few props, if you can: books, a pillow, a phone, and so on. Ask them to open and close the books, fluff the pillow, answer the phone—the activity doesn't matter so long as it's something that frees them to think what the character might be thinking, sensing, or wanting and therefore to behave as the character would behave. Try having them do the same physical activity so that the differences in their assorted characters will become more apparent.

You could send a few girls up to be shopping. Set up two chairs as a clothes rack or two as a counter. Use different Whos—ask them to be snobs, gang members, designers, potential thieves, daydreamers, clerks. Or you could assign Whos with different senses: One who loves to touch and feel things. One who is sharp eyed. One to whom everything smells bad or good, or one who hears an inner rhythm or has a sour taste in her mouth.

Start by suggesting the different Whos they can be, but by all means let them think up their own if they wish. Take advantage of their creative impulses. (In almost all the exercises we describe it's a good practice to allow the kids who are watching to give ideas to the ones doing the exercise.)

As Barbara Finamore has observed:

> Asking the kids who are watching an exercise to give suggestions and directions to those onstage is an excellent way to keep the attention of the group. All are involved. And for the person onstage, it's the first step in getting over the fear of being in front of everybody. They all know they're not going to be on the spot up there. It's just going to be fun.

Then the stage, or whatever your performance location is, becomes a place to relax. It becomes a place to think of things. It becomes a place where you and your young actors solve all the problems together.

The Inner Who

Actors must examine their characters on a deeper level, too. For example, a person's posture toward others can be helpful to an actor. Often a person is said to have an "attitude"—meaning a pejorative or hostile view of or response to another person, place, or group. But the word also means the way a person feels about something; it could be admiring, cautious, or accepting. Encourage your young people to explore this quality. Try the Physical Attitude exercise above.

They should also probe the difference between what they think is expected behavior and what is really going on within their characters—their feelings, thoughts, and sensory experiences. This can help them develop the insight to tell the difference between the truth and a lie, or generalizations and realities. Robert Coles, the child psychiatrist and teacher, said, "Character is how one behaves when no one else is looking."

The answer to this question, "What would be the character's behavior when there's nobody looking?" could lead to more insight into the role and might give some clues to a character's inner life.

Actors have to work to find reasons for people's behavior. They see that we are what we do and we are not always what we seem to be. This has to do with the answers to Why, which we cover later.

A choice of Who is also determined by the attitudes of the other characters onstage. In life we all play the roles in which we are cast. We try to meet or exceed the expectations thrust on us by our friends and others. As a director you can often use this principle to establish the Who.

A Way with a Walk

Many theater exercises designed to define a character were dreamed up by the Broadway actor and director James Brennan. Once he asked his teenagers to "borrow" someone else's walk and bring it into the meeting. He reflected:

> It's an excellent way to show that an actor is an observer and, like a good reporter, inquisitive. Actors try to see the unusual or quaint things that people do. Various kinds of walks became helpful methods in identifying the Who of any one character.
>
> A girl in this inner-city group began walking back and forth, obviously a very provocative walk. Some of the guys reacted accordingly, but they all discussed it in the normal way and agreed it was certainly a female. We dissected it, and it became a very serious discussion. When asked who it was, the girl said, "It's the prostitute on the corner where I live."
>
> The kids' imaginations reflected their lives in their own neighborhoods. One of the rules in the class was that there were no wrong answers. We were not authoritarian. We were very interesting, though.

Relationships

Suppose an actor simply walks onto the center of the stage. If everyone bows down, chances are he's a king or nobleman of some sort. If they drop to their knees, maybe he's the Pope. If they respond in awe and wonder, pointing to the person's legs or going up to touch her, crowd around her, or lift her up, maybe she is a formerly crippled person who's just been miraculously cured.

James Brennan had a great idea for one of his students. Some of the girls were shy, and one of them, Maria, whispered most of the time. On a day when they were doing improvs, he suggested, "In this scene, we want you to be your father." There was some grumbling from the group about asking someone to cross genders. Maria just stared for a while, and James suggested a simple, domestic situation. After more hesitation she brought her father into the scene; she re-created him. Needless to say, it was a very different personality from her own, and it amazed everyone.

From then on she steadily improved. By the end of the sessions she stood up in class and was heard; she explored situations and enjoyed them. Of course, we can't generalize from this. Maria was a unique individual, but her experience touched the others, and many profited from it.

The group often used parents after that, not only to explore the Who but also the What and Why. One day James offered this suggestion to some of the kids:

> I'd say, "Let's see how your father and mother behave when they come home from work. What do they do? What do they see in you at the end of the day, and what do you see in them?" If we fed the kids a whole scenario, they would do what everyone expected. If we kept things specific but open, with only a few limitations, they invented.

A Famous Funnyman Finds a Who

The actor Robin Williams, before he became famous, did an improv with another actor in which they were delivery men carrying heavy furniture and a heavy plate glass window. Mr. Williams endowed his muscle man with great culture and talked on and on, as they were working, about Greek philosophy and famous Renaissance paintings. The paradox was hilarious and the clarity of the Who was impressive. (After the class we told him we wished we could invest in his future career.)

To find out the way others in the show, or sketch, feel about a character and the attitude of that character toward other people in his life, a theater game we used in our own group was called Find the Relationship. We split up into small groups and sent one member of each group out of the room. The remaining children decided on the relationship they would have with the outside member. Then he (or she) was called in, and the others went up to the front with him. Using gibberish, they gave hints to the chosen member about their relationship. He listened and watched until he had the answer. Who are these people and who is he to them? The group had to behave in a way that would reveal the answer, but by using only gibberish, la-la-la, instead of words. Some kids find gibberish hard. If this is the case, have them repeat a phrase like "many, not many" or "before and later" or "books and letters" or simply repeat some numbers, "40, 60, 80, 40, 60, 80," etc.

For instance, the group decided that a girl was a lawyer reading a will to a grieving family. Sniffing and sobbing, they showed her to a chair behind a desk, gave her a sheaf of papers, and motioned to her that she should read what was on them. They sat in a row of chairs in front of her, leaning forward respectfully to listen. They occasionally consoled one another or directed severe looks at one another. When she responded in any way, even with her own gibberish, they responded with pleasure, anger, tears, or stoicism. It didn't take long for her to know who she was and what her relationship was to the others.

Some other situations we used were:

A cop is taunted by a crowd of pickets.

An individual becomes a desert mirage, and the others, gasping, drag themselves across the floor toward him with desperate hope in their eyes.

A girl is hoisted off the stage by rescuing firefighters.

A boy is a snowman that children are making.

Other examples of these can be found in the Additional Exercises, Improvs, and Games section at the end of the chapter.

A different but popular procedure is to give members of your group slips of paper on which they each write a personality trait of someone they love, fear, admire, or dislike. Ask three or four volunteers to draw one slip each, not revealing what is written, and to think a moment about how to assume the written trait. Then tell them to start an improv together. Give them the circumstances: Where they are, When, What they're doing, and Why. For instance, they are in a store after school buying a music CD because it includes a new hit song. But there's only one left, and they all want it right away.

When you call a halt to the improv (perhaps to save the room from destruction), you can get everyone to discuss which person acted which personality trait, which kind of Who. You can send up another team to do the same improv but with different slips from the hat.

Adjectives vs. Verbs

A word of caution here. There is a small trap when you're working on Who. Make it a habit to translate adjectives into active, actable verbs. Adjectives are impossible to act with any kind of reality or truth. They lead to vague posturing or what we call "indicating" in the theater.

For instance, no one can really play the adjectives *shy, kindly, tough,* or *important* and make them work. The audience will clearly realize that the character is shy or kindly only as a result of what the actor does and says.

Since acting is doing, you must ask yourself, "What does that type of person do?" And put it to the children in the same way, not with an adjective but with a description of what a character *does* in any given circumstance. "This is the kind of guy who…"

A shy character is the kind of person who tries to avoid meeting other people's eyes.

A gentle person is the kind who tries to make peace, or simply shares a sandwich.

A self-important person expects to be treated with deference

A conceited person looks for admiration.

Though we all think of adjectives when we are developing a character, it is crucial to accept that an actor cannot play an adjective by assuming a general attitude. Suppose, for instance, a young actor named Gerry is playing a character who displays great anger because someone on another team cheated and he's being made to take the blame. Gerry is perhaps too timid to create the character's real feelings here, so you need to give him direction.

General, weak direction based on an adjective: "Gerry, you've got to be madder here." Gerry might just tense his jaws and fists to give a general idea of "madder," but we won't see specific action.

Better direction using verbs: "Gerry, make this guy listen to you. Don't let him get away with it. Blast him/Threaten! Roar! Tear up the stage with your eyes and your voice!" This time Gerry might try slamming a towel against the bench to get rid of some of his excess rage.

Those verbs lead to behavior, not just to general attitudes and posing. Think, for example, of Margaret Hamilton in the film *The Wizard of Oz*. She succeeded as the Wicked Witch of the West because she fiercely pursued getting the ruby slippers. She concentrated on *doing* that, not on "being wicked."

What
Malcolm X once gave this advice to an audience of youngsters:

> I think each of you young people, especially nowadays, should learn how to see for yourself and think for yourself. Then you can come to an intelligent decision for yourself.

Intelligent decisions about what you are really doing or should be doing are almost as important in a show as they are in life.

The question What is the most important and requires the most concentration and work. Celebrated actress Marian Seldes says, "Every second onstage there always has to be something you want." Professional actors use terms like "objective, intention, motivation," etc., but those might be confusing to kids, so we simply use the word "What" to encompass those. As the Broadway director Robert Lewis exclaimed, "It doesn't matter what you call it. You could call it 'spinach.' Just DO it!"

Actors onstage must be aware of what their characters are trying to accomplish at every moment, what they are doing in their thoughts, and what they want. That's what makes a story active. People try to accomplish something. They face a conflict or an obstacle, and they succeed or fail. This is relatively simple for kids when they are playing games of sport. They may throw the ball, kick it, hit it, catch it, serve it, get it through the basket; but the final purpose, the answer to What they are doing is: trying to win. In professional actors' parlance, the kicking, catching, and throwing are "pieces of business" done to accomplish an action, objective, intention, or goal—in this case, to win. In the theater, a piece of business is almost any physical action done on a stage by an actor, such as moving a chair, picking up a prop, or looking out a window. But these pieces of business are done to help achieve What the character is really trying to accomplish.

The important lesson: An actor must do what his <u>character</u> wants to do, not what <u>he</u> wants to do to show off.

I, Lenka, was called in to audition for the role of Gramma Rosie in the upcoming Broadway musical version of the film *The Wedding Singer*. My agent e-mailed me the scene to read and a new song composed for the show. I had only one day to prepare and, of course, no way to hear the song before I sang it for them. I could only plunk it out on my piano. But I knew they wanted it to be funny. In the song, Rosie is singing about her past "sowing of wild oats" to her beloved grandson, whom she has raised since his parents died when he was six years old. The scene and the song take place the day before his wedding. The song has many tricky rhythms and double entendres. Now, even in heels, I am so short that third-grade boys brag about being taller than I am. I also have white hair and a wrinkled Kewpie-doll face. So I thought that coming out of me, raunchy, low-down physical behavior, like a few bumps and grinds, would make them laugh. And since doing European accents is easy for me I thought it would be fun and make me feel more comfortable to play her as if I were Dr. Ruth, who is my size and age. WRONG. In the preliminary round of auditions, the casting director asked me to sing it again but this time as simply as possible. "Otherwise she'll just seem like some kind of kook." I was truly taken aback. I thought, "For heaven's sake, I'm not practicing what I preach!!" So, I sang it again, this time as if I were just trying to help my grandson by suggesting a few ways he could make his bride happy on their wedding night, because I love him deeply and want him to be happy.

Result: I got called back to read and sing for the director, producers, and writers. They laughed at all the right places, applauded, and thanked me profusely.

The bottom line: Actors and singers...first, play the WHAT! (the intention)

Other examples of what we mean by What:

In the various parts of Lewis Carroll's stories about Alice in Wonderland, the heroine tries to satisfy her curiosity, to fulfill her need to know, to discover where the White Rabbit went, or to learn what's on the other side of the looking glass. In legends, Robin Hood tries to help the poor. Peter Pan tricks Captain Hook in order to save Wendy, John, and Michael. Huck Finn's friend Jim tries to escape from slavery. John Henry tries to win the contest against the steam drill with his own hammer, and he succeeds—but dies in the effort. Pocahontas tries to save the life of Captain John Smith.

We have seen how acting involves making choices about character. Once the actor has made a clear decision also about what the character is doing, his or her acting can be illuminating, and the audience will understand. Some years ago, our daughter, Glynnis O'Connor, then an angelic eight-year-old, played a street urchin we had invented for a scene from *Oliver!* in which she entered a loft filled with the miserable boys in Fagin's gang. Today, she recalls, "All I did was react to the situation in Fagin's den and say the line." She had decided she wasn't afraid of any of them, and she came in to take over. She marched in with all the confidence in the world, took a wide stance, fists on hips, looked each of the boys over with disdain, spat on the floor, and belted out her line, "Coo, you'd think it was me mother's funeral in 'ere!" It brought down the house.

We recently watched, with great frustration, a school play on a local access cable channel. Much work had been expended on the production by parents, teachers, and students. The costumes were impressive and obviously expensive. But each time a young actor spoke, both arms came up, too often just from the elbows, and then went down. It was as if every speech was accompanied by some kind of offering to the gods. That was the only action or movement, and it was pervasive in the entire cast. No one had challenged them with the What, or suggested they use their own imagination in deciding pieces of business and body movement to make clear what their characters were trying to accomplish in the story.

As a matter of fact, most people on a stage don't know what to do with their hands, feet, face, or voice—children, especially. Without a real context, they are embarrassed, bored, ill at ease, rigidly droning their lines at one another or the audience. But help them figure out what they (their characters) are really doing there, discuss it, spend a little time rehearsing it, and they'll fly into action.

It wouldn't be a bad idea to put a few kids up on the stage and whisper to each of them a Who and a What, such as "You're an irritable, impatient person who tries to get everybody to hurry up and do what he wants them to do," "You're full of wonder and joy. You keep stopping to look or touch or listen to things," or "You're a very suspicious person who doesn't want anyone near you and keeps trying to stay by yourself." And ask them to use their hands to illustrate what you suggested. Then ask those watching if they can tell what you whispered.

What Exercises

Remember, in these exercises, the What question we are concerned with does not refer to simple physical activities like those you've given the kids in exploring Who. It refers to a character's goal, what the character is *really* doing: trying to escape, to learn, to insult, and so on. A person setting a table might do it hurriedly and poorly *in order to* get to a meeting on time, or might set it slowly and carefully *in order to* make it impressive to the guests.

Try these exercises with your kids when dealing with the question What. We suggest silent exercises at first because too often kids will substitute words for behavior. Consequently real acting suffers.

I: Ask two kids to cross the stage and, without using words, shake hands with each other. Then suggest the following ideas about what they are trying to do. Have them repeat the handshake with each new suggestion.

> They are trying to restore their friendship after having an awful fight.
>
> One, who has just won a scholarship, is sharing his triumph with his buddy, who is trying to hide his disappointment at losing it himself.
>
> As spies, both are trying to determine what the other is up to.
>
> One, a shy child, is trying to get up the courage to greet a great-uncle whom she fears.

II: Ask five children to pile up three or four books. Give each child one of the following Whats:

To straighten up a mess	To get rid of angry feelings
To challenge someone's belief	To figure out which ones to buy
To protect them from a flood	

III: Send a child to one part of the stage and three or four others to the opposite side. Ask the first child to huddle down and pretend to cry. Ask the others to cross, one at a time, to the sad child, saying his or her name and using any gibberish they choose. They should each do one of the following:

Comfort the child	Find out what's wrong
Try to stop the crying	Distract the child

IV: Send four kids to the stage. Ask each in turn, speaking only the numbers 1-2-3-4, to do one of the following Whats:

Lead a cheer	Exercise
Try to avoid exploding in anger	Conduct an orchestra

An exercise we call What, Without Moving consists of a child simply standing still in one place onstage, not "frozen" or stiff, but relaxed and without any deliberate movement. Tell her (or him) and the whole group, what you want the child onstage to be doing *in her mind only*. Give her one of these tasks:

> Figure out which way is north, or which fork in the road
> to take in order to get somewhere.
>
> Listen hard to pinpoint a cry for help.
>
> Hold still so that the animal nearby won't attack her.
>
> Watch a rescue operation after a plane crash.
>
> Resist tears so that the group won't know how angry she
> is that she was not invited to go with them on the trip.

The barest minimum of natural movement while remaining in that one spot may be allowed only if it is the result of concentrating on the action you suggested. But do not allow any unrealistic indicating that is not the direct result of the given action. Ask the children watching the exercise to raise their hands as they start to believe that the young actor is doing what you asked her to do.

This exercise provided one of the most successful, and even moving, experiences we had at the Seven Angels Theatre Camp. All the young actors became completely quiet and focused as they concentrated. They believed their fellow actors when they became totally real, alive, and committed; they observed this even if no deliberate bodily movements were made onstage. And they wound up thoroughly understanding the point of the exercise.

The transition from nonverbal to verbal is natural and logical. As babies, all of us learned to move before we learned to talk. As adults, our bodies normally respond to a situation before we find the words for it.

Once the children are at ease doing simple exercises one at a time, or in small groups using minimal sounds or gibberish, get them working together using their own words. They could be pushing a broken-down car, or working as chefs in a crowded kitchen, or arriving at a disaster site to rescue the injured. They can begin to act out conflict situations by devising opposing Whats. Of course, you will spell out simple ground rules to avoid injuries: *If they do any hitting, pushing, or tripping, these must be faked, not real.* Obviously, if things get too rough, the game or improv should be stopped.

Here are some more examples of conflict situations for the kids:

> Cops trying to control workers on strike
>
> A customer in a hurry trying to pass a dawdler in a narrow
> supermarket aisle
>
> Individuals representing the President, the Senate, the House,
> the Pentagon, and so on debating budget cutbacks, or
> debating whether to invade another country
>
> Athletes challenging an umpire's call

In our production of *Annie Get Your Gun*, the Buffalo Bill and Pawnee Bill teams were always in competition, so we decided to have the members of those teams do the "Anything You Can Do, I Can Do Better" song, instead of leaving it to the two leading players. We sent the Buffalo Bill troop onstage to gloat over a big poster of their upcoming show, followed by the Pawnee Bill troop, which sparked dispute. They challenged the others to Indian wrestling matches and bragged about their broad jumps, then huddled in the corner. Just then a Pawnee Bill cowgirl taped a "Kick Me" sign on the back of a Buffalo Bill cowboy. This started a great rumble out of which the song followed naturally, with each actor getting to sing a line, each trying to out-brag the next.

In the Young Angels Co. production of *The Lottery* by Shirley Jackson, we developed other characters as we were adapting the story. One of the characters was the rebellious sister of the politically slimy mayor. That enabled us to have a strong conflict scene near the beginning, which set up the story more clearly.

In a Christmas show we developed for P.S. 128 in New York City, the kids created a conflict situation by bringing in a group of street gang members who started a snow fight on the street, during which a girl was hit by a car and hospitalized. This allowed the two opposing groups to come together, apologize, make peace, and then do a Christmas show for her in the hospital. This then gave all the cast members a chance to sing, recite funny poems, and do break dancing and silly skits "to make her happy because they had no money for Christmas gifts." All this evolved from improvs the kids created.

Listening Is Doing

As you move into more advanced improvs, games, and skits using more dialogue, you will see that the actors who have no lines also have an agenda. They must know what they're doing when they are onstage listening to another character. So they must determine what their own characters need and what they want to accomplish.

When teaching students who later became fine successful actors, Robert Lewis, the well-known director and author, discussed the critical importance of listening. He said: "Listen for clues, *for the way the speaker feels,* for the truth of what is being said, for what is missed, for what to answer, for what to refute." Often the audience learns about what is really happening onstage by *the way the actors listen and behave in response.*

This may be over the heads of young children, so perhaps we can clarify it with an example. Members of the Theater Camp in Waterbury, Connecticut, were excited about an improv in which they played a family preparing Thanksgiving dinner. Producer Semina DeLaurentis assigned parts: a pair of twins, a grandmother, a father, and a mother. As they created and played the scene she sent others in to join the improv: two policemen looking for escaped convicts, three lost foreigners who didn't speak English, and a couple of creatures from outer space.

The improv went so well they wanted to repeat it. But the next time, they were too eager. Everybody talked at once as they set the table. The doorbell rang, they opened the door, and they dropped the turkey all at the same time. It disintegrated into chaos. Finally, one girl stopped and said, "It's not working."

We replied, "You're right. It was fun watching you, but we really couldn't tell what was going on in the scene." So we all sat down together and soon decided the scene failed because they *weren't listening* to one another. No one was paying any attention to what the others were doing, and the audience would not know where to look and what to listen to. They wouldn't be able to find the focus of the scene. We canceled what we'd planned for the rest of the meeting and concentrated on the listening exercises described below.

First, we asked one person to describe the events of a recent day with as many details as possible, but to decide privately whether some or all of them were true or "made up." That is, the speaker decided beforehand which it was to be, then tried to convince everyone that everything was true. We then polled the group to determine who thought the speaker was telling the truth, a lie, or a partial truth.

It was very satisfying at the end of the session to point out how well they had all concentrated on listening and, especially, on thinking as they listened. We then compared that with what had happened in the Thanksgiving scene. We commented on some of the interesting behavior we'd observed in the exercise as they listened and as the speaker had tried to convince everyone that the story was true.

You can complicate the exercise later by asking everyone to engage in an activity such as painting a wall, sweeping the floor, or folding towels while only one of them is talking. When the children are doing a show and working from a written script, they already know what they're going to say, but they must not just wait for their cue to speak, or take their turn to speak. As the actor Alan Alda has said, "Listening means being able to be changed by what you hear." Listening includes being aware of your feelings as you are listening. They must still keep their thoughts going. Thinking is doing, too—it is also a What.

Thinking, an actor can:

Evaluate what the speaker is feeling.

Determine what the speaker really means.

Decide which of the words he hears makes him want to reply.

Send signals of agreement or distrust to the speaker.

Keep trying to interrupt.

And—very important—pay attention to how what he's hearing makes him **feel.**

Encourage the kids not to allow awareness of the audience—"counting the house"—to distract them from the plot when they are onstage. Emphasize that they must concentrate on the other actors and listen to what is being said. Of course, there will always be those who say, "Gee, I'm having enough trouble remembering what my next line is." You can tell them that if they're really listening, they won't have so much trouble remembering, because what they feel in response to what they're seeing and hearing is what will cause them to behave and speak as their characters do in the play. If it doesn't, stop the rehearsal and find out why not.

Getting Deeper into Scrooge

In a production of *A Christmas Carol* at the University of Nebraska, the actor playing Scrooge decided his character was not just a cruel, decrepit old man. He and the director found other traits in the book, in the author's life, and in their imaginations that had an effect on the way he played the role. For example, as a boy Scrooge had been neglected and rejected, and in later life he tried to shield himself from any warm human involvements. They decided there should be a slyness about the old man; the actor's behavior toward Cratchit sometimes seemed more like game-playing and trickiness than cruelty, and at times he was testing and playing with Christmas Past, Present, and Future, rather than groveling in front of them. Thus, at the end of the play, his transformation was more believable.

The Underlying What

As we suggested when investigating "the inner Who," characters have intentions that lie under the surface of what they're doing. When the children grow more sophisticated in this process, some will become adept at finding the truth underlying the character's behavior. What is that person really up to?

The toughest challenge professional actors have is determining what their characters are *really* doing, deep down. What are the actions that this character would normally exhibit? What are the character's intentions and needs? What's really going on inside that head?

It's just as easy for kids to act truthfully as it is to fake it. When they approach their character with skepticism and curiosity, with your help they will learn more about that character.

Why

Now we come to the most important W...the one that involves feelings that impel behavior. Every parent knows how often children ask, "Why?" Over and over, that word comes from the toddler. It's a sure way of learning, of becoming more involved in life. In the theater, asking Why is a way of becoming more engaged in the action.

The reason why a character is trying to accomplish something is what gives passion to the imagination and vitality to the actions and behavior. The answers to "Why?" usually supply the energy that drives the scene, pushing the action forward until something is accomplished or, for some characters, impeded. So once your young actors know *What* they're really doing in an exercise or scene and the circumstances—Who, Where, and When—ask *Why* they're doing it. We place the most importance on *Why with feelings* because that's what is the most actable. Feelings are really what most propel behavior. Actors must pay attention to their characters' feelings and make them their own. Often the Why feelings are determined to a great extent by the Where and the When. If it's excruciatingly hot or freezing, or after an accident, or ridicule, or in a secret or forbidden place, or during a war or a period of puritanical zeal, behavior will change accordingly. After all, most of us do what we do either because we want to continue to feel good or want to change from feeling bad to feeling better. So, even if there are otherwise apparent justifications, look primarily for the feelings that make the character do or want to do something.

The more we see, hear, and think about it, the more we realize feelings are such a huge factor in determining our actions. Actors use feelings when they act. That's what acting is all about. BUT we mean *real feelings*. Not what we call "indicating"... phony acting. You can't just put expressions on your face, or do some weird physical thing like clenching your teeth or stamping your foot or pretending to cry. You have to think about what makes you feel that way and what the feeling makes you want to do. And then do it; or if the play demands, try to hide it. Kids are pretty good about this. We talk about feelings to them, and they almost always say something like, "It makes me want to push him down." Or "It makes me want to run away and hide." We love to talk to them about what the senses feel like when they have certain emotions. They'll say, "It makes my stomach shake" or "I can't breathe" or "It makes my fist go like this." That's great. As long as they don't just make faces. The truth is that a lot of us react in very different ways to different feelings. When some people see something that's really awesome, they laugh. When some people are very angry, they freeze. We just want the kids to be honest.

When you ask children why a character does something, it's much easier for them to respond to suggestions like:

"Because he was scared of getting caught," or

"Because she felt like she couldn't wait to find out," or

"Because he didn't want everyone staring at him, he was so embarrassed," or

"Because she was so happy she couldn't hold it in," or

"Because they were totally confused and furious," or

"Because they were too cold, too hot, too tired, surprised, amazed, etc."

Those are actable Whys; much more than plot-line Whys like "Because the school was closed," "Because there was no one else there to do it," "Because everyone was waiting," "Because Dad lost all his money," etc. See what we mean?

Michael Frayn, the playwright who wrote *Noises Off*, *Copenhagen*, and *Democracy*, among others, said, "Everyone, even the most inflexible among us, is a squirming knot of contradictions." If you try to discover the Why for a Shakespearean character, you'll find a wealth of complicated feelings behind his or her actions, rather than a motive that simply meets a narrative demand.

Answers to Why can often be found in the Who answers and can enrich them when the character's *values* are clear. Values can include money and power vs. kindness and compassion, or brawn vs. brains, to name a few.

Notice the change that a shift in Why will cause in a scene:

A police officer asserts authority one way if keeping a mob away from a celebrity, and quite another if keeping a mob away from the scene of a murder...because he feels differently about it.

You might say good-bye to a friend in one way if she's going on a long journey, and quite another if she's just going off to work...because you feel differently about it.

A Senator might argue in one way if supporting a bill she passionately believes in, and quite differently if she's serving a special interest group...because she feels differently about it.

The Whats and Whys often depend on each other, sometimes sound like each other, and may duplicate each other. As a little boy, Forrest Gump ran until his braces fell off. What he was trying to do was to get away from the bullies. Why? Because his girlfriend told him to do that, and he obeyed her. Why? Because his Mama told him he should always obey. So he *felt safer* if he was being a good boy and obeying, and so on.

The Whats are all tied up with wants, wishes, dreams, and goals. The Whys are the reasons, *the feelings*, behind these things that make it urgently important to achieve or experience them. Whys are tied up with frustrations, needs, fears, environmental forces, anxieties, joys, and sorrows.

Where

"I loved it," remembers Barbara Finamore, a former member of our Dramatics Club, "when we'd play the Where game."

> One kid would get up and start doing something that gave hints about his location. And as soon as you knew where he was you could run up and start doing something in the same space that he had set up. Pretty soon we'd all be up there. It was great fun, and all the kids wanted to do it right away.

One summer, in one of our first sessions at Seven Angels Theatre Camp, we explained the exercise, asked one girl to go up to show us where she was by acting it out, and asked the others to join in as soon as they knew where the place was. Within a minute or so, we had a whole stage full of window washers.

Where exercises can be made richer if you do a good relaxation exercise with the whole group first. Ask them to think of a place without naming it aloud. Direct their imaginations to all the sensory elements you can by asking them to think of the answers to:

> Is it light or dark?
> Are you up high?
> What's the temperature?
> What's the strongest smell?
> What do you hear?
> Is there anything you can taste?
> Is there anything to eat or drink?
> Does the air make your mouth dry?
> Are the objects in the space heavy, light, hard, soft?
> Do you hear music, or is it strangely quiet?
> Do you like being there, or hate it?
> Do you feel comfortable there?
> Do you feel nervous being there?

With this kind of work preceding that first game at the theater camp, our "window washers" might have found even more interesting behavior. They might have been buckling their safety belts, pulling themselves up on their "platforms" with "rope pulleys," teetering precariously, "splashing" one another or feeling queasy as they looked down ten floors. They might have had sore shoulders or cold hands. They might have done battle with "pigeons" or climbed into an "office" to use the "phone." Interesting behavior almost always follows good questions.

Playwright Rosemary Foley has worked with a group of about eight physically or mentally handicapped children at the Art Center in Pelham, New York. Her purpose in teaching theater to these children was "to prove to them that they were capable, responsible, and that much was expected of them." After the last session they put on two original shows with all the kids in each cast. One was about a baseball team and another about a girl working at a lunch counter. Rosemary approached the kids as if they were pros and "only helped them to help themselves." She began with the question Where.

A lunch counter. Where are the stools? The girl gets an order for a peanut butter sandwich. Where's the bread? Where's the jar? Where's the knife?

She did the same with a baseball field, even with someone selling popcorn as the children's eyes watched the ball hit into the bleachers.

Of course, the children will always want to do a Where such as a circus, supermarket, or school, because there are so many things to do, so many pantomime possibilities that cause their minds to race. That's fine, but just keep urging them to use their senses. The more they can really try to see, touch, hear, smell, and taste, the better and more believable they will be.

Another way to help children develop awareness of specific sensory Where elements is to suggest a place and assign a fairly small group to move around the playing area. Ask them to describe the elements in the imaginary place as they think of them, and as they see, touch, hear, smell, and (sometimes) taste them.

For instance, someone in a "cave" might say:

> I feel a stalactite. It looks like an icicle coming from the ceiling.
> And here's a little opening. If we crouch way down, we can crawl
> through. Careful, we're at the edge of a deep hole, and it looks as
> if there's bubbly water down there. Oh, there's a dead bobcat...or
> something...I can see its teeth! Let's get out of here!

A variation on this is to send one child onstage, suggest a Where, but ask those people watching to give the actor specific directions to follow as they tell him or her what to do. Directions such as, "You're slipping on ice. Your scarf blows off, and your ears are freezing. You see a big crack in the ice in front of you. Your skate gets caught in it, and you yell for help. Everybody's over at the bonfire, and no one hears you." It's a good way to initiate many of these exercises.

One former member of our Dramatics Club observed:

> We would send one person up and then choose some kids in the audience: "Okay, Joachim, tell her where she is," or "Charlotte, what's her body temperature, and what is she feeling?" or "Darren, what does she see, and what should she do now?" The person onstage acts out what they're telling her (or him) to do. Those in the audience don't have to feel too responsible because they're not being watched. But they do have to think of something, come up with some ideas, and it teaches them how to justify their actions.
>
> It also makes the child onstage much more comfortable being there. She becomes a puppet, loses the fear of being in front of everybody, and can then go on to the next step of taking total responsibility for what she's doing.

When

Most actors, directors, and teachers ask themselves and others only three of the W questions: Who, what, and where. Too often the When is left out, though it can be just as conclusive in the understanding and development of a story. The When often crosses over and combines with the other questions. Are you young and eager to learn everything right away, embarking on a new career, or overwhelmed and weary from a lifetime of responsibilities? These issues of When also pertain to Who. The actor cannot ignore them.

How, for instance, can anyone be onstage telling a story with the body and voice and not pay attention to When it occurs? A woman can go straight through a narrow doorway with ease today, but in previous centuries huge side panniers or hoop skirts made it difficult. Just as the historical period of the story must be explored, so must the time of year. Being outdoors is not the same on a cold day as on a warm one, or as you watch a tornado approach or stare at your brown grass after a drought. The time of day is also important. Is it morning when you are full of energy, or late when your eyes are burning from doing homework? And don't forget the time in the social life of your community. Is it a Fourth of July celebration, a pre-holiday rush, Election Day? Is this the week the circus is in town or a period when a crime wave has the whole neighborhood scared? Time of month, of year, the seasons—all are very important to the director and actor.

Actors should ask critical questions about what has happened to the character in the recent past, and what is expected to happen in the near future. These contribute to asking When.

If an actor comes onstage to reveal an important piece of news, the audience should know from the actor's behavior whatever is pertinent to the When of it. Has the character just heard it (he can't wait to tell it), or has he forgotten it for two days? The audience needs to know whether the character has been chased by an angry mob, just awakened from a sound sleep, or if it's been three days since her last meal. Is it right after a heavy lunch or vigorous exercise?

All the When exercises can be fun. Send two to four actors onstage and give them a Who, What, and Where. Let them decide on the When. Ask the others to guess the time frame of the improv. Or vice-versa, let those watching call out various Whens for the actors to play. (They could also change the Who or What, or both.)

For instance, the setup could be:

Who	Two leaders from opposing factions
What	Arguing an issue
Why	They want power. They feel insecure.
Where	In front of a big crowd
When	In a prehistoric era—as cavemen, or Before the time of Christ—as Roman senators, or During World War II—as dictators, or During the last election campaign—as politicians on TV

It's easy to see how games and exercises focusing on When can be used success-fully in school classes. Greg Tully, an HFDC alumnus, now a PhD in Psychology, remembers how proud he was when a history teacher asked him to write and present a Civil War scene with some other Dramatics Club members for a class period. They did so with great success, and all really learned that day's lesson. We will be exploring more uses of acting techniques in school in Chapter 10.

The When question can often be the seed for varied skits and the door to a lot of good ideas. More examples of When exercises appear at the end of this chapter.

HELPFUL TIPS

You can invent an endless array of games, exercises, and improvs using the ten ele-ments. The five Ws and the five senses can be gathered together, built up, combined, and recombined, one at a time, one after the other, or all together. Begin with a simple activity—moving a chair or a couple of props, perhaps a cap and magnifying glass. Send six or eight kids to the stage, singly, in pairs, or in groups, to work with the props. Call out one of the five Ws to start and watch their imaginations work.

One good rule that James Brennan always follows is that no one doing an improv is to stop it themselves. Only the leader makes that decision. That way they won't quit on you when they're coming up dry. Use your own judgment here; try not to stop an improv until something has been accomplished.

Be Specific
Urge the children to make the answers to the five Ws more and more specific as they do the games and exercises. An answer to "When," for example, is: "It's a lovely day." But a better answer is: "It's sunny and beautiful." Best of all might be something like:

"The air is so clear and the sun so bright, the light seems to bounce off the pavement and onto my body." This last one is full of specific sensory perceptions and prompts one's whole being to respond.

Find the Humor
Exploring humor and using surprising contrasts are useful techniques. There are disparate theories about what moves people to laughter—exaggeration, bizarreness, an unexpected twist are some of the explanations offered. For an actor it's useful to search for the answers in the play or the character, but it is perhaps more valuable to know that we can all be laughable. Sharing laughs is one of life's most healing activities.

We suggested to the kids that laughter occurring in the theater or anywhere else could really be just a very rapid series of sighs of relief that derive from the feeling "Oh, thank goodness, I'm not alone. I'm not the only person who does jerky or klutzy things. Nobody's perfect, thank God." Even the pompous VIP in a top hat can slip on a banana peel. But, of course, we must emphasize that hurting or humiliating someone by laughing *at* him or her is *never* condoned.

An old theatrical aphorism says it succinctly and with humor: Take care of the characters and the jokes will take care of themselves.

Use the Children's Own Experience
Encourage the children to find answers to the five Ws in themselves, the people they know, and their environment. Ask them to explore why they do certain things, what they're afraid of, what they love, what they long for. Let kids ask themselves, "How would I feel, or what would I be doing if I were that character?"

Try to set up an improv to use all five Ws, helping the kids become more involved in their own experiences. Create the Who, What, Why, Where, and When. Here are two examples:

> Three kids and a cop: It's a crowded city street, late on a hot, rainy night. The kids saw a mugging, but a cop won't believe them. He thinks they are up to some mischief.

> A group of students: In a classroom, the last period of the day in early spring. The teacher is late, and the kids are planning a joke. They want to be admired for their daring.

Using their own experiences offers another advantage: The more the youngsters believe they are bringing facts to you about their own lives that are new to you and that give you insight, the more they will welcome receiving information and directions from you.

Discussions
As you work through the five Ws with the children, we recommend that you gather everyone together after your group has completed some exercises or skits and discuss

the work. You should be cautious with this because it can be very tricky and counterproductive. Be careful to hold to a constructive track: "Did it work?" or "Did it do the trick?" Never use comparative or qualitative terms such as, "She was better than he was," or "That wasn't as good as the last one."

During a general discussion after a skit, one kid said that another's skit was better. We seized that moment and turned it into a discussion about how one skit is not better than another skit. We were not competing; we were all just trying to do our best.

Keep the Values Straight

Encourage the children not to go onstage to impress anyone, pass some kind of test, or be better than anyone else. Tell them that the primary task is to find the means with which to tell the story in the fullest, clearest, most interesting, exciting, and believable ways. And to tell it in their own ways. They can all help one another to do that.

Your Own Homework

Here's a small confession in the hope that it will help you. When we're relaxed, sitting in our living room, it's not hard at all to think of dozens of games, exercises, and improvisations. But there have been many times when, standing in front of an eager, energetic bunch of kids who are raring to go, the imaginative powers evaporate. Especially when shortness of time, discipline problems, or concerns about an excessively shy young actor are making it hard to concentrate. That's when we appreciate the time spent preparing for the meetings, as every teacher knows. For those of you who have no experience in teaching or have not managed the kind of sessions we've described in this book, here's some advice:

Think clearly about how you want to order your meetings and how to keep order in your meetings. Decide which technique works best to quiet your group down when you need to have them listen and stick to it. Since our first edition was published in 1997, we've heard more and more teachers complain about how much more difficult it is now to keep order and a certain amount of discipline in the classrooms. Many good teachers use clapping in different rhythms, which the kids must then follow and then stay quiet while they're listening to you or one of the actors onstage. A teacher in Dublin said she takes up a ridiculous pose physically and holds it. As the students see her, they must imitate that pose and keep very still. We confess we often used a whistle. Some use a bell. But don't use shouting. One teacher simply starts whispering. Believe it or not, it works. One young man simply stops and says, quietly, "Everyone who heard what I just said, raise your hands." If necessary he repeats that until they're all quiet, but he told me he usually only has to repeat it once. It's important to keep your agenda moving rapidly so that you don't lose the youngsters' attention.

Playwright and youth theater director Richard Carter is careful to establish work times and play times, as well as work spaces and play spaces. He lets his cast jabber or play for a few minutes before starting, then says, "O.K., it's time to go to work. If you're not in this scene and you need to talk, you may go outside." Decide what rule you want to make and determine to stick to it.

Before your group gathers, whenever you have the time, be your own teacher.

Start off by doing a relaxation exercise and let your ideas begin to flow. Think of what the kids like to do, what they talk about, what their big concerns, goals, and dreams are. Phrase them for yourself in terms of the five Ws and senses, and set up situations for the young people to play out. You can throw them out to the group and let the kids expand on them. If you want to develop them into scenes or skits for the following meeting, plan to ask one or more people to go up front with one goal to achieve, an intention, an action to perform—in other words, a What. Then send another person or group up front with an opposing What and consider the result. For instance:

> One group wants to plant a tree to beautify the neighborhood, but the other wants to widen the sidewalk to ease the crowding.

> Two or more football players are arguing with the referee about a penalty.

As we've said, opposing Whats usually lead to conflict situations, which are the essence of drama.

Next, review in your mind a couple of relaxation and warm-up exercises that work well. You can create some or look up new ones in this book. Also think of a skill that needs strengthening. You'll find examples of those in Chapter 3. Jot them all down on a card. Or you can check out the Leader's Guide Addendum at the end of this book.

If you are planning to begin work on a show soon, ask yourself some Who, What, Why, Where, and When questions about the characters in the show and their individual situations. Jot down some of the things you know about the story from reading the text and also the things you don't know, such as what has happened to the characters just before a scene begins. This will help in filling out or justifying the situations, the dialogue, and the actions of the characters. At the next meeting, toss all these jotted thoughts out to the kids to use as the basis for their improvs. If your children have been part of the search for answers and the finders of solutions, they won't forget them, or resist them, when the show is in production.

With all that done, write on a couple of file cards the agenda for the next session so that when your mind goes blank you can refer to the "safety net" in your pocket. You'll find some helpful lists in the back of this book. Of course, you must be prepared to forgo that agenda and go with what's working well at the moment.

Etienne DeCroux, the famous French master of mime, said that setting limits, rather than giving total freedom, is what leads to creativity. Peter Sellars, the opera director, has said, "The nightmare of all art, as well as of all politics, is generalities." If you simply tell the child to go and play, the child is lost. But give the child a dozen objects with which to create a village, and play begins immediately. Mary McDonnell, actress, observed (while playing a role in a wheelchair):

> I love requirements; the more the better. Great characters develop
> out of restricted situations. When people feel the limitations of
> life, something else takes over that's specific and colorful. We all
> become individualized by boundaries, not freedom.

In our Dramatics Club, we limited the options, spelled out the boundaries, and suggested specifics, giving each child a ladder with which to reach that imaginative plateau.

Let the suggestions in this chapter be a springboard for your own imagination as you seek ways to evoke the best acting your kids can do. (In Chapter 3, we'll discuss ways to sharpen your actors' skills.) Ultimately, aside from all the other perks you'll receive together, the shows you do will be a joy for you, the kids, and the audiences as well.

Additional Exercises, Improvs, and Games

FURTHER SENSORY EXERCISES

1. Wake up the five senses with suggestions.
Pretend it's 105 degrees in the shade and you can feel the sweat running down your back.

Try to see a tornado coming as the sky darkens quickly across the horizon. Do you hear a scream from that direction about a block away? Is it coming closer? Can you smell the dust swirling around in the air?

Where is the smell of that freshly baked pie coming from? Your own kitchen?

Eat an ice cream cone that is so cold it makes your teeth hurt. Can you taste chocolate bits in the ice cream?

You have been out in the very cold wind for more than three hours. Where was the wind hitting you? How strong was the wind? How did it sound? Where did it come from? What was the coldest body part? Chin numb? Toes aching? Fingers stiff? What body part starts warming up first? Does anything ache? Where? Do you find it impossible to move fast yet? How slowly does the body relax? Where first? Next? And so on.

2. Use the senses to develop a Who.
Send *five* children into the acting area. Each in turn is to enter and cross the stage from the far corner diagonally down to the near corner on the other side, but stopping a

moment in the center. Before each one enters, someone in the audience calls out Who the actor is to be.

Goal: To make the Who real to themselves by imagining and using the sensory elements involved. For example, the first boy is told to be an arthritic old man. Several senses come into play, as follows:

> Sight: His vision is poor.
> Hearing: Sounds seem muffled to the old man.
> Touch: He feels painfully stiff and dry in the mouth. Every joint
>   hurts when he moves.

The actor's behavior possibilities: He might walk slowly and carefully, not flexing his ankles. He might pull his shoulders up to his ears. He might strain to see the traffic signal. He might keep opening and closing his mouth, running his tongue over dry lips.

Extend the same exercise with five different young people, suggesting an activity or piece of business. (Reminder: In the theater, a piece of stage business means sitting down, opening a window, sweeping a floor, and so on.) Then explore the What and Why in turn.

Try asking the kids to enter one at a time and sit down, and to pantomime picking up a phone to make a call. The group gives the first girl in line a What and Why: For instance, she is calling the fire department because her house is on fire. The senses that come into play here are:

> Sight: Seeing flames at a window, smoke from under the door,
>   paint blistering off the walls
> Hearing: Flames crackling
> Smell: Heavy smoke, not as heavy near the floor
> Touch: Feeling extreme heat, shortness of breath, hands shaking

The actor's behavior possibilities: She could crawl to a chair, miming a towel over her mouth and nose, and coughing. Her eyes could open wide at the sight of flames. She might lift her head sharply at a loud sound and collapse for a moment before crawling off the stage.

An exercise like this can be extended by asking each child in turn to build upon what others have established before or by directing each person in turn to add a W or change it. You can give the tasks to whole groups, letting them create together. You can develop conflict situations by sending others onstage to use the same Where and When but acting out different Who, What, and Why answers.

3. Use the senses to develop a Where

This is a good exercise for younger children. Send about six youngsters up front at a time. They can start without words or by saying only their own or one another's names as they are walking, or by reciting the alphabet or a nursery rhyme—whatever releases them from having to think up words to say. Give them a Where that has strong sensory elements. For example:

In oozy mud	In a pile of dry leaves
On a hot beach	On a bed of sharp stones
On top of a mountain	In a haunted house
In a forest	In the Fun Palace
On a slippery sidewalk	In a shallow, rocky stream
On a train or subway or bus	In an approaching tsunami wave
In a snowstorm or rainstorm	On the second floor of a burning
On a roller coaster	building
In an old church	

EXERCISES USING THE 5 Ws

Here are various approaches to the five W choices, and some ways to present them, consistent with the age and skill of your young thespians. Use them as springboards for exercises, skits, and improvs. You can also build on them with other Ws.

Who

1. Bizarre characteristics

This is suitable for quite young children. Assign a child to play someone who:

Can move only in straight lines, or only in circles
Always wears long clown shoes
Is really a robot
Can't actually talk but can only growl or giggle

2. Extreme characteristics

This is also suitable for quite young children. Assign a child to play someone who:

Has no hands or feet	Knows no real language
Was brought up by apes	Is as big as a Sumo wrestler
Talks like a duck	Has a body that is made of water
Can only walk sideways	Can't talk, can only hiccup or growl
Keeps getting smaller and	
smaller, or taller and taller…	
like Alice In Wonderland	

Often young people's extreme shyness can be overcome by giving them certain strong or outlandish characteristics to play.

3. Animal traits

When director Moni Yakim was staging the opera *Gianni Schicchi* at the Metropolitan Opera Studio, he asked the singers to base their characterizations on animal observations. One strutted like a rooster, others twitched like a squirrel (good trick!), lumbered like an elephant, or prowled like a lion. It's a fun exercise for kids.

4. Sensory elements of character

Give the kids a character to play based upon a pronounced sensory element. For example, the director Lonny Chapman, who often gave his casts sensory ways of eliciting character traits, asked an actress who was playing a self-centered patronizing socialite to imagine she was bestowing her perfume on everyone who approached. He asked a man who was playing a lumbering boor to imagine that he was twice as heavy as he really was, and that his body extended out a foot beyond its real boundaries. This helped him to become clumsy, hostile, and overbearing.

5. Fantasy

A popular springboard for exercises is to encourage kids to play with fantasy, magic, and myth: King Midas, Tom Thumb, the Wicked Witch of the West, Puck, or Narcissus, who fell in love with his own image in a pool. From the movies come the figures Harry Potter, Superman, Darth Vader, Edward Scissorhands, Matilda, the girl with mean parents and teachers who could make things move magically, and countless others.

6. Clown faces and bodies for character ideas

Ask each young actor to draw a clown face with its own special feature and a clown body, and use that image in an improv or rehearsal. His or her clown face might have one highly raised eyebrow, tears trickling down one cheek, or a big lopsided grin. The body could have huge thumbs, a pointed head, massive shoulders, or stilt legs.

7. Hypocrisy

Assign the kids to play characters who do exactly what they abhor in others or engage in the very things their jobs are designed to fight. For example:

> A public groundskeeper tosses a candy wrapper behind him
> as he scolds people for littering
> Parents punish a child for cheating on a test, but evade
> income taxes
> The head of an agency appointed to erase corruption is guilty
> of using public funds to take vacations

8. Finding power

To help a young person play someone with power or a masterful personality, suggest that he or she:

> Treat everyone else as if they were only four years old.
> Teach a dog to heel.
> Pilot a space shuttle, concentrating on a computerized
>   control panel.

9. Shadow self

Ask two or three children to do an improv or skit with which they are already familiar. Then ask them to repeat it, while someone else onstage with them "shadows" one character, following him or her but saying aloud what he or she thinks the character is really thinking. The shadow should also do or nearly do what the character secretly wants to do.

For instance, Aaron, Kyle, and Amaury improvise a birthday party. Amaury, opening a gift, smiles and says, "Thank you, very much. That's so nice." But Kristine, the shadow, might say, "Yuk! Another crocheted pillow?! Kyle knows I need a new basketball!" Kristine might then try to shove the pillow back at Kyle. Shadows can go much deeper, but it takes time, trust, and insight before they do. Don't be afraid to let kids use their dark sides, to express fears, resentments, or rage.

10. Magical realism

This exercise can lead to joyful discoveries. It follows natural laws of realistic behavior but inserts one or two elements of magic into the story—for instance, everything a character touches sticks to his hand or starts to burn. In the movie *Big*, the only magical element is the granting of the boy's wish to be as big as a man. But then, what wonders ensue! Young people can use their "if only" dreams with soaring results.

11. Myths

The famous director Peter Brook said, "The distance to the audience is bridged by the energy of the actors." He strongly advocates exploring myths in exercises and improvs, and urged members of his international troupe to transform and to endow objects with magical or mystical qualities. Examples of magical objects abound in myths: the golden egg, the Holy Grail, the Sword in the Stone, and so on.

Give your actors an object and suggest they make up a skit that endows it with magical qualities:

> A girl puts on gloves that can heal people's wounds.
> A boy discovers a magnifying glass that allows him to read
>   the minds of tiny insects and frogs.
> Children feed the hungry with a food basket that magically
>   never empties.

There are many more ideas to be found in the ancient myths and in literature and films, especially fantasy and science fiction.

12. Contrasts
Have the kids improvise in pairs as highly contrasting characters:

> One feisty, the other timid
> One sleepy, the other raring to go
> One indecisive, the other bossy
> The jock and the librarian
> The enraged shopper and the bored clerk
> The slob and the neatness fanatic

13. Paradoxes
Let the kids explore contradictions within one Who, such as:

> A tiny person who wants to be a big boss and run
>   everything
> A straight-laced executive who tap-dances when she's alone
>   in elevators
> A hefty, muscular 200-pound wrestler who's afraid of mice

14. "What if"
You can do a variety of these, which invite the kids to act characters beginning with certain suppositions:

> What if each of your joints is rusty?
> What if you're invisible?
> What if you're a sumo wrestler?
> What if you can read everyone's mind—or you're afraid they can
>   read yours?

15. Old age
To help a young actor play someone who is very old, ask him or her to repeat an action such as moving an object, doing knee-bends, or flexing the arms, legs, back, and so on, until utterly tired out. Then ask that actor to translate that fatigue into the entire body as he or she walks across the stage.

Or ask her to imagine she's looking through dense fog, or trying to hear nearly inaudible faraway bells.

Or imagine that he's very, very lonely and hasn't talked to anyone for days. (Every person needs connection with others—not admiration necessarily, or approval, just some kind of anchor—and the very old often lack this.)

Or ask her to endow a body part with a bad toothache—like her knee or hip or neck.

16. Different ages
Ask the kids to do some activity or handle some object. Each actor, or group of actors, must pretend to be a different age: an infant, a first grader, a teenager, and so on through the early twenties, middle age, and the senior years. They must deal with the object accordingly. For instance:

> An infant puts the object right into its mouth.
> A first grader tries to get credit for sharing it.
> An elderly person contemplates it or tries to remember whose it is.

What
1. Repeating one's name
This sounds silly, but it does work. The actors' task is to repeat their own names as many times as necessary while playing a strong action, until they feel they've really tried hard to accomplish it. They could act out the following:

> Looking for a relative among the missing
> Signing their name over and over to get through red tape
> Trying to get chosen for a job, a team, or a privilege
> Trying to regain lost memories

2. Using one's name once
The actors say their own names once as if they were:

> Giving their name to a doctor or nurse
> Deciding whether to tell the truth or not
> Entering a beauty contest or a spelling bee
> Meeting the president or a movie star

See also Session 5 of the Leader's Guide.

3. Exchanging names
Here, the actors speak one another's names in the following situations:

> Explorers in a pitch-black cave trying to find one another
> Movers handling a large glass window
> Spies meeting in secret to share information
> A politician heckled by a citizen
> Fashion models entering a runway
> Homeless people fighting for a spot to sleep
> Two thieves in action
> A judge and the accused

4. Conflict situations

Strong intentions and the obstacles that get in the way give rise to workable improvisations. The same is true of a full-length play, in which conflict is essential. Set up conflict situations for the kids by giving someone a strong action to play—a What and an obstacle to overcome before he or she can accomplish it. You can often send someone onstage to play an opposing character. Here are some situations:

> One actor is trying to reach a drowning person while swimming
>   against a strong current.
> One actor is trying to catch a train as the suitcase breaks open.
> An employer refuses to give an interview to a job seeker.
> A cop won't listen to a suspected law-breaker's explanation.
> A bus driver won't let a passenger on because she is short a
>   nickel for the fare.

5. Hiding an object

For this easy What exercise, try giving the students a single object, one at a time, to take onto the stage with a direction to hide it, as if:

> One is setting up a surprise for her mother's birthday.
> Another is destroying evidence.
> A third is preparing to run away.
> A fourth is trying to get even with a bully by hiding the bully's
>   favorite object.

Why

1. Why with feelings

Use any of the Whats in the Hiding an Object exercise, but add a Why feeling. Adding this new factor will lead to a more complex character and action, such as:

> Setting up a surprise for mother's birthday because she feels sad
>   for her mother's loneliness
> Destroying evidence because he is terrified at being imprisoned
> Running away because she is furious at her father's neglect
> Getting even because he's hurt and ashamed

2. Extending the Why questions

You can ask an actor to keep repeating a scene refining the answers to Why in terms of plot development.

For example, in a scene, a boy approaches an older person to confront him or her.

> Why? To declare that he's innocent of an accusation.
> Why? Because he'll be kicked out of school if found guilty and
>   his father will be furious.

Why? Because the father always thinks the boy is a no-good.

Why? Because the boy could never stand up for himself.

Why is he able to do it now? Because his girlfriend is watching him. She knows he is innocent and won't let him take any more humiliation. He feels ashamed in front of her if he balks.

And so on and so forth. Many background sources can be explored. *But it almost always comes down to feelings.*

3. Using secrets

Ask the kids to print on slips of paper their secrets, things they'd never tell a soul because the secrets made them feel too ashamed, too embarrassed, too guilty, too vulnerable or too fearful of consequences—things they're afraid of, things they've done that were wrong, thoughts they regret, and so on. Tell them not to sign the slips—just drop them into a hat and then pass them out blindly. Each actor then draws a slip and uses the secret written on it to build improvs or skits with the anonymous Whys as reasons for behavior or character elements. You can call on two or three actors to get together to create a skit by creating the Whos, Wheres, and Whens. Or you can give them the place, time, and activity and have them improvise a scene based on the secret Whys they have drawn. For example:

Actor A draws a slip that reads "I hate my father." And actor B draws a slip that reads, "I don't think anybody likes me." They might get together and in a few minutes come back and improvise a scene in which "B" plays a father who is pushing his son "A" to join a team, club or activity, so others will admire him or so that the father will be esteemed. "A" resists because he doesn't want to do anything his father wants him to do.

Or Actor "C" draws a slip that reads "I am afraid of heights." He then creates a skit in which his buddies try to get him to dive off a high tower.

4. Facial Expressions

As we have said, feelings are usually what cause people to do or at least try to do certain things, that is, certain Whats. On the following page are drawings used by deaf people, or hearing people signing with deaf people. The drawings help to communicate words for feelings or emotions. They are so amazingly expressive that we can't resist putting them into a theater game for kids. No, Marlon, we don't want to teach kids to "indicate." We just thought it would be fun to use.

Copy the drawings onto individual cards. Ask two to four kids each to close their eyes and pull out or choose one face, then get into a huddle, and give themselves the Whos, Wheres, and Whens. Then have each one take on that feeling expressed in the drawing and start to DO whatever that feeling makes him or her want to do within that situation with those others. For example: suppose Dan draws "ecstatic," Aiden draws "mischievous," Lisa draws "disapproving," and Mandy draws "anxious." They might decide that Dan, Aiden, and Mandy are students and Lisa is a teacher. They are in a school hall near the lockers before

HOW DO YOU FEEL TODAY?

  AGGRESSIVE AGONIZED ANXIOUS APOLOGETIC ARROGANT BASHFUL BLISSFUL

BORED CAUTIOUS COLD   CONCENTRATING CONFIDENT CURIOUS DEMURE

DETERMINED DISAPPOINTED DISAPPROVING DISBELIEVING DISGUSTED DISTASTEFUL EAVESDROPPING

ECSTATIC ENRAGED ENVIOUS EXASPERATED EXHAUSTED FRIGHTENED FRUSTRATED

GRIEVING GUILTY HAPPY HORRIFIED HOT HUNGOVER HURT

HYSTERICAL IDIOTIC INDIFFERENT INNOCENT INTERESTED JEALOUS JOYFUL

LOADED   LONELY LOVESTRUCK MEDITATIVE   MISCHIEVOUS   MISERABLE NEGATIVE

OBSTINATE OPTIMISTIC PAINED PARANOID PERPLEXED PRUDISH PUZZLED

REGRETFUL   RELIEVED SAD SATISFIED PARANOID SHEEPISH SHOCKED SMUG

SURLY SURPRISED SUSPICIOUS SYMPATHETIC THOUGHTFUL UNDECIDED WITHDRAWN

64 All Kids Can Act

lunchtime. Aiden might think up a prank, which delights Dan, who urges him on, but Lisa suddenly appears and catches them at it. Mandy sees it happening and is afraid that the boys will be punished. Since Aiden is her brother, she is anxious about what her parents will say and tries to draw the teacher's attention away. Then we'll see what happens as the improv skit proceeds.

Or Sally could draw "guilty" while Marissa draws "hurt." Sally could be trying to apologize to Marissa for insulting her, but Marissa is too hurt to forgive her. So—will she or won't she?

Where

1. From familiar to imaginary places

This is suitable for quite young children. For instance, you may begin with a girl on a big ship rolling on the ocean. But if she has never been on a ship or at sea, suggest that she start with what she knows, such as the feeling of trying to get her balance on a bicycle or Rollerblades. Then add the unfamiliar, imaginary elements: the salty taste in the air, the feel of the wind, the foamy whitecaps visible from the railing on the deck, and all the rest. Give her a simple activity, playing shuffleboard or carrying drinks. Ask two or three others to join her.

2. Paintings or news pictures

For those more advanced, begin with a famous image—Edward Hopper's nighttime lunch-counter painting, *Night Hawks*, for example—or use a picture from the newspaper—the Astrodome in New Orleans after Hurricane Katrina, an anti-war demonstration outside, president Bush's ranch in Texas, the White House or the Capitol steps, the site of an earthquake in Kashmir, a gate where strikers picket in front of a factory, the finish line of a marathon. Have a few kids go off to prepare a skit using those people in that place.

3. Circus

Set up a scene with each child in the role of a different member of the circus; each should concentrate on just one sensory element of the Where. For instance, the animal trainer could concentrate on the sounds of the animals. The ringmaster could smell the sawdust underfoot. The tightrope walker could concentrate on the feel of the rope under her feet; the clown on the feel of a rubber nose or big floppy shoes; the vendor on the weight of the hot dog tray, and so on. Then signal the kids to exchange roles and find more sensory elements in the new character they've chosen. They should do all this as they improvise behavior and relationships with one another during or before the circus.

4. Emotional relationship to a place

It's good to encourage emotional expression whenever you can, but without letting it threaten anyone's privacy. One approach is to ask the children to name places that make them sad, curious, or mad, or that fill them with wonder, disgust, or fear. If you see, as they name and describe the places, that others are responding positively, have them start an improv set in that place. Prompt them to answer the other W questions for one another.

5. Familiar places
In this exercise the Where is the child's own home. Have him or her pretend to come into a room still very sleepy and see something unexpected that wakes him or her up with a jolt. (The kids are apt to get a little silly on this one, but let them have fun.)

6. Absurdities
Here, one young actor talks to another:

> In a church or funeral parlor—but as if they were in an amusement park
> At a box office ticket window—but as if the ticket seller were a big star
> On a short flight of stairs—but as if they were climbing a mountain

7. Where people gather
If you want to involve a large group of kids all at once, suggest scenes taking place at auctions, sales, demonstrations, trials, town meetings, rallies, football or basketball games, or prizefights, and so on.

When
1. Time of day
Put a couple of actors onstage who respond in opposite ways to the time of day. For example, the early morning eager beaver versus the one who just can't face the day after awakening, much less talk to people.

2. Season
Prepare a wintertime skit about the Polar Bear Club in which brave souls go swimming outdoors. Others could be standing by, wrapped in jackets and scarves, begging them to stop or cheering them on.

3. Historical incidents
To help children with their history lessons, choose stories from their history books, such as:

> At a meeting between the leaders of two opposing armies, one of them surrenders.
> Gold miners working in the Black Hills of South Dakota try to force the Indians off their land.
> Suffragists marching for the vote are arrested by policemen.

Thomas Edison explains his lightbulb to people who have
tried to blow it out like a candle.
Two people trying to find their child after the tsunami hit,
or children trying to find their parents.

4. What if?
Set up improvisations that might have changed history:

The Spanish queen Isabella refusing to give her backing
to Columbus
Someone stopping John Wilkes Booth before he kills President
Abraham Lincoln
Frenchmen deciding not to follow Joan of Arc into battle

THE FIVE Ws IN COMBINATION

Most exercises and games can be developed into improvs simply by making additional choices based on the five Ws. A list of them follows later to stimulate your imaginations when needed. Here are some introductory exercises:

1. Line up five or six children.

2. Ask each one in turn to do a simple activity such as moving a chair, with a different What in mind. For example:

Prepare for a meeting
Fix a lightbulb
Get away from a mouse

3. Ask them next to move the chair in order to fix a light bulb, but this time as if they were each a different Who:

An anxious clerk
A weakling
An arrogant movie star

4. Continue this way with the rest of the Ws. Tasks can be done one at a time or in groups, and combined and built upon. Start simply and gradually add complications.

5. You can use a sensory element as a springboard for an improv. Ask three or four actors to imagine a ticking sound. When you ask the group observing them what

the sound is, they may say, "A time bomb." Then ask them who the actors should be. Someone may answer, "Newspaper reporters." Ask what they are doing. "Covering a revolution." Why? "They want to get the story" and so on. That is, keep throwing out questions, continuing with the five Ws.

6. Using the same approach, build improvs on any other sensory element or a combination of them. For example:

> Taste: One person bites into something bitter and hard, another into a sweet, gooey roll, and so on.
> Smell: One sniffs bacon, another smoke, newly cut grass, and so on.

7. Build up the five Ws, one on the other: Ask the same actor to do each one, or a different actor can add an element when his or her turn comes. Some further ideas to toss out:

> Who: An arthritic old person
> What: Trying to get help
> Why: Afraid to cross the street alone
> Where: A busy intersection
> When: Just before Christmas
> Who: A parent
> What: Disciplining the children
> Why: To make them take more responsibility
> Where: In the garage
> When: A morning when you're late for work
> Who: A teenager
> What: Trying to find shelter
> Why: You're scared, cold, and hungry
> Where: Near railroad tracks
> When: A January evening

8. Have five or six kids do the same W, but keep refining it as each one takes a turn.

9. Keep one actor onstage and have each of the others enter, bringing a new idea.

10. Tell several kids to go on at the same time with the same task, like painting a fence, but with each one displaying a different Who and Why.

11. Getting more specific is almost always possible and lots of fun. You can, for instance, assign an activity to a group with four of the Ws. Then ask the kids in the group to zero in on the one W that's been left unanswered to make the activity more

detailed and specific. For example: Ask someone to move a chair and suggest the following Ws:

> What: Vacuuming the floor
> Why: To make money. Afraid of poverty.
> Where: A rich old lady's house
> When: End of a long, hard day

Now, zero in on the Who. Give each child, in turn, another specific detail to add to what the previous child did when he or she played the house-cleaning person moving the chair. Each one thus adds to the characteristics that have already been played; for instance:

> The person has trouble breathing…
> Has a sprained ankle…
> Hates the work…
> Mutters constantly, and is…
> Compulsive about cleaning up every speck.

If the last child to do the exercise still remembers all the different elements of the Who, he or she certainly won't be playing a one-dimensional or "cardboard" character, and all those character elements will be seen in the way the actor moves the chair.

Another exercise is to ask them to be themselves and zero in on the Why, Where—or any of the other Ws—in a similar way.

Ideas for Improvisations
Still emphasizing the five Ws, set up scenes for the kids to act out based on the following situations.

1. Give two actors a problem to solve, like trying to get across a big puddle, and give each an opposing word for the type of Who to play from the examples below. When the actors choose their opposing words, remind them that they must decide *what* that type of person *does*.

hot/cold	movie star/fan	smart/stupid
bold/timid	optimistic/pessimistic	impish/serious

2. Hand three actors different objects with which to improvise:

> A hat, a ball, and an apple
> A cup, a towel, and a pillow
> A book, a key, and a mask

3. Do a scene around a character who can't hear, or see, or talk. Here you can let the group choose the five Ws. Discuss the senses and what it would feel like to lose them.

4. Invent skits based on family rituals—birthdays, holidays, beginnings of vacations, and even Dad's or Mom's daily return from work.

5. Invent skits based on problem situations to solve. For example:

> Who: Three friends
> What: Trying to gather enough money between them to buy
> sodas
> Why: They're poor and very thirsty
> Where: A small grocery store
> When: A 102-degree summer day

6. Make a list of extreme traits and create improvs based on them. Three or four children each choose a different one to play:

biggest	tiniest	speediest	slowest
strongest	weakest	coldest	hottest
smartest	most stupid	most dangerous	

7. Here are lists of disparate choices from each of the five W categories. Place any three objects in the acting area, such as a book, a comb, a cap, newspapers, cloth, a phone. Call on two actors. Let each choose one item each from the Who list, one item together from the What list, and one item together from the Why list so that they are two different people trying to accomplish the same thing for the same reason. You select one item from the Where and When lists for them to use. Tell them their only dialogue will be the poem "Jack Be Nimble," or any other nursery rhyme. They should keep repeating that as dialogue while they are picking up and putting down or handing each other these three objects, or somehow using them, imagining themselves in a situation developed from a combination of these W choices.

Who:

Bully	Striker	Scientist
Homeless person	Cop	Escaped prisoner
Beggar	Politician	Rebellious kid
Show-off	Crash victim	Carnival barker
Lawyer	Preacher	Cheerleader
Very old person		

What:

Getting warm	Solving a problem
Escaping from jail	Reassuring a teammate

Keeping people away	Soothing a depressed friend
Breaking off a friendship	Denying an action
Deciding on a law	Denying blame

Why:

Wants to survive	Wants to become famous
Can't understand	Feels humiliated
Needs to know	Wants to escape responsibility
Needs approval	Overwhelmed by work
Concerned about others	Needs to prove courage
Feels jealous	Feels scared
Feels hot and exhausted	Feels weak and starving
Feels strong and powerful	Feels rewarded
Wants power	Feels ashamed

Where:

In a supermarket	At a hotel
In a kitchen	In the principal's office
In a hospital	In a control tower
In a sewer	At the U.S. Congress
At a carnival	In a museum

When:

At midnight	After hearing a secret
A cold winter	While lost in a jungle
A hot August	After being shipwrecked
After winning a prize	The last quarter of the game
Before making a speech	After being chased by a mugger

Later on the young people will drop the nursery rhymes and create their own dialogue.

8. Nonsense sentences are described in Session 6 of the Leader's Guide. Here are four dialogues for the kids to try that can make sense in many different ways depending on choices the actors make—that is, they take their meanings from the situations invented by the participants. Give three pairs of actors a set of cards with some of the nonsense sentences typed on them. One child is to be "A," the other "B." Each pair in private makes up a situation using any of the five Ws and the senses. Then they perform the nonsense dialogue. The last of the four examples here is mostly numbers:

A: I want you to take this.	**B:** Why?
A: It will help.	**B:** But I don't want it.
A: Now, please. Cooperate.	**B:** But I have been.
A: So, keep it up.	**B:** I can't. I'm sick of it.
A: Do it!	**B:** No!

A: Is that right?	B: Yes, I think so.
A: Are you sure?	B: Sure, I'm sure.
A: I wish I had as much confidence as you.	B: I don't know what you mean.
A: I mean I'm just not as certain.	B: Everything will be okay.

A: So?	B: Take a deep breath and begin.
A: You first.	B: No, you go ahead.
A: Really?	B: Sure. I'll follow you.
A: Now?	B: Now.

A: 158	B: 64
A: 96	B: 172
A: 172	B: What?
A: 172	B: Can't be.
A: It is.	B: It won't work.

It's fun to create more yourself, or ask the kids to do it. Just come up with some ideas for Whos to use with nonsense dialogue, and let the kids onstage or the audience suggest the What, Why, Where, and When.

9. For the next meeting, invent the first and last lines of a skit to create. For example:

First line: "What are you guys doing here?"
Last line: "So just forget it. I'm telling you, forget it!"

Chapter Three
Developing Skills

USING THE BASIC SYSTEM we've been describing will, of course, be even more rewarding as your young actors sharpen some important skills. As their voices become clearer, their bodies more flexible, and their concentration stronger, their work will be better. And as they learn to trust you, one another, and themselves, and to follow directions with ease, they'll have more fun doing shows.

VOICE

One of the amusing paradoxes about doing shows with children is that there is a constant battle to lower the volume level of the group and to raise the volume level of the performer. Insisting that anyone who is speaking in the meetings as well as on the stage must be heard by everyone else is a necessary rule.

If you are a singer or voice teacher or can conscript one to help you, you should teach some of the basic good vocal practices to the kids for singing and speaking. Otherwise, keep reminding your charges to take deep breaths; relax the shoulders, necks, and jaws; and remember that their best friend in the back row wants to hear them. Assign various children as monitors to sit far away from the stage and let you know when they can't hear or understand something. Generally, when your performers have heard "Louder! I can't hear you" five or six times, the volume and clarity will improve. They'll begin to project in self-defense.

An actress who was working in the Pulitzer Prize–winning play *Look Homeward, Angel* on Broadway some years ago, remembers that Anthony Perkins left the show after playing the lead for a year or so, and his replacement lacked experience in large theaters, so his vocal projection was weak. The director, George Roy Hill, sent the actress to the back of the theater to rehearse an entire scene with the actor, who remained standing on the stage. It worked, and it might work for you.

How well a voice can be heard depends a lot on where it is directed. If a girl is standing near the front edge of the stage (the "apron") with her back to the audience and is talking to another actor near the back wall of the stage, she reduces her chance of being heard by half, or more. The same applies if she's looking at her feet or a prop on the floor.

Actors should, whenever possible, "open out" to the audience, turning their bodies a bit toward the audience even if they are addressing another character directly to their right or left. This helps the audience to see and hear better.

When you're directing a show you can solve problems of audibility in the way you "block" the show—that is, by directing the movements and positions of the actors. One of our Dramatics Club members, Tony Vairo, recalled this episode:

> When we were rehearsing *South Pacific*, several sailors and nurses were onstage when their Captain was about to make an entrance from stage left. One of the little sailors was supposed to yell "Hey, here comes the Captain!" But we could never hear him, so the director asked another sailor to read the line. Suddenly all the kids became quiet as they shuffled around nervously, and one of them said, "You know, that's the only line he has." So, of course, the little sailor retrieved his line, and we found another way to focus the Captain's entrance. Two sailors looked offstage left and ran over to the other nurses and sailors. Then the little sailor ran over to the group, turned left, and saluted.

In other words, if you can't direct the audience's attention by sound, try it with movement. We will deal with that in more detail in Chapter 6.

In skits and exercises the actors can begin to learn the skills of helping themselves. That girl with her back to the audience could find a reason to walk upstage where she could face the audience and address the other actor. Or she could have motioned him to come down to her. Or she could have looked back, addressed him briefly, then turned downstage as if trying to picture what she was saying in her mind as she was saying it. This can be performed quite naturally. At the Trinity Repertory Theater, in Providence, Rhode Island, director Adrian Hall reminded us that people do not always look at the person they are talking to. They look occasionally, perhaps to check the reactions. The listener more often looks at the speaker, because we listen with our eyes as well as our ears, by watching the speaker's face and body language.

We simply tell the children: "If we can't see you, hear you, or understand you, we won't know the story."

Children's vocal power or lack of it often has more to do with their sense of themselves than with physical ability or learned technique. Remember in Chapter 2, for example, the girl's change in confidence and vocal presence when she was asked to play her father in an improv.

If young people understand that the way they use their voices helps them to tell the story, they become freer in the sounds they make.

You can help them by devising games primarily for the voice. Give them a nursery rhyme such as "Jack, Be Nimble." Ask them to say it and act it out in different ways:

> With a voice as big as the sea
>
> With a voice like a machine, a typewriter, or a hammer
>
> Like an English butler
>
> Like a ghost
>
> Like a loudspeaker announcer or sports commentator
>
> As if talking with a deaf person who reads lips.

We often began the meetings of the Young Angels Theatre Company by having half the members go to the "back of the house" or the auditorium, and the other half up onto the stage. The ones in back were to raise their hands as soon as they could hear the speaker onstage clearly. Then one at a time each actor onstage had to keep repeating a tongue twister until all those in the back had raised their hands. We later extended the exercise by adding "as ifs" to the tongue twister, such as "As if you're blaming someone for a bad mistake," or "As if you're a detective lining up clues."

BODY DEVELOPMENT

If actors are nimble and relaxed, they can move more smoothly and quickly onstage and will be less prone to injury in energetic scenes.

Stretching, loosening, and shaking exercises are good ways to begin your sessions. So are light aerobic exercises—jumping jacks, running in place, or arm and leg stretches. Ask any physical education instructor, athlete, or physical therapist for advice about some safe exercises to do regularly with your group. Many videotapes, pamphlets, and books are available on the subject.

If yoga or t'ai chi is your thing, they're great. Pass on what you can of your knowledge. Any kind of balancing exercise is good for strength and concentration. Isometrics, even simple ones such as pushing one hand against the other, are helpful.

Also, dancing and moving with strong rhythms are usually a joy for the kids. Put on music and ask everyone to move around the room shaking, wiggling, and dancing in any way they want. It's a productive way to warm up at the beginning of a meeting.

No matter how strong or physically adept anyone is, relaxation remains the most necessary ingredient of good bodywork. Not a falling-asleep limpness but a gentle awareness and alertness are the goal. Perceiving things in an intuitive manner, a valuable skill for actors, is achieved most often when they are relaxed and tranquil. A television director once observed that when Marlon Brando moved his head around now and then, even in a scene, he was often doing it just to relax.

James Brennan had this to say:

> When the kids find out these relaxation skills are effective ways of unwinding, in tests and sports as well as theater, they will go to great lengths to practice them. On the other hand, this is a sensitive area because if the kids suspect anything artsy or phony from those they perceive as "dabbling dilettantes," they will go to great lengths to avoid them.

Physical Expressiveness

"I don't know what to do with my hands!" This is often said by amateur actors and often thought, but not admitted, by professional actors. The problem occurs because many of us are not always physically expressive. Normally we only speak with our voices and sometimes our faces, but not with the rest of our bodies—at least not when we're on a stage or in front of a camera.

The exercises and techniques we have described usually lead automatically and logically to physical expressiveness while playing a role. But when there's time, additional exercises can free the body so that it can help us tell the story. Some teachers suggest that acting students do exercises or scenes in masks or, as we mentioned before, in gibberish, so that young actors discover they must use more of their bodies to make a scene clear. We often suggest that they imagine the audience is deaf or speaks a different language. If you know sign language, it would be great to teach it to the members of your group. Many new classroom teachers are using it as a teaching tool even with hearing students. Actors must make clear what is happening, but without "indicating" or "playing charades."

One of the dead giveaways of inexperienced acting is the tendency of many kids to hold their elbows close to their bodies and gesture up and down with their arms and hands outward together. It's usually the result of feeling an impulse to move but not knowing what to do or fearing to do it wrong. We've never seen anyone in real life gesture that way. Sometimes a person may move with just one arm from the closed-in elbow, but almost never both at the same time. Urge your young actors to use one or both WHOLE arms. Bring them away from the body or let them be still.

An exercise that's fun for physical expressiveness is to isolate individual parts of the body and then apply an adjective and a verb: happy feet that dance; worried shoulders that tense up; nervous fingers that drum on the table; and so on. (One fifth grader suggested, "How about tired butts?")

Problems people have with physical expressiveness are commonly found at opposite ends of the spectrum: they do too much or too little. Professional directors have been known to stand in the back of the theater calling out, "Make it bigger!" or, sitting in the front row, they urge, "Keep it full, but tone it down." A good professional actor can make the adjustment and still keep doing what the character should be doing. But this type of direction is hard for kids to follow, so keep in mind the advantage of giving them examples by transforming adjectives into verbs and actions.

The objective should be to keep the acting honest whether you're in a large auditorium or a small room by adjusting the size of the physical expressiveness to fit the space. The Mobile Statuary exercise is excellent for developing this skill (see page 81).

CONCENTRATION

A lack of concentration by an actor is commonly seen in films when the scene involves a driver and a companion in a car. Zooming along, the actor in the driver's seat often turns his head to talk to his companion, taking his eyes off the road for such a long time that he surely would have hit someone or driven off into a ditch. The actor who rarely looks in the mirror or to the right or left when he turns shows a total lack of attention to the details of what one really does when driving a car.

Luciano Pavarotti once said, "Concentration is a big skill in opera." It certainly is in acting. So what is it?

It is not staring intensely at a spot on the wall. It is taking in the detail, not just looking at it. It is the result of a passionate desire to know the answers to questions and a desire to accomplish something, to test yourself, or to win. It is paying attention to what's happening at each moment, not kicking yourself for something you did five minutes ago or worrying about something that might happen five minutes from now.

Think how easy it is to concentrate on a murder mystery when you're dying to know who did it. You want to stimulate the curiosity of your young people. Give them a passionate need to know, to solve, and thus to create. (Think how much you concentrate on the tennis ball as it speeds toward the racket.) Then inspire them to win. And help them become so specific about the story they're telling that concentration is natural and powerful. Discipline will automatically follow and better acting will be the result.

Of course, acute observation is the partner of good concentration. The famous actress and teacher Stella Adler told her students that when she was a little girl her father would come home late at night and wake her up to demand that she describe to him six people that she saw that day, and describe head to toe what they were wearing. Now that seems a bit extreme, especially to do to a child. But training yourself to remember everything about at least three people you saw the day before will surely help your acting.

Most theater games and exercises we have already discussed will lead to better concentration, particularly those involving work on the senses. But some, like Mirror and Slow Motion (see Session 2 in the Leader's Guide) are especially helpful. You probably know many concentration games or will make up your own. We have provided a few more at the end of this chapter.

Again, make sure that relaxation precedes these exercises, for tension is the enemy of concentration. Lee Strasberg, director of the Actors Studio, often observed that you cannot think when your body is tense. If you're trying to move a heavy piano, you can't think about multiplication tables without risking a broken foot. So, at the very least, remind everyone to keep the shoulders down and do a quick "muscle check" of the whole body to ensure that no muscles are tight and rigid anywhere.

When the whole group is relaxed, all focused on the same goals, you can arrive at the ideals of trusting in one another and achieving excellent ensemble work.

WORKING AS AN ENSEMBLE

The dictionary defines *ensemble* as "a group constituting an organic whole or producing together a single effect." Good ensemble acting is not easy to achieve, even with professionals, but it delivers a big payoff. It means that everyone is equally important and pays close attention to what others onstage are doing and saying. It means everyone is working together to tell the same story for the audience and to make it interesting, believable, enjoyable, and clear. And nobody steals the spotlight.

Safety in Numbers

Good, strong ensemble work can often save the show. One of our eight-year-old boys landed the role of a mischievous South Sea native who makes an uptight nurse so mad she chases him all over the stage. In the first performance, after learning that the school principal was in the audience, the youngster became so nauseated from stage fright that he ran to the bathroom just as his cue came up. A mother who was posted backstage grabbed another child who had a nonspeaking part in the scene: "Maureen, you do it; you've seen it in rehearsals." So Maureen played the whole scene for him. And Debbie, the nurse, picked up the scene without a blink. She immediately understood what had happened and knew Maureen could do it. The young actor made up for it in the other three performances—when the principal wasn't there.

An excellent exercise that helps to develop a tight ensemble is in Session 3 of the Leader's Guide; it's called Circle: 1–50. We strongly recommend using it.

Trust

Trust may not be correctly termed a skill, but it is necessary when children are doing shows together. The actors need to feel safe with one another. The ability to trust can be developed, and it is particularly essential to good ensemble work. But never push a child who resists the trust-building exercises, and remember that trust is a very difficult thing to revive if it is broken. No child should be forced to do an exercise or game he resists or fears. It could turn him away from all the benefits of the process.

A basic trust exercise is based on a game that children often play. One child in the center of a tight circle of friends closes his or her eyes, turns around, and falls backward into the arms of whoever is there. The exercise, Relaxation and Trust, is described in detail in Session 7 of the Leader's Guide. James Brennan described extensions of that exercise with some fourth- through eighth-grade children:

> When the kids were a little older and more adept, we invented a production of *Alice in Wonderland* requiring careful preparation and rehearsal. In the beginning, the scene was bucolic, and then Alice began chasing the rabbit all around the area and up a ladder. The entire company ran onstage and with a spotlight only on her, she leaned out to see the rabbit and did a "forward roll" into space and was caught in or on the arms of everyone in the company. It became an ensemble piece as she rolled on, all the way across the stage and down to the floor. It was very physical. She was not an acrobat, not even a dancer.

One chilly October afternoon, our family was in a stadium watching a football game. The Penn State mascot was dressed as a lion. Each time Penn State scored, the lion jumped onto the raised hands in the first row of the student section. Prone and stiff, the mascot was lifted row after row all the way to the top of the very high stadium and all the way back down. Total trust.

If you plan to involve your kids in any kind of activity like this but have no experience with it, it is clearly necessary that you seek professional guidance, perhaps from a local gym teacher.

The Actors' Trust Fund

Trust isn't automatic, but it can be learned by example and through experience. Actors must be able to trust one another just as dancers, acrobats, and surgical teams must. An actor needs to know that a door won't be opened in his or her face, that a staged fight won't inflict pain, and that everyone onstage will fulfill their obligations to the play.

An actress we know was on camera during a live broadcast of a soap opera when a fellow actor totally forgot his lines and simply walked off the set. She had to improvise alone for the five minutes left in the scene. She ad-libbed it well, but that breach of trust made her wary about doing live television after that.

If actors cannot trust one another, they can't relax and concentrate. And without concentration the reality of the acting suffers and the audience tunes out.

James Brennan climbs, leaps, and dances from one elevated space to another in his Broadway shows, but he always tries an activity himself before asking any of his student actors to do it. Then he carefully coaches them through it. Kids are nearly always brave and eager; they want to try everything. But they are sometimes careless. Having established trust, never attempt any unusual physical activity unless you have total confidence in what you are doing.

THE ABILITY TO FOLLOW DIRECTIONS

There may be several reasons why people don't follow directions. Perhaps they don't hear them, because the director isn't loud or clear enough, or there is too much other noise, or they simply aren't listening. Knowing your own group of kids and what works best for them, you'll be able to deal with those problems.

Perhaps they don't understand the directions. Some actors might protest that they don't see the reason for a direction. "Why would I go over to the table and around the couch?" You're the director, and they are kids, not experienced actors, so most of the time you may have to explain the reason. But when you think the child can handle it, just say, "You have to figure out a reason. I've got to get you over there to draw the audience's attention."

In the early days of the Actors Studio, the director Elia Kazan made it clear that the actor's job is to follow direction and justify it, to make it real and reasonable to the audience—even if the director is only using it to balance the stage picture or change the focus of the audience. To help us learn to do that, he gave his actors the Justifying Three Moves exercise. One person would make three arbitrary, unrelated movements—for example, a kick, a turn, and a handclap—quickly and without pre-planning, and then repeat them in the same order and justify them by putting them into a context of logical behavior. You'll find a description of this exercise in Session 10 in the Leader's Guide.

Be aware, though, that it's hard to avoid planning moves ahead, as well as the justification for them; doing that, of course, negates the reason for the exercise, which is to develop the ability to follow directions quickly and spontaneously and make them seem real.

We overcame that trap by asking the other members of the group to give the performer the moves that he or she must make and justify. If, in the first few attempts with this exercise, the performer is stymied and can't seem to come up with a reason or justification, be prepared to suggest a few: looking for something, being mad at yourself, exercising, trying on clothes, dancing, and so on. Or better, ask those who are watching to begin supplying the justifications. The children will all want to do it because it's fun and takes the pressure off everyone.

A refinement of this exercise may help a child to follow a direction. Name a particular sense—Sight, Hearing, Smell, Taste, Touch—and then ask the actor to justify the three moves in relation to the chosen sense. As we've said before, being very specific or placing a limitation on the actor often helps. For example, the actors could do the three moves as if they were feeling too hot or dancing to some music they were hearing or seeing something they can't reach. It's amazing how, when you're trying to make a certain sensation real to yourself, almost any bizarre movements seem to fit the circumstances.

Still, this exercise is not easy. It might be best to try it only with kids beyond the fifth or sixth grades. Perhaps if several of them try it at the same time, they won't be intimidated by it.

People who are born actors, even the youngest one, will instinctively do more than just follow directions. They will justify the directions themselves and make them their own. They will add their own ideas to the directions and fill them out with their own thoughts. But not everyone has that instinct, so we made up the Entrances game which is described in Session 5 of the Leader's Guide.

Now, having built trust and a sense of working together, let's go on to what all the kids want, all the time, the "meat and potatoes" part: putting on the show!

Additional Exercises, Improvs, and Games

VOCAL AND PHYSICAL EXPRESSIVENESS

1. Sound and motion

Let the children pair off and face each other. Without planning ahead, person A does a movement, person B produces a vocal sound. Then A starts moving in various ways while facing his (or her) partner, perhaps starting by tapping his fingers together, suddenly throwing open his arms, and then slowly gyrating down to the floor. Person B must make sounds that simultaneously match her partner's movements. At first Person B might just do small rhythmic "tsk-tsk" sounds followed by a sudden yell as A throws open his arms, and a sliding groan as A sinks to the floor. Next, reverse the procedure. B starts making sounds that A must match with movements. The whole group can do this exercise all at once if you like.

2. Mobile statuary

Mime artists tell an entire story using only their bodies without broad exaggeration and without sacrificing truth. At the Actors Studio, Etienne DeCroux taught this exercise: Begin by standing in a neutral position, weight on both feet, arms down, and face forward. Then slowly and carefully, keeping good balance, move each part of the body. Start with the eyes, moving them up to the right corner of the room. Follow by turning the head up and right, then the chest and shoulders, the arms, waist, hips, and, finally, the legs and feet until the whole body is turned up and around in a graceful spiral.

We developed a variation for actors asking each student to begin with a simple phrase such as "I can't!" "Stop!" "It's hot!" "I love this!" or "Get out!" Think of a situation that evokes the phrase, and ask the actor to keep saying it while moving (not necessarily rotating) the body, starting with the eyes and continuing slowly and deliberately as more and more of the body is involved in the expression of the phrase.

For instance, a girl might be given the phrase "I'm not going!" First, give her a strong situation. Some of her friends want her to trespass into a place that is filled with danger. Let her think of the particulars first, visualize her friends, the place, and the consequences. Ask her to use all her senses to make it as real to herself as possible. She might start with her eyes, by glaring up at her friends, clenching her jaw, thrusting her head forward. She might square her shoulders in preparation for a fight. Her chest might pull up in defiance, hips thrust forward into a stronger position. She might cross her arms over her chest in denial. She could step forward in challenge and stamp her foot.

Or she could look down and away from her friends and turn her head aside. Her shoulders might rise in fear, her chest might cave in, and her hips contract. She might then move her arms into an entreaty as she drops to her knees.

She could, in the end, stand her ground or capitulate. But if each move is built up one by one, the actors will learn how to involve their whole bodies without skipping any steps along the way, which might result in a phony performance.

CONCENTRATION

1. Who started the motion?
This game devised by Viola Spolin is very good. One person is sent out of the room while the others sit in a circle and decide who will lead the body motions. The first person returns and goes to the center of the circle, watching them all so he can try to determine who the leader is. The designated leader then begins to move slowly and carefully as all the others do the same in imitation of the leader. It is the task of the whole group to stay together without giving away who the leader is. Sometimes they can fool the person in the center by looking at and following someone else in the group who is watching the leader, and by shifting around their focus of attention.

2. Object throwaway
Fifteen kids stand in three lines—call them A, B, and C—stretching from the front of the stage to the back. The person at the head of line A pantomimes using an object, such as a ball or bat, names it, "throws it away," and moves to the back of the line. Then the person at the head of line B, followed by line C, quickly mimes and names a different object and "throws it away." The point is that you can't use an object that has already been thrown out. If you can't think of a new object, you're eliminated.

Eliminations become more frequent after two or three run-throughs. It all goes very quickly, and the kids should try to remain relaxed as they make the quick decisions.

3. Observation
Ask each child, one at a time, to look at a tray containing about six to eight different objects. Cover the tray and tell the child to name all the objects. Keep repeating until

he or she can remember them all. Change the objects on the tray for each child. This activity, obviously, requires a little preparation.

4. Here and now

At the Actors Studio, the director Arthur Penn often stopped his students in a scene rehearsal and said, "Here and now!" At that signal, the actor he'd addressed had to stop and say, "Here and now, I…" and continue by verbalizing exactly what he or she was thinking or feeling at that moment.

If the actors were indeed thinking their characters' thoughts, they verbalized them. If they were noticing something in the other character or the surroundings, they would remark on that. If their concentration had shifted to something totally unrelated, or they were worrying about how they were doing at the time, they confessed that.

The point was simply to get actors to be aware of what they were thinking and feeling at each moment, to accept it, and either to continue it or correct it and move on. It helped to avoid being caught in a groove of fear, tension, or self-flagellation.

This is a good rehearsal tool when you are already working on a play, scenes, or monologues.

DEVELOPING REACTION SPEED

1. Pitcher and batter

Have people form two lines facing each other. First person in line A "pitches" the first part of a line to a "batter" in line B who "hits" the rest of the line back. The players pantomime pitching and batting as they say the lines aloud. For example: The pitcher says, "One of the things that drives me crazy is—" and the batter immediately hits back with "people who crack their knuckles in the library." Or the pitcher says, as he pantomimes pitching the ball, "Yesterday I thought I'd just—" and the batter pantomimes hitting the ball as she says, "skip school and go swimming." However, make the rule that the parts of sentences must be more than just two words long. Otherwise it's too easy. Particularly for the batters.

2. Alphabet exercise

The Berkshire Theatre Festival apprentices used improvised dialogues for training. In one "alphabet" exercise the first actor starts a line with a word beginning with the letter "A." The other actor must answer with a line beginning with a "B" word and so on through the whole alphabet. For example Actor 1 says "All I want to do today is relax." Actor 2 answers, "But you've got a lot of work to do." Actor 1 says, "Can't you stop nagging me?" Actor 2 huffs, "Do you think that's all I ever do?" etc.

Another improv skill-training rule they insisted on was that the actors never answer in the negative, no matter how bizarre the initial question or statement. The answer or following line had to begin with the words, "Yes, and—." It's a great exercise because the surest way to kill a good improv is to answer "No, I can't" or "No, it isn't."

3. Automatic lecture

Rosemary Foley used to have her fifth graders in Mount Vernon, New York, give one-minute lectures on a subject they had drawn blindly from a stack. One boy drew "desert" and had a ball, but one girl drew "auto mechanics" and ranted about how much she hated it when their family's car broke down and she had to walk.

WORKING AS AN ENSEMBLE

This is a variation on the Relaxation and Trust exercise, mentioned earlier, in which one falling child with eyes closed was safely caught inside a circle of other kids. This new one is called the Lift:

One person lies on the floor with four kids standing on each side of her and one at her head with hands under her head. The four on each side then put their hands under the one lying down and slowly lift her up to waist height. Led by the end person who is holding her head, they swing her three times, like a pendulum, and on the third swing they lift their arms straight upward, full-length.

The responsibility of the prone person is to remain relaxed. If she tenses up, it will be too difficult to lift her steadily, and she will feel uneasy and nervous. But if she is totally relaxed, it's very easy for the nine people to lift her (she should be about the size they are), and she will have a pleasant feeling as she is lowered to the ground.

This exercise goes to the heart of ensemble playing, which is all about trusting the other players. Chances are, the kids will all want to do it. But as we've said, if children ever hesitate to participate in a trust exercise, at least trust them. That is, don't push them; simply accept their decision with respect.

THE ABILITY TO FOLLOW DIRECTIONS

The purpose of this exercise is to learn to follow directions fully and even extend them. Have six or eight members line up outside the acting area. Each in turn follows the direction given him or her and justifies it. Each actor must personally add something to the direction—an answer to one of the W questions or a sensory element.

For example, the director says, "Run onto the stage." The actor decides Why—he's being chased by a crazy mugger. He runs on, looks back in fear, runs back to his point of entry, and mimes locking the door.

Or the director says, "Walk to the center of the stage and stop short." This actor decides Where. She's in the darkened Hall of Mirrors at a carnival. She stops short because the lights have suddenly come on. She looks around in wonder. She laughs at her different images in the weirdly shaped mirrors.

By using the five Ws and the sensory elements that they make up for this exercise, your actors will need your guidance, but they'll be able to use those inherent in the script. When doing a show they'll often surprise and delight you with their own ideas.

DEVELOPING PHYSICAL BEHAVIOR IN A SCENE

One-line Improv

First, split your group or class into teams of two or three people. Give each team one word or one short line. Their task is to develop a short skit using that line, word, or phrase so that their physical behavior will reveal the situation in which the line is used. They may add additional lines or phrases, but they should try to make it more fun by not verbally giving away the situation. The rest of the group must try to guess the situation. Here are some examples of short lines, along with potential situations:

1. "Believe me, I didn't."
A girl could be standing, arms folded in front of her, with a guy on his knees. Or a shopkeeper could be running out of a store shaking his fist, gibbering in a foreign language at a shopper standing in front of the store's fruit stand, trying to deny that he had just eaten a piece of fruit from the stand.

2. "Quick. Hide!"
A surprise party. Or thieves. Or seeing unwanted guests approaching, or kids using their father's computer, or little girls using mom's makeup.

3. "Get out of there!"
An angry parent or pet owner to kids or a puppy hiding under a table.

4. "Oh, no. I can't believe it!"
A person who has lost keys or important papers, or dropped a gift of candy all over the floor.

5. "What did I do?"
A driver pulled over by a cop, or a child seeing a parent approaching with a paddle, or a girl ostracized by friends.

6. "What a time for this to happen!"
A bride spilling tea, coffee, or juice on her own gown just before her wedding. Or a dancer spraining an ankle just before a recital or show.

7. "Now look at yourself."
A hairdresser or a makeup artist to a client. Or a photographer showing proofs.

8. "Go ahead. You can do it."
A kid scared to dive off a high board. Or afraid to give a speech or learning to ride a two-wheeler.

9. "I am so sorry."
A funeral, or someone accidentally stepping on another's foot, or knocking an old lady down, or comforting a "losing team."

10. "Where do you want this?"
Moving men. Or a husband holding a large painting.

11. "Where are we?"
In a car with maps, or walking in a dark woods, or fancy adults finding themselves at a rock concert on a hill. Or new employees at a big business meeting. Or generals studying a large map.

12. "Hold still."
A photographer, or a dress fitter, or a friend seeing a mosquito on another's back.

13. "And the winner is…"
Oscars or Tonys, scholarship announcement, or a wrestling match.

14. "Where is it?"
A cop pulls a driver over. The driver can't find his license.

Part II
The Show

All Kids—and You—
Can Put on a Show

Step by Step to
Your Production

Chapter Four

Choosing or Creating a Show

LET'S PUT ON A SHOW! But what show? If you haven't already been handed a script to do, your first question is: Shall we do a play that's already written and published, or adapt one, or create one ourselves? Should our first effort be a few skits or scenes for the parents to see?

The final decision on what show you choose will depend to a great extent on the cast size, abilities of the performers, the space you have for the performance, and the production help available to you from parents, teachers, and friends.

SOURCES FOR SCRIPTS

You, the children, and fellow playwrights can prepare your own scripts and create your own characters, especially for short scenes and smaller shows. Or you can look into various script sources. The Internet, local libraries, and bookstores will be your first stops. Sometimes community Parks and Recreation agencies can supply material or point you in the right direction.

Richard Carter, the cofounder and artistic director of Community Shakespeare, has written plays for third- through twelfth-grade actors, and original adaptations of Shakespeare's *Comedy of Errors* and *The Taming of the Shrew* for middle school children, and abridged versions of *As You Like It*, *All's Well That Ends Well*, and *Love's Labor's Lost* for middle and high school students. See his Web site in our bibliography.

There is a monthly drama magazine for young people called *Plays*, (see Bibliography), published from October through May. Each issue contains eight to ten plays for children and young people to perform. Each play is accompanied by production notes regarding cast, age levels, playing time, costumes, props, sets, and lights. Often, the issues contain plays or extended scenes especially geared to the time of year, such

88

as Washington's birthday, Thanksgiving, the Fourth of July, or Martin Luther King's birthday.

Subscribers to *Plays* may produce plays they find in any issue without having to pay a royalty fee, if their subscription is current at the time of the performance and if the performance is part of the regular school or drama-club activity. If you're not a subscriber, you must apply in writing for permission and royalty quotations. You must also do that with any other published play you choose, unless it is in the public domain.

You can also call or write to the 52nd Street Project, Samuel French, Inc., Dramatists Play Service, or The Drama Book Shop, all in New York City, or Leigh Curran's Virginia Avenue Project in Los Angeles. Information on how to reach them can be found in the Bibliography. The Drama Book Shop, for instance, has an Express Bibliography of Educational Theater. The plays for children listed in it include about eight versions of *Tom Sawyer*, four of *The Lion, the Witch and the Wardrobe*, as well as *The Night of the Pterodactyls* and the *My Sister Makes Me Sick Musical*.

One problem with many of these extensive lists is that they are classified as "Plays for Children." That often means plays produced for an *audience* of children, with or without some parts for children. The scripts in the magazine *Plays* are specifically created for child and teenage actors. They vary considerably in quality, so enlist the guidance of the staff at your children's library, as well as the publishers themselves.

After a few weeks or months of meetings with kids, you'll be familiar enough with your group and their increased capabilities to judge which plays they can do well. The main thing is to try to do a show or group of shows that can include everyone who wants to be involved. As one of our Dramatics Club alumni, Michael Finamore, wrote:

> What we appreciated most was that everyone got a role. If there were not enough acting roles, some kids sang, or they danced or worked on the crew—but they were in that show. Each of us would feel just as important as the others.

This leads to a welcoming, nurturing environment, a sense of belonging, acceptance, and teamwork. Clair Walcovy, one of the parents we mentioned earlier, observed:

> We found that the older kids were very good to the younger ones. Everyone helped each other. Of course, they were excited and often unruly and noisy. But the basic spirit of cooperation and mutual joy was pervasive.

DRAMA FORMS

A brief description of the six forms of drama may be helpful to some of you and guide you in avoiding those forms less likely to be suitable for children's productions.

Tragedy

One generally accepted definition of tragedy is "the story of a relatively great and good person who has a weakness or flaw, such as willingly succumbing to a serious temptation, the result of which is punishment." Most tragedies are too grim, forbidding, and demanding to be appropriate for children.

Serious Drama

Serious dramas contain a serious action in which "greatness" or the tragic flaw itself is missing, or the hero "gets off the hook" and is not punished. Examples of this form include melodramas, soap operas, suspense thrillers, and detective and spy stories. Simple melodramas without complicated plots might well be acceptable for older children.

Nineteenth-Century Melodrama

An exaggerated form of melodrama, this form is based upon a struggle between Good and Evil. Typically, it features a heartless villain and a heroine who is rescued in the nick of time by the hero. Good always wins out.

Often called "melerdramers" or "potboilers," they are easily within the reach of teenagers. Though often taken seriously in the nineteenth century, today this form strikes us as funny and borders on farce. It must be played very broadly but earnestly.

Farce

The first comic form, farce is usually the story of a foolish person with a material flaw who succumbs to the flaw and is punished. Farce can sometimes be savage. It is typically played very fast, and is associated with the slamming of many doors as characters run furiously on and off the stage. The Marx Brothers? *Noises Off*? You bet.

The danger in farce is that your young actors will begin thinking of themselves as clowns. But they must learn to regard the characters as real and very serious about what they are doing, despite the fact that what they are doing is often hilarious.

Comedy

Compared to tragedy, the definition here could be "the story of an ordinary person who has a flaw or temptation from which, in the nick of time, he or she is saved." Comedy is "all over the place." There are satiric, social, dramatic, domestic, psychological, and ironic comedies and probably a few dozen more, including tragicomedies. The simpler comedies are good candidates for children's productions.

Fantasy

This is not necessarily a fairy tale we're talking about, but typical examples are James Barrie's play *Peter Pan* and the movies *The Wizard of Oz*, *Harry Potter*, or *The Lord of the Rings*. Most kids would love to be characters like Gandolph, Frodo, or even Gimly, the dwarf. And they'd think being someone like Albus Dumbledore or Hagrid, the giant gamekeeper would be cool. Fantasy is relatively easy for children to grasp, and is always fun for them to play.

Musicals

American and British musicals contain a vast source of materials for children's work. In fact, musicals offer the best way to introduce children to the stage after they have had some basic experience with the games and exercises described in this book.

Musicals need not be produced in their entirety; they can be severely edited. You can limit your production to three or four scenes or numbers, if you wish. But it's always more rewarding and fun to do the entire story with selected cuts to control the length.

Again, with any copyrighted material, you must take care that you have the right to produce plays or musicals or any part of them.

ADDING CHARACTERS

Often you will have many more children than there are characters in a script you have selected for your show. You may not be willing to go as far as we frequently did to invent characters and ensure that everyone got a part. In *Annie Get Your Gun*, we had Sitting Bull, so we also wrote in Geronimo. We tripled the number of Indian names and added them to the cast. Toni Vairo played one of the Indians when she was eleven. When she was older and went to see a professional production of the show, she was astonished that her character, "Mrs. Bickering Bird," was not in it.

In our Dramatics Club production of *The Sound of Music*, we must have had at least a dozen Von Trapp children; twenty-seven nuns, postulants, and novices; and twenty-three convent students. In *My Fair Lady*, Colonel Pickering shared his part with his friend, Lord Rickaby Hackaby. And Henry Higgins's household had at least eight maids. Others chortled that we'd threatened to pad the parts in *A Christmas Carol* by adding "The Ghost of the Day Before Yesterday." We weren't the only ones who do this. Recently we heard of a kindergarten class that performed a production of *Snow White and the Twenty-Seven Dwarfs*.

However, do this only when you are presenting the shows, free of charge, for the school or just parents, to be sure you do not run into trouble about getting permission.

Some directors try to solve the problem by double-casting—that is, two actors are cast for each role, and they play it in alternate performances. Others feel that this can lead to bad feelings of competition and comparisons, and is also twice as much work for the director. We tend to agree with the latter view.

ADAPTING OTHER MATERIALS TO FIT YOUR CAST

If you can't find a ready-made script for a scene or longer production suitable to your cast, adapting one from a book, a biography, an epic poem, a story, an article, or even a cartoon in the newspaper can be a solution.

Carolyn Kennedy Graupner, a professional actress and writer, created and directed a big new musical, *Greek... To Me!* She used *Aesop's Fables* as her base, imagining Aesop traveling in a sort of time machine, and did an adaptation of each fable in a different time period. She enlisted a friend to compose and conduct the music. It was warmly received, especially by all the children and adults who were in it.

If you decide to produce a musical such as *Oliver!*, and then find that you need to expand the cast, it would be a help to go back to Charles Dickens's novel, *Oliver Twist*, on which the show was based, and find ideas there for creating new lines of dialogue. Investigating books about the lives of Londoners in the nineteenth century will help you add more characters and thus more parts for the children.

We avoided exact adherence to the written script. Adapting the show to make sure it was interesting, involving, and exciting for the kids resulted in a higher-quality performance.

Although we did fit the scripts to the talents and personalities of the cast members, sometimes we also turned the children's limitations into assets for the show. One little girl had previously worked very hard on props, and we wanted to give her a part of her own for a change. But she was very shy and seemed uncertain and vulnerable when she stood onstage. So we decided to create a part of a blind girl who was the best friend of one of the other girls. That way her "friend" kept holding her hand to lead her around, and addressed many lines to her for affirmation. With that security, the shyness disappeared, and a gentle sensitivity and awareness of hearing, smell, and touch made her character quite poignant.

One little boy in another show was eager—let's say he was supremely eager. He was in a lineup in front of the curtain with about six others who were to do a rapid-fire introduction to Act II, each delivering one word at a time. But he got rattled and could never get it right. So we asked him to repeat the last word of each sentence the others said, but with a little extra pizzazz. He found that easy and fun to do, and when they came to the very last word of the introduction, everyone repeated it loudly with him, and it got a huge laugh. He was overjoyed.

Occasionally, we wrote scenes and added them to the script, just because we wanted them in the show and we had extra people who could play them well. One of those scenes came out of an incident reported to have occurred in a Bronx school. An angry teacher had chased a little boy all the way down to the basement. When she finally caught him and backed him against a wall, he cried, "Go ahead and hit me. That's all anybody ever does!" The teacher did not hit him, but hugged him instead. It was so moving we wanted it in the show. We asked a few younger children to improvise some pranks that would make a nurse, one of the characters, furious, and with their help we came up with a scene that proved to be very effective.

Actually, we adapted most of our shows to fit the understanding and abilities of our casts. Roy Finamore, a former member of our Dramatics Club and, today, a popular author of several cookbooks, such as *One Potato, Two Potato* (Houghton Mifflin, 2001) wryly observes:

> I guess my acting was okay, and at twelve years old I was the tallest
> boy available, so I was cast as the hero in a musical. But there was
> a problem. I was tone deaf. I'm sure ours was the only production
> in which the mascots and overture singers sang the big number
> instead of the hero.

We routinely cut almost all the romantic and love scenes that children find difficult to play. Then we added big group scenes, fights, contests, rallies, parties—events the kids loved to do. Once, a bunch of third- and fourth-grade boys were dying to be in one show, so we wrote in some lines for them as London street urchins. They performed along with an older group by alternating the verses and imitating the "big guys." They all joined together for the last rousing verse.

How to Adapt Materials

If it becomes necessary to adapt a play or musical or change scenes to fit your particular circumstances, involve the kids as much as you can. Let's say your script is to be based on a news story, historical event, or a classic book. Look at the original as a source for more dialogue, and underline all the dialogue you could possibly use. Later, you'll choose from these as you write the final script.

Use the five-W system: determine Who your characters are, What they are trying to accomplish and What the obstacles are, thus determining the conflict. Search for the best Whys for each of your characters' needs. Decide on only a few Wheres, in order to reduce the number of locations and sets. Then carefully explore how those Wheres affect the characters and the action. Find out everything possible about When it all happens and how the When affects everyone in it. Use all the dialogue you have underlined that is appropriate and understandable, and use any descriptions of the locations, characters, and time.

Create the rest of the dialogue with improvs involving the children. (Often, even Hollywood's feature-film directors will use lines the actors have improvised in rehearsal.) Do as many as you can and write down the best ones. Tape recorders, camcorders, and computers are very handy tools for this, but we have "made do" by using many children with notebooks, pencils, and good memories. We provide an example of a scene we wrote this way, later in this chapter.

As you write the script, begin with scenes that inform the audience about the situation. Build up any conflicts, move irrevocably toward a confrontation or crisis, then resolve it so that you can send the audience home satisfied.

WRITING YOUR OWN SHOW

When you are creating your own show or scene from scratch and without resorting to other books or plays, you follow the same general process. In this case, you make it all up together—that is, by brainstorming with the children. Find out what they are most passionately interested in doing and nudge them on with many questions. It's best to begin with some kind of theme. Then invent your characters. Find out:

> What trouble they might be in...

> Whom they're trying to help, or...

> What problems they have in realizing their dreams.

Just as an actor endeavors to determine the "spine," or main theme, of the character—this would perhaps reflect the character's overall lifetime intention—the director and actors try to find the theme of the overall show. It has been said that the better the play, the better the chance of reducing the theme to one word, such as jealousy, as in *Othello*, or revenge, as in *Medea*. Some other possible themes for kids might be Loneliness; Friends; Popularity; Gangs; The Outsider; Kids vs. Parents; Class Clowns; Class Hero; Ideal Teachers vs. Not So Ideal; Dangerous Hikes; Neat Inventions, The Catastrophic Party, Facing a Hurricane, Tsunami, Earthquake, Flood, or a Group of Insurgents.

Finding Ideas

As the basis for skits or short scenes, not full-length shows, we have found *Bartlett's Familiar Quotations* and similar publications helpful springboards for ideas. So are ancient myths, superstitions, predictions, heroes and heroines, and even proverbs such as "A rolling stone gathers no moss" or "A stitch in time saves nine." Don't forget news stories in your local newspaper; these often suggest current social problems. You can do several skits combined into a short production on one theme.

If your agenda is a lesson you want the kids to understand, you can start by saying, for instance, "You've just had a peaceful revolution and your old country is being split into three. You guys are meeting in the parliament building trying to figure out how it can be done without hurting any individual or segment of the population. You need three constitutions now instead of one. You, Nicky, are the leader who represents country number one. You, Danielle, are number two. And the third country has no leader, but the citizens are represented by six of you. Now let's take it from there, and see what kind of story we can develop."

The younger kids you work with, especially, will want to use popular TV and film characters and situations. They love to imitate and feel more secure using something they've seen that they know people like. But we try to discourage that, if possible. Children will grow more if they use their own imaginations.

They will also want to imitate the actors on "Whose Line Is It Anyway?", but save that for your game sessions, not your show development.

Warming Up Their Imaginations

One thing is very important: if you are creating or adapting a show with your group and have not had any of the meetings or exercise sessions we describe in the previous chapters and in the Leader's Guide, please take some time to go through at least some of that process first. Those sessions help students realize just how fertile their imaginations are. The improvs give them a chance to warm up their creative juices. Otherwise, they might be overwhelmed at the prospect in the beginning. When they learn to create what they didn't even know was in them they'll be wiggling with ideas.

Most of the time with younger kids, you will be acting as a sort of reporter writing a news story after a press conference. But when you are working with teens, after they have done some work with already-written scripts and know the form, they will want to, and can, write their own scripts—with a bit of tweaking from you. Remember, too, that you can stimulate kids' creativity by setting limits. As stated in Chapter 2, the more limitations given to an actor, the more the imagination thrives.

We keep in mind Willie Reale's 52nd Street Project, in New York, and Leigh Curran's Virginia Avenue Project, in Los Angeles. They have been successfully helping inner-city children write and perform their own shows. With the assistance of people from the film community and the professional theater, and using teaching methods described by Daniel Judah Sklar in his excellent book, *Playmaking* (see Bibliography), adults team up with the kids. Sometimes the adults help kids write shows in which the adults perform. Other times the adults write scripts in which the kids perform, or they combine all their efforts. Each season they decide on a theme for a series of short plays or skits, such as Tomorrow, Today, or Second Thoughts, or Lost Luggage or Earthquake. One year members of the Virginia Avenue Project did a group of skits based on the theme, Heaven Sent. One eight-year-old wrote a play about an angel who does good deeds but is persuaded by a space alien to do bad ones until she starts having nightmares. A thirteen-year-old wrote about an angel on the day she finally grows up and gets her wings...only to find they are leaves and she is on the wrong planet. Another thirteen-year-old wrote about a boxing kangaroo and his boxing guardian angel who gives him the courage to believe in himself.

Each year the organization City at Peace-New York brings together a cast of seventy youngsters, ages thirteen to nineteen, from over thirty-three various schools and centers in all five boroughs to write and produce an original work of musical theater drawn from their own lives. They meet regularly in absolutely private creative training sessions to share the challenges of their lives...the joys, the pains, the betrayals, and the abandonment. Together they develop scenes and songs from their own experiences that become part of the show, but they never play themselves in the final production. They all play roles in the others' stories. Thus they are ultimately engaged in making positive changes in their lives and communities.

These theaters have found ways to help kids discover their creative powers despite the often discouraging effects of their surroundings.

Lunch Bunch

In twenty cities throughout the country, professional actors read to and discuss books with lower-grade children as members of BookPALS, a branch of the Screen Actors Guild Foundation. They have been helping to raise reading levels considerably, especially in inner-city schools. We started a chapter in New Milford, Connecticut, and followed the reading with theater games related to the books we read. It was such fun that we formed a "club" of third graders, the "Lunch Bunch," who met with us once a week to do theater games and acting exercises during their lunch break. Last spring the Lunch Bunch members ended the school year by performing a play called *The Missing Dog and the Creepy Guy*, which was entirely based on their ideas and suggestions. It probably wouldn't win a Tony, but the cheers of their classmates were ample reward.

After spending several months doing improvs based on the ten elements of acting, we told them that in the spring we wanted them to do a show they had created themselves. We then urged them to come in with their own stories to read aloud as their chosen "cast members" acted them out for the group. Each week we did a few more, took notes, collected their stories, outlines or just notes, and transcribed some of the spoken lines that emerged. We asked them what locations they wanted for their play. We shared ideas of what kinds of characters they wanted in the script. And after a couple of months we wrote a script by putting all their ideas together, ideas that included a creeper, a missing dog, a kidnapping, a haunted house, swimmers, football players, cheerleaders, teachers, policemen, and a narrator. We made up "try-out sheets" with different lines we had heard in their improvs. Then we had them take turns reading the lines for us and writing down which character they wanted to play. They showed us some special talents they wanted to display as part of the show, like cheerleading and a sort of rap singing of songs they wrote. Finally we cast it, rehearsed it scene by scene and presented it in June for the rest of the school's third graders and the cast members' parents. Next year we'll try for the Pulitzer.

A Self-Created Scene

What follows is "Spark of Liberty," an example of a scene that we developed from an incident in American history. We wrote this after researching a few history books, recalling some details from a documentary film, and adding a few lines of our own dialogue. You're welcome to try it with your kids. We have also provided lists of props and technical needs and a rehearsal schedule for a production of the scene "Spark of Liberty" at the end of Chapter 7.

Who
PAUL REVERE A silversmith, age thirty. Physically strong, intelligent, brave, a crafty opponent of British rule. He has worked long and hard for the rebel cause, even befriending influential Loyalists and Tories, spying on their plans and movements.

SAMUEL ADAMS A steely leader of the infant American revolution. Now in his fifties, Adams is ill with palsy and has trembling hands. He lost most of his money to poor investments and now relies on John Hancock for financial help.

JOHN HANCOCK A wealthy (by inheritance) revolutionist in his thirties. Vain, ambitious, and selfish.

REV. JONAS CLARK A preacher in his forties. A great friend of Adams and Hancock, he is anxious to help the resistance movement.

MRS. CLARK The minister's wife, in her forties, also devoted to the cause.

DOROTHY QUINCY Pert, pretty twenty-year-old, engaged to John Hancock. A loyal rebel, eager to help, but not at the expense of her wedding.

SGT. MONROE A heavyset, tall man in his thirties. A minuteman in homespun clothing.

WILLIAM DAWES A short, powerful man in his twenties. A great horseman and a brave patriot.

What
For **REVERE** Finding out where the British are in order to tell the people and get the news out as fast as possible.

For **ADAMS** Controlling the quirky Hancock and getting out of town.

For **HANCOCK** Putting on a show of bravery and then getting out of town.

For **REV. CLARK** Getting Adams and Hancock out of town and the British out of America.

For **MRS. CLARK** Getting her guests out of town well fed.

For **DOROTHY** Getting her fiancé, John, out of town.

For **SGT. MONROE** Protecting his leaders.

For **DAWES** As Revere's backup, sharing his mission.

All the characters are facing large and potentially dangerous events that are about to occur. They are making brave and possibly risky decisions that could affect the rest of their lives.

Why
A revolution is brewing. The government of King George III of England has lost patience with a colony that defies its orders in the streets and dumps British tea in the ocean. The colonists are disgusted with an empire that imposes high taxes on them though they are not allowed to be represented in the British parliament. They hate the King.

Where
Rev. Clark's house near Lexington Green, in Lexington, Massachusetts. Some baggage sits by the wall and in the corners, some bags empty, some packed. There is a fire in the fireplace and hot food and rum on the table.

When
April 18, 1775, at about 10 P.M. It is an unusually cold night.

SPARK OF LIBERTY

> A sentry stands extreme stage left. The rest of the stage is the living room of the Clark house. **REVERE**, entering from left and breathing heavily, is stopped by the sentry.

REVERE: Let me pass. I have news for Hancock and Adams!

SGT. MONROE: (*Guarding the front door, musket ready.*) They've all retired for the night. They want no noise out here.

REVERE: (*Shouting.*) Noise? You'll have noise enough. The Regulars are coming out!

HANCOCK: (*Crosses the living room where the others are gathered and opens the door.*) Come in, Revere. We are not afraid of you.

ADAMS: What's happening, Paul?

> (**REVERE** *enters, crosses to the fireplace, and rubs his hands to warm himself.*)

HANCOCK: Yes, what do you mean—they're coming out?

REVERE: (*Tensely.*) Coming out. The Regulars—a whole contingent on their way to Concord. You've got to go to Woburn where there are no British.

Marine officers are out ahead of the main body—I barely escaped them near Monotomy. But you're the two they are really after.

MRS: CLARK: I think Mr. Revere can use some food and drink. (*Crosses to table, pulls up a chair, fills a plate, and pours rum.*)

DOROTHY: Why Concord?

ADAMS: Our ammunition and supplies. They're out to destroy them. How many men and officers on the road?

REVERE: Don't know the actual number, but they are well-armed—a serious threat to our purpose. And they are looking for you, Sam, and Mr. Hancock. (*Goes to the table and begins to eat.*)

HANCOCK: We've got to stop them. Right here in Lexington.

ADAMS: We may do them harm, but we can't stop them.

HANCOCK: We will. I say we will. And I'll be there on the green with our patriots. (*Goes for his coat.*)

REV. CLARK: John, John—you must not expose yourself to capture. (*Puts his coat out of* **HANCOCK's** *reach.*)

DOROTHY: (*Runs to him and holds him.*) You'll give it all away? Our days of work? The planning? You have more important things to do than carry a rifle and shoot at soldiers.

HANCOCK: My dear, I must not let our men down. (*Crosses to the door and opens it.*) Sergeant Monroe, fetch my rifle. I'll join Captain Parker on the green!

ADAMS: (*Slams door shut.*) John, you're the one who usually holds me back from doing foolish things. This is not wise, or expedient. You and I must leave immediately for Woburn.

HANCOCK: Sam, I've got to be with them. This is our sacred obligation and I will not be absent at the first trial.

ADAMS: (*Quietly, but very firmly.*) Our Continental Congress will sit in Philadelphia next month. We need you there. That's where our job lies, not on Lexington Green shooting balls at a professional army and risking almost certain capture. That would be a brilliant success for the British and a damaging loss to our cause.

DOROTHY: (*Really upset.*) John, you are not going to fight the British army. You are not equipped for that. Your place is in the Congress. (*Turns away from him, then quietly.*) Furthermore, I don't want a dead groom.

HANCOCK: Sam, I don't believe this. I thought you'd be right there with me.

(*A heavy knock on the door.* **REVERE** *opens it and* **WILLIAM DAWES** *enters, out of breath. He is followed by* **SGT. MONROE** *with a rifle.*)

REVERE: Willie Dawes—what news?

DAWES: The Regulars are hard on the road. They are heavily armed—both marines and light infantry. Houses are burning in Monotomy. Revere, we must be on our way to Concord.

MRS. CLARK: (*Hurrying to him.*) Mr. Dawes, before you go, do have some quick food and drink. There's plenty from dinner.

ADAMS: She's right—hot food and hot rum. It's a brisk night, and you have hard riding before you're done.

(**REVERE** *returns to the table, along with* **DAWES**.)

REVERE: Come on, Willie. You'll need a bit of this.

(**REVERE** *and* **DAWES** *eat as* **DOROTHY**, *still distraught, pours the rum.*)

ADAMS: All right, John, which is it? An adventure on the green, dodging rounds from the king's own Regulars, or do we leave for Woburn to fight another day?

HANCOCK: (*Looks at* **DOROTHY**, *pauses, then reluctantly:*) Well, Sam, I suppose you're right. We must think of the bigger plans. (*Paces a bit.*) Sergeant, put the rifle inside the carriage. (*To* **DOROTHY**.) All right, dear…please make haste now.

(**SGT. MONROE** *hurries out with the rifle.*)

DOROTHY: Thank God!

REVERE: (*Hurriedly eating and drinking.*) Go straight north, not west. Stay clear of the Concord area.

REV. CLARK: (*Peering through the window.*) The horses are all hitched and I'll make sure the carriage is ready.

(**REV. CLARK** *exits.* **HANCOCK** *and* **ADAMS** *follow with packed bags.*)

REVERE: Thank you, Mrs. Clark and Miss Quincy.

DAWES: Much obliged, ma'am.

(**REVERE** *and* **DAWES** *exit into the cold night.*)

MRS. CLARK: (*Stuffing blankets in an empty bag.*) Dorothy, get your bag. I'll clean up. Take only the one bag and this. I'm sure you'll be back soon. (*As* **SGT. MONROE** *returns:*) Jonas, come get some food for the guards outside.

(**SGT. MONROE** *hurries to the table, fills his arms with bread and a pitcher of hot rum. Exits.*)

DOROTHY: Mrs. Clark, what is to become of us?

MRS: CLARK: God only knows. It's twelve miles to Woburn, so for now, get your cape, just keep warm. And pray. Here, have a last drink of hot rum.

DOROTHY: Oh, I've had enough rum, thank you.

MRS: CLARK: (*With a wink.*) Behave yourself in Woburn. Maybe you can get married up there.

DOROTHY: (*Wrapping her cape around her.*) Would Reverend Clark come up there to perform the ceremony?

MRS: CLARK: Is the British king a villain?

> (**DOROTHY** *laughs as she exits.* **MRS. CLARK** *walks over to the table, picks up her cup of rum, looks at it, hesitates, and then downs it.*)

CURTAIN

Depending on your sense of humor, that may or may not be a funny ending. Since we don't know what Mrs. Clark did as Dorothy left, you can edit those last few lines any way you want and write your own ending.

When they are reading this scene and rehearsing it, lead the children through the process we described in Chapter 2, using the five Ws and five senses to guide them.

When you are doing full-length shows, don't let the individual scenes stretch out, even though you want to give everyone a chance to shine. Children can't maintain the action too long. The outside time limit for an entire show is about an hour and a half. Remember, the longer the show, the fewer may be the benefits.

Here's another short script, also written by Dan O'Connor. It would be fun for a small group of youngsters to play. It only requires one set, a couple of tables and chairs, and if possible, a cabinet of some sort for the "kitchen," a carrot, and two witch costumes. Just mark the stage for an outside and inside door.

THOSE WITCHES

Who

A family made up of a mother, father, one son, and two daughters (all young teenagers).

What

The kids reveal a secret from the past.

Why

They want to play a trick on their mother.

Where

A house in a small town southwest of Boston.

When

Sunday morning after church.

The following description may be used as an introductory narration :

NARRATOR: Once upon a time, many years ago, there were, in a number of countries around the world, small groups of people who were referred to as witches—by themselves and by others. They were good people, in the beginning, but eventually they changed as some of them did things that most people considered unsanitary, unsatisfactory, insensible, and, by many, immoral and illegal. This is a short scene depicting what could have occurred at one time decades ago, or perhaps only a few years ago. In it you will discover that they were not all evil people.

FATHER: All right, children, time to change your Sunday best for work clothing.

ELLEN: But Father, this is Sunday…and we're not supposed to work on Sundays.

FATHER: Well that's true, Ellen, but I think the Minister would overlook some labor since there's such a mess in the barn. We can all fix it up in no time.

MOTHER: Your father's right, children…and I'll fix something really good for dinner. On with you now.

(**MARIE** *enters, chewing on a carrot, and goes to* **ELLEN**. *She pulls her downstage away from her* **MOTHER**, *who is preparing dinner.*)

MARIE: What's up?

ELLEN: Dad wants us to help him clean up the barn—it's a mess.

MARIE: Really?…Hmmm…I've got an idea. Let's put on our costumes.

ELLEN: What costumes?

MARIE: You know…the ones with the silly hats…come on, it'll only take a minute.

ELLEN: (*Obviously anxious to do it.*) That's a terrific idea. (*Pauses.*) Wait a minute. Will Mom be offended?

MARIE: Mom's got a good sense of humor. You know that. Come on! (*There's a pause and they hurry off stage left. Their brother,* **BENJAMIN**, *enters from stage right.*)

BENJAMIN: Mom…. Where is everybody?

MOTHER: (*Comes out from behind a cabinet.*) Here I am. How was football practice today?

BENJAMIN: It was really good. Did I tell you on Friday they gave us my favorite lunch at school? Frogs' legs.

MOTHER: Come off it! You don't like frogs' legs.

BENJAMIN: You're right. We had a chicken sandwich. But there's something I didn't tell you. I don't know why. I guess it was bothering me. But… anyway…the teacher brought a woman into the classroom. She was dressed in a fancy-looking outfit, and she told us about a special group of women.

MOTHER: What women are they?

BENJAMIN: Witches…they live in a Wicca…and they help poor people.

MOTHER: WITCHES?!?!? (*She grabs the nearest chair and collapses.*)

BENJAMIN: Mom? Are you all right?

MOTHER: (*Takes a deep breath.*) Yes, Benji. I'm all right . . . Benji, not all witches are good people, and not all of them are bad or evil. I have something to tell you.

(*At this moment,* **ELLEN** *and* **MARIE** *rush into the room, dressed in what are obviously witches' outfits.*)

ELLEN and MARIE: SURPRISE!!!

(**MOTHER** *almost faints again.*)

ELLEN: We found these in the attic, Mom. Are they really witches' dresses? They sure look like it. Why do we have these in the attic?

BENJAMIN: That's the same kind of a dress that the woman at school was wearing!

(**FATHER** *enters from the barn. On seeing his two daughters, he stops, finds the nearest chair, sits, and laughs, enjoying every bit of it.*)

FATHER: Mother, they finally found them. I thought they were locked away in the trunks.

MOTHER: So did I. Well, children. We will tell you the whole story. Many years ago, when I was very young, my mother, your grandmother, suggested that I might want to join a group of young women who were doing very good things for poor people and orphans.

ELLEN: You don't mean witches!?

MOTHER: Yes, but in those days, and even today, many of the witches were kind and generous persons. So we joined and attended church services with them and helped the poor.

MARIE: Then what?

MOTHER: Well, when we learned what a few witches were up to, we packed away our dresses and your grandparents told us never to mention any of this to anyone.

FATHER: Except to us! Now, what do you think we should do with those costumes? Burn them? Frame them and hang them on the wall? Or give them to Goodwill?

ALL THREE CHILDREN: Put them back in the attic!

ELLEN: And we can tell our children about them!! And they can dress up like the **good** witches!!

THE END

Additional Exercises, Improvs, and Games

When choosing and creating your show, there are some exercises that are specifically helpful in preparing the kids for a larger production.

1. You could start with a Where. Let's assume you're planning to do *My Fair Lady* or a shorter adaptation of it, or even one scene. Ask a group of kids to go onstage. Take your situation from the script. Tell them it's raining very hard on a London street outside a large concert hall in the early 1900s. There is a crowd of people. A "swell" insults a flower girl. See what happens.

2. Try an improv that leads into the joyous celebration of the "Rain in Spain" number in *My Fair Lady*. Choose a group and tell them they are in a living room waiting for news of a contest they've entered. When you clap your hands it means they've just gotten word that they won a million dollars or a trip to Disneyland or whatever you know they really want. Then see how wild they can become. They will probably have all the emotional energy they need to take off ecstatically with Professor Higgins's line "By George, I think she's got it!" and then fly into the song.

3. Set up the five Ws for an improvised scene that might have happened just before one of the real scenes in your show. For example, in *The Sound of Music* the nuns in the convent hide the Von Trapp family from the Nazi officers. Or getting the party started at Fezziwig's in *A Christmas Carol*. Or Annie telling her brothers and sisters why she is crazy about Frank Butler in *Annie Get Your Gun*.

4. Make use of the phrase "What if." Set up an improv in the form of a scene from the show, but insert your own "what if" idea that would change the story. For example, in *The Sound of Music* scene above, what if the officers found the Von Trapp family in the convent before they could escape? Ask your young thespians to improvise what might have happened. It helps to raise the importance of Why—the reason they're hiding: they're terribly afraid of being caught and sent to a concentration camp or killed.

Chapter Five
First Things

CASTING—THE AGONY and the ecstasy! It's ecstasy when you've got just the right show for your group, you know you've got people who can really do it well, and there are parts or crew jobs for everyone. It's also ecstasy when the quiet, chubby little kid becomes "Mr. Personality" as soon as he's given lines to say, or when the tall, bespectacled girl suddenly fills her lines with passion and then looks a bit surprised at herself.

AUDITIONS

The first task you face is to announce the dates, times, and place for your tryouts. One director prefers to use the term theater pros use, "casting calls," which seems to make the experience a little less intimidating. One of our fourth graders and her friends happily divided up the parts among themselves when they heard we were going to do *The Wizard of Oz.* They didn't realize they had to audition.

Write out some lines from the show on index cards and make a few copies. Choose short scenes or a few lines that represent each character best, and mark the main character's name clearly on the tops of the cards. Or create your own lines for the audition cards.

Monologues for auditions are okay, but it's better to ask two or three kids to read a short scene together, then watch how they relate to each other. If the parts are unequal in a given scene, create additional lines just for tryout purposes, to give the children a better chance to show what each can do.

They don't necessarily have to be considered only for the part they are reading. We often asked everybody to read for the major characters and then cast them in roles we thought would be good for them. The results of this process could be endearing. When we were casting one show, we asked Michael, a fifth grader and the only boy there at the time, to read the leading man's lines with four or five girls who wanted to play the leading lady. He was about a foot shorter than the girls. We put him up on a round piano stool facing them, so they wouldn't feel foolish looking down at the leading man. Michael read very well, with intensity, but every time he made a point, shaking his finger at the girl, the stool began revolving, leaving him pointing at thin air with the girl behind him. But Michael remained in character throughout.

Releasing the Genie

When we began auditions for *The Wizard of Oz*, our first big show, it was a brand-new experience for most of the children. We were distressed because so many of them followed familiar classroom patterns of standing still with blank faces and reading in a monotone. But a fourth grader, Darren, who had been a regular club member for two or three months, asked to read for the Tin Man. He stiffened his body and moved each part separately, as though they were on rusty hinges. His voice squeaked occasionally. His movements were mechanical. Clearly, he was made of tin. But his heart was in the pink, even though the Tin Man thought it was missing.

This inspired all the new kids, and the readings improved. It was as though their imaginations were the genie let out of Aladdin's lamp. This illustrates not only that children prefer to do shows, but also that they'd rather see shows done by their peers. That seems to be what they love and what gets them excited.

Have plenty of copies of your audition cards so hopefuls can look them over while the people ahead of them try out. We usually stationed one child at a school desk on each side of the stage to hand out the cards and announce the candidates' names. We had lots of volunteers for those jobs. One little girl was rather officious. She made out "passes" for people who wanted to leave for a drink or go to the bathroom.

Have the children line up, two or three at a time on each side, and await their turns to read and sing.

Directing Auditions

Whenever a child finishes reading the first time, it's prudent to make some sort of comment or suggestion, then ask the youngster to try it again. This gives the kids a chance to overcome any nervousness, and it gives you a chance to see how well they take direction. Most of them will give a better reading the second time. Naturally, you shouldn't make destructive comments, but you don't want to be phony either. If you can't honestly say "Wonderful" or "Very good," try saying something like "Nice going," "Good try," or "That was very brave."

Next, give your auditionees some adjustments and directions—for example:

"Next time make sure everyone near the back wall can hear you.
You can face me more and still talk to your partner."

"I'd like to see you make her so mad she wants to slap his face."

"Now, do it again, but this time remember that he's late and was running hard for fifteen minutes."

"Take your time. You don't have to rush. Give yourself a chance to think."

Even if some of the actors are just right, give them some direction so that the others won't feel singled out or inadequate. You might only correct a word or two. One girl chose for her singing audition a song from *My Fair Lady*. She very carefully sang, "Oh, so loverly sitting absolutely blooming still," instead of the witty original: "Oh, so lover-ly sittin' abso-bloomin'-lutely still." We had her try it again.

If you have time and not too many people trying out, you can have a second round of auditions on another day to give them the chance to think about the scene and make improvements.

Audition Anxiety

Auditions can be a trial, full of anxious moments for the kids. Two of our favorite audition stories will serve to illustrate.

We asked all our Dramatics Club members to write their name, address, phone number, and so forth on index cards, and we used the backs of the cards for abbreviated comments on their auditions and what roles they might be able to play. One afternoon, a sweet little girl who had just auditioned couldn't wait to find out what we'd thought of her. As we worked with another child, she pulled her card out of the file box, and we heard an anguished cry. We'd written "VG" (because she was Very Good) but had scribbled it so quickly that she thought it said "Ugh." She quickly got a big hug and reassurance.

Paul Sheils, now an executive at Aetna and then an eighth grader, remembers being mortified because when his singing audition came up, the only song he knew from the show was "I Could Have Danced All Night." But when he sang it, and sang it very well, his buddies sitting in the front row hooted and threw erasers at him because he was singing a girl's song. Publicly, we reprimanded his buddies. Privately, we chuckled.

CASTING DECISIONS

Once all the tryouts are finished, the hard part begins: your decisions. Gather whatever production staff you have who were at the tryouts; arm yourselves with coffee, pencils, papers, cast lists, and all those valuable index cards; and start considering each aspiring young actor.

Usually, you start by narrowing it down to those who are physically right for the various roles. But occasionally casting the opposite way ("against type") can yield fascinating results. Sometimes the little guy can be a much more frightening villain than the big guy. Or the lanky cutup will reveal a tender side that's marvelous for the strong hero.

Often girls can be cast to great advantage in boys' roles, but occasionally you just can't avoid casting a leading girl who's five feet, six inches and a leading boy who is only five feet. Since the disparity is very common around ages eleven to thirteen, you have to adjust when you're staging the show. You can find ways to have one of them sitting while the other is standing, or one up on a platform, or kneeling, or on the opposite side of the stage. The cast will help you.

Physical considerations taken into account, you'll choose those whose auditions were best and who also understood and followed directions well. Also consider dependability and willingness to work. Some of our alumni remember being given parts or having their parts padded just because they were always available and often volunteered to do more work. We also gave students who were graduating first choice for the leading roles, because it was their last chance. But that's up to you.

Once you have the necessary roles cast, you can add characters and jobs to use more of the auditionees. Whoever is left over can fill the ranks of overture singers, understudies, prop gatherers, scene painters, assistants, and callers…even ushers, if necessary.

Barbara Finamore remembers:

> In one big show, I was on the sound effects crew. All I remember is breaking glasses every night. We just adored breaking those glasses. We had our own little group backstage, and as part of that important group, I didn't miss not having any lines.

When all assignments are finally made, set the date to announce your decisions to the cast and crew. You can be sure nobody will be absent from that meeting. One director wisely precedes the announcements by saying, "If you are disappointed you are allowed one day to grieve or feel bad. After that we work as a team." Usually, if you have a part or a job for everyone, you'll witness no jealousy or disappointment—just a lot of happiness and back-pounding. But when you announce it all, be sure to stress that singing in the overture or working on the sound crew are some of the most challenging and essential parts of the show.

When we were casting one show, we decided to cast one group of actors in "walk-on" roles as high-society children in rich families, and another group as street urchins. One little girl, when her father asked her, "So, what part did you get?" replied, "I'm a street walker!" You may find that some kids are just too good to cast as walk-ons (even respectable ones) or to leave out altogether. Your next task, then, is to make the necessary adjustments in the script to accommodate all those people. As we've said, this often results in marvelous scenes because they are now tailor-made to fit your cast.

PRELIMINARIES

To make rehearsals easier for you and your new cast, it is important that you prepare a complete outline of your script. (A sample outline is at the end of the chapter.) Spell out each scene, what happens in it, when it happens, and list all those involved in that scene.

Then make copies of the outline for everyone involved and extra ones to pin up on the bulletin boards and tape onto the backstage walls, dressing rooms, hallways, and prop rooms. If you have very large casts, as we often did, it helps to divide the actors into groups of people: maids, policemen, nurses, sailors, cowboys. Assign a dependable person who is part of each group to be the leader.

The leader's responsibilities during rehearsals are:

> To make sure that the kids stay together in the waiting area to which they're assigned when they're not onstage
>
> To get actors ready for entrances on time
>
> To check that all the props and costumes are accounted for and complete
>
> To know when and where rehearsals are and report to you when someone is absent

These may sound like rather heavy duties for the kids, but in our experience they have always handled them very well.

Prior to rehearsals and during the rehearsal process, you will meet with the people who will be helping you with sets, costumes, and props, as well as lights and sound equipment, if you can get them. Usually your helpers will be a supportive spouse, an older sibling, and friends and parents. If you are in a school, you may be able to lean on some teachers and staff members for help.

Ideally for most productions, in addition to the director, the following individuals would make up the creative and production staff:

A *producer*, whose very important tasks are:

> Preparing script copies, programs, prop lists, and costume needs
>
> Soliciting advertising for your programs (if desired)
>
> Securing publicity by preparing announcements, sending out invitations, and contacting the local news media
>
> Making sure that royalty fees are paid and insurance is in place

The *musical director*, whose responsibilities range from simply playing the piano and coaching the singers to directing a small orchestra behind the scenery or in the pit, depending on the scope of the production.

The *choreographer*, whose duties range from helping a few kids in a ballroom sequence to creating and directing full production numbers.

The *stage manager*, who is the director's right hand, marking all the cues, blocking, and so on in a master copy of the script; calling out the cues for actors, light, and sound during rehearsals and performances; and directing traffic backstage.

Sound and *lighting designers*, whose duties can range from handling one spotlight and two sound-effects cues to presiding over a full sound and light console.

The *scenic designer*, who presides over set design and construction. In the professional theater this person directs a crew of carpenters, prop people, and stagehands. But in our world it might be one local carpenter building a platform for your big number. Parents and kids will do the rest.

The *costume supervisor* (also called wardrobe mistress or master), who acquires and cares for all the costumes and makes sure they are available in the right place at the right time.

A *production assistant* or *secretary* will be helpful to the director and producer for correspondence, note-taking, sitting in for absent actors, or being a general "gofer."

SETS, COSTUMES, AND ALL THE REST

On large productions you will need scenic, lighting, and sound designers, a prop master, and a costume supervisor, along with crews who will be busy during rehearsals organizing, gathering, painting, and building the production. On smaller shows all these people may be just you wearing different "hats" whenever you can find the time. If you are going it alone, keep your project small. Let the size of your undertaking be determined at the outset by the amount of help you think you can muster when it's needed.

And never underestimate the power of the kids! They'll come through in any crisis. They'll think of things and work very hard to meet their deadlines.

Tom Woodruff, an established and acclaimed artist, remembers:

> When I was twelve years old, I already loved art. Doris Fugazy, one of the mothers helping us, said, "Tommy, you can paint the mountain for the backdrop." She gave me several huge pieces of brown paper. I didn't think I could do it, but everyone said I could, so I developed fearlessness and did it, the whole thing. It was that kind of atmosphere, imbued with confidence, in which nobody ever felt stupid.

The technical aspects of your show need not be overwhelming. Keep all the production elements as simple as possible. We never had a real door, archway, or window of any kind in any show. We never even had a full-sized painted backdrop. We did build a few levels with wheels to move onstage when needed—levels can be invaluable—but that requires a good carpenter.

It should be apparent to you by now that most of this depends on how much money there is in your budget, if you have any at all. Many things can be rented from theatrical equipment companies, and there is hardly a limit to how far you can go— with money. All we ever rented was a spotlight to point up a singer or dancer or project patterns on the curtain or wall with cutouts. With only that, instantly it all became a little more professional.

Without full sets, we used only set pieces that could suggest, not replicate, a locale: a large sheet of drywall mounted on braces, with a painting of train windows on it to suggest a train interior, or wallpaper that looked like stained glass pasted on cardboard to identify a scene in a church. Palm trees were made out of decorated poles or posts topped with paper leaves hanging down from all sides. They were all well done insofar as our resources allowed, but they were far from professional. It didn't matter. Staple guns come in VERY handy.

Besides, a realistic set on which a lot of money was spent can overwhelm the actors. Kids do very good work on the stage, but they are not professionals and are still very young. They are the important things onstage, not the sets. Every spring our backyard was filled with children painting sets on cardboard boxes or sheets of styrofoam, draping old furniture with older curtains, and making papier-mâché props.

In our groups all the kids were responsible for their own costumes. Costumes can be easy to come by. Attics, closets, and dresser drawers in any home can produce a treasure trove of wardrobe items for almost any production. The less valuable items can be adapted for use with the help of mothers and fathers who know how to use a sewing machine. A next to last resort are tag sales, rummage sales, or eBay for great bargains. One resourceful costume director bought prom dresses at $15 each, used them for the "royal" characters, then rented them out again as prom dresses.

The Bibliography lists a few reference books for costumes that can help, as well as texts on scenery construction and theatrical makeup. Many pictorial history books should be available at your library to reveal facts about clothing worn in other times and places.

SCHEDULING REHEARSALS

It will be your task now to prepare a reasonable *rehearsal schedule* for the full rehearsal period. Make plenty of copies for everybody involved and post them all over the place. On each day of this schedule, show clearly which scenes are to be rehearsed and which actors or groups of actors are needed. The schedule should also include the time and location of each work session for those involved in other aspects of the production: finding or making props, sets, and costumes; copying script changes; writing programs and announcements; designing flyers; planning publicity, and so on.

How long will all this take? Our schedule for large shows that were produced once a year with grade school and junior high children will give you some idea of what might be involved. We held our auditions in January. After the cast was set, we began writing or rewriting the script and started preplanning, enlisting help, and preparing for rehearsals. Rehearsals usually began around mid-March, and the play or musical was presented in mid-May, on a date that did not conflict with tests or graduation.

As you can see, it took a long time. This was because of relatively short rehearsal periods after school, lasting two to two and a half hours at the most, and because of the adults' responsibilities to jobs and domestic concerns. Smaller productions, of course, will require much less time.

When they estimate the total amount of actual rehearsal time needed, some directors allow an average of one hour per page of script; others feel that's much more than is needed. You can always adjust as you go along—the last version of your rehearsal schedule will probably look much different from the first. But try to allow at least two or three days for catch-up toward the end as a safety margin.

In your initial rehearsals, you want your cast to simply read the script out loud, making no attempt to act it. The amount of time you spend in these reading rehearsals depends on the difficulty of your script and the concentration capabilities and age groups of your cast. Reading rehearsals are very important, but, by far, most of the time will be devoted to staging, blocking, and scene rehearsals (see Chapter 6); and on final run-throughs, technical rehearsals, and dress rehearsals (see Chapter 7).

It's difficult to forecast which of these two later rehearsal periods will take more time. Here again, much depends on the age and abilities of the kids. As with any enterprise, good planning brings you most of the way toward the goal. You can calculate the full production time as approximately two months for a large production of an hour-and-a-half musical, and less time for smaller productions. Once you take the children through many of the exercises, improvs, and games discussed in earlier chapters, you will have a clearer idea of the children's abilities and will be better able to apportion your time.

Others who work with junior and senior high-school kids spend as much as two and a half to three months, rehearsing three weekdays after school for two and a half hours, then two weekdays in the evening for the same time. This allows time for other after-school activities and leaves weekends entirely for the family. Closer to the show date, one or two weekends might be required.

A sample time schedule for the short scene, Spark of Liberty, is at the end of Chapter 7. Although it only spans the ten days required for rehearsing a short piece, it has all the elements described above and can be expanded and used as a guide for a larger show.

REHEARSAL BASICS

Now that you've selected, adapted, or created the show, cast it, locked in your schedules, and assigned your crew jobs, and now that you've met with your creative and production staff, agreed on the various ideas, defined tasks, and delegated responsibilities…*now* you are ready to begin rehearsing.

First, let's consider what happens the first day of rehearsals for a Broadway musical. We did not do all the same things in our Dramatics Club; neither were we fortunate enough to have most of the facilities described here. You will be in the same situation with your group. But here's a procedure that works for the professionals and that you can use as a guide for a large production.

The Broadway musical's rehearsal space might be a large conference room in a hotel or other building, but more often it will be a professional rehearsal hall with a good floor, mirrors and bars for dancers; a piano, plenty of chairs and tables for scripts, music, props, designers' drawings; and helpful background information such as photos and articles relating to the historical time and place of the story.

On the first day, after everyone has been identified, they are shown the costume and scenery sketches and a model of the set. Next, the musical director plays and sings the music for everyone. The producer greets everyone assembled and describes the journey they will all take together in happy and hopeful terms. The stage manager will spell out the rehearsal times and explain the floor plans and all the rules necessary for a smooth operation. The schedules for costume and wig fittings and for music and dance rehearsals will be posted on a wall.

A well-prepared stage manager and his or her assistants will have already put strips of variously colored tape on the bare floor, accurately defining the size and shape of the actual stage where the play will be performed. Other lines of tape will demarcate the set's boundaries: the walls, doors, steps, trees, windows, entrances, counters, and so on. This is done to acquaint everyone with the floor plan—director, actors, and designers. They also will have set out temporary props and furnishings to use for rehearsing, such as chairs, stools, cups, bags, hats, canes, and even a large wagon or table on wheels to simulate a car.

Most directors will spend at least a couple of days with the cast just reading the script, talking about it, and reading it again before they start "putting it up on its feet"—that is, before they begin staging. Very simply, staging and blocking are terms that mean directing people to move around on the stage as they will eventually in performance. The actors still have their scripts in hand, marking each move as they listen to the director. We'll go into detail about blocking in Chapter 6.

Again, that's the way the professionals do it. Of course, they have a lot of resources and experienced people. You can adjust their procedures to fit your own operation. Maybe this will involve only you and a few actors sitting around your kitchen table playing cassette tapes to see what, if any, music you want to use. Or trying to remember what furniture might be in your various attics that will fit into the set. If you have a bigger group involved early on, your adult helpers and most of the production staff will go off to do the technical work while you and the cast begin readings and rehearsing.

Finding an Approach
All professional directors have their own rehearsal patterns. Robert Lewis, for example,

who directed the original Broadway production of *Brigadoon* among many others, sometimes read the whole script to the cast himself on the first day of rehearsal, so that the actors, following along in their scripts, would get a sense of how the audience would perceive the show before they began to concentrate on their individual parts. His intention was not that the actors copy his line readings, but only that they gain a feeling of how the whole story develops and how the pace within it varies and builds.

Ray Fry, a director at the Actors' Theatre of Louisville, asks members of the cast to read their own lines aloud together, then discuss and work on them for several days before staging begins. On the third or fourth day, limited blocking might begin, followed by another reading. The procedure continues to rotate blocking and reading sessions until it's time to attempt complete "run-throughs"—rehearsals of the whole show from start to finish. This rehearsal method allows the actors to alternate their concentration on words and meanings with their concentration on movements and staging. One reinforces the other and ensures a growth in the actors' understanding.

The director Arthur Penn has used another approach in his first rehearsals: he'd ask the actors to read their lines aloud and the stage manager to read all the movement and set directions. After a short break, the members of the cast turn their scripts over to the stage manager, regroup at the table, and begin talking through the play without the scripts. They say what they remember of their lines and describe what happens as well as they can on the basis of the read-through. The director then returns the scripts to them, and they repeat the whole process as often as it is helpful and as time permits.

Penn's procedure is especially valuable for very complicated scripts because it helps to define what is happening, and when it is happening, throughout the entire show. The story and the characters then come together with more clarity and logic.

Choose any method that seems to be most beneficial for your cast. Keep in mind that at least one thorough and complete reading rehearsal is essential.

WARM-UP EXERCISES

If you have not had the time to conduct a few sessions in which to do exercises, improvs, and so on, we recommend some warm-up exercises before you begin the reading rehearsal. These will demonstrate to the actors that there are many different ways to speak their lines. It all depends on the situations and the thoughts behind them. Try this "As if" exercise: Ask someone to say "I love it" a number of different ways, as if…

It's food that tastes awful.	It's food that tastes good.
It's a surprise gift.	It's an unwelcome gift.
It's an evil idea.	It's a beautiful work of art.

There are innumerable ways to say those three simple words through speech and body movement. Or, use any other phrase, such as "What are you doing?" "Just a minute," or even just "Hello," answering the phone as if you're in a hurry, or have been waiting for this call, or as if to mean "stop bothering me."

Other exercises, including Truth and the ABC Game (explained later in this chapter) are superb ones to do before any of your rehearsals. If you move to using the real lines too quickly, that's all you'll get—no physical behavior. You risk getting just the deadly recitation of words.

FIRST READINGS OF THE SCRIPT

However you decide to order your rehearsal procedures, tread carefully, especially on those first days. They're very important because the directions given then are the ones that stay in the actors' memory the longest. This is the time to keep everyone focused on questions instead of hard-and-fast decisions.

In the first reading, seat all the actors around the table, and explain that their purpose at the beginning is to learn everything they can about the show and not to worry about performance. As one director used to say, "Just see how the words feel in your mouth."

After the first reading, talk about it. At first, ask a lot of general five-W questions, such as:

> Who are the characters?
>
> What is happening to them?
>
> What are the main characters trying to do?
>
> Why are they trying to do these things? What feelings are making them want to do them?
>
> What are the others trying to do, and why?
>
> Where is it taking place?

Talk about some of the sensory details of the setting. Don't forget to discuss the time. When does it all happen—what time of day, what year, what season? Ask what happened before the play started, and even what made that happen. Finally, ask simply: What is the play really about?

Avoid trying to answer *all* the questions at first. After all, asking questions, finding out together what behavior the answers suggest, and then choosing what works best for the show—these activities will be your primary approach, at least until you get into run-throughs and technical rehearsals. In order to arrive at the best collaborative results you will be constantly using phrases like:

> How about...?   What if...?

Why don't we try…?   Did you feel…?

Suppose you…?

Doing a production of *Into the Woods*, Kathel Brennan used the "As if" approach in directing an eighth-grade boy whose character's mother had just died. She asked him if he'd ever had a dog, and he said, "Yes, but he was killed by a car." Kathel suggested he recall that experience: how his body felt, what happened to his breathing, how the skin on his arms felt, what he wanted to do when it happened. She said, "Although the death of the mother would be a much bigger loss than the death of your pet, when you play the scene you can play it *as if* you were going through the same experience again." The young actor played the scene very well after that.

The Gossip Game

If you have time, do another read-through of the whole play and tell the actors you're going to try the Gossip Game afterward. We learned this wonderful approach to working on characterization from an excellent teacher, George Morrison, and have used it to advantage with children above third grade.

Ask the cast (or at least most of the principal players, if the cast is very large) to sit in a circle. Working strictly from the script and all the things that will have been inferred so far from the script, ask each person, one at a time, to speak as his or her character would, verbalizing the character's thoughts about each of the other characters in the play. Ask each one to start by spelling out what he or she does not like about all the other characters, one by one, perhaps with:

> "What I really don't like…"

> "What I can't stand…"

> "What I really hate about…"

Then the actors should begin telling what they *do* like about each of the other characters with:

> "On the other hand, what is great about…"

> "What I really love about…"

> "A redeeming factor about this guy is…"

Again, each actor expresses ideas based solely on the script. Everyone should concentrate on what the others say about his or her character. It may seem complicated, but we assure you, it is a shortcut in characterization. It speeds up the work on the Who question, as each actor digs into his or her character's reactions to all the others. It leads easily to very colorful and specific behavior and much clearer relationships.

Recently Marla Truini, the head of the drama department of Westover, a Connecticut teenage girls' boarding school, was directing a production of *Fiddler On the Roof*. Not an easy task—to help young, modern, mostly American girls to understand the feelings, values, attitudes, and behavior of Russian Jews in the early 1900s. So one day the whole cast played the Gossip Game. In playing it, the girls really had to search their characters' feelings about each other character in relation to that specific time and place—what kind of behavior won their approval or disapproval, what they feared or condoned, what they dreamed of achieving or resented in others' achievements or disloyalties. They found out which characters wanted to lead in rebellion, and which felt safer to follow or submit. They learned how important tradition was to most of them, but which ones ached for change. And it made a big difference in the whole show. It kept the girls from caricaturing. The audience was amazed at how completely they believed those young actresses, in difficult roles.

After the Gossip Game, read through the play again, but slowly. Stop occasionally as needed to talk about the five Ws as they apply to every aspect of the show, each scene or character. As the individual emotions of each character appear spontaneously in the children's readings, you can talk about them. However, don't push the actors to show them. Otherwise, they might be pressured to fake their feelings.

Finally, ask your actors to examine how their characters are both different from and the same as themselves. For instance, the girl playing Eliza Doolittle might say, "Well, Eliza has a lot of guts and speaks right up to Higgins, but I don't think I would dare to do that myself. I'm too shy. But both Eliza and I love to learn things and like to be good at something."

Personalizing the lyrics to songs in a musical can deepen their meaning and effectiveness substantially. In *Fiddler on the Roof*, the cast sings the sad song, "Anatevka," about their grief at being forced to leave their beloved village and the ordinary, mundane things—a pot, a pan, a book, a broom, a hat—that are so meaningful to them. In the first rehearsals of the song, those were just words until Marla Truini, the director, stopped the girls to ask each one to tell about an object that was very special to her and would break her heart to lose. After a few minutes of quiet thought, each girl revealed her own private, well-loved object: a plush toy, her own room, a stuffed animal, her little sister's blanket. When they sang the song again, the words were filled with a sweet pathos, and in the performance they made the audience weep.

Working on Dialogue

We don't recommend stopping or slowing down too much during the readings in order to figure out what the words mean and what their context is. However, at this point you can stop the actors' reading *occasionally* to paraphrase some lines of dialogue to make their meanings clearer. Or ask the actors to do the paraphrasing themselves—that is, put the lines into their own words to make sure they know what their characters are really saying.

Suppose Charlene, in the title role of *The Little Mermaid*, a play by William

Glennon, has the line "Your Prince—does he ever sail off in a tremendous vessel with huge white sails?" That might be too stilted or formal for some fourth or fifth graders. To make it easier for her, ask her to paraphrase it by putting it into her own words such as: "Tell me about this Prince. Does he ever take off in a cool, humongous boat?" Then she can go back and say the written line more easily.

Also, it's helpful occasionally to suggest an unspoken thought that the actor, as the character, might be thinking before she says her line. This might lead her to say that line in a certain way. For example, Charlene, above, might have been thinking, "Is it true?" "Are you sure?" or simply, "Wow!"

As the director you want to encourage the actors to find the best way to interpret the dialogue themselves. Under normal conditions you should not give "line readings"—that is, try not to say the lines for them the way you think they should be read. As one of our former members said, "That can turn them into dead wood." Occasionally, a young child will need that kind of help. Most of the time, however, just giving the child a good, strong "as if," mentioning the character's feelings, will put him on the right track. Generally you want to avoid achieving the right results too quickly or having the kids reach performance levels right away. Let their own ideas form and "cook." Otherwise, something important could be overlooked.

If someone's line reading doesn't make sense or sound right to you, use the five Ws to help identify the important, or operative, words in the speech, the ones to emphasize. Amateur actors sometimes tend to read punctuation instead of meanings. The periods at the ends of sentences do not necessarily mean the voice should drop off on the last word of every sentence.

Consider the possible operative words in these lines:

"Go fight *City Hall*."

"A stitch in time saves *nine*."

"It is the moon and Juliet is the *sun*."

"Dedicated to the proposition that all men are created *equal*."

Often, though not always, the last sentence of a speech may be the important one that the previous sentences lead up to. So, too, may the last word in that sentence be an important (operative) word.

While you're all still at the table reading the script, before you get your actors up on their feet to stage the show, the next big step, recap your discussions about the five Ws of the story and the sensory elements on which to concentrate. Having these things in the forefront of their imaginations will help them make sense of the blocking you'll be giving them and will even stimulate them to initiate good ideas for movement themselves. It will tie the dialogue and movements together and make them eager to start acting with their whole bodies. And rather than mechanically following directions, they will keep their behavior real throughout the rehearsal process.

DEVELOPING CHARACTERIZATIONS

One of the best ways for actors young and old to work on characterization is to stay entirely in character during rehearsal periods, not just when they are saying their lines but when they talk with the director or the actors about the script, movements, or anything else.

It is also important that every single one of the characters has a name. Often the smaller roles and members of the chorus or ensemble aren't assigned proper names in the script. The late director Mike Ockrent, when he was rehearsing the touring company of *Crazy for You*, a musical, remedied this situation when he met with each member of the ensemble privately for fifteen or twenty minutes. During that time they decided on a name for the character and thoroughly discussed the character's background, hopes and dreams, relations to the other characters, and function in the play.

For instance, one singer-dancer decided that his character fancied himself a poet and journalist. It was a neat touch on the stage to see him in the background of the seedy, one-horse town of Deadrock, Nevada, writing down ideas in his brown leather notebook, showing it to another character in the background, and then shoving it into his pocket when a dance or other routine came up. Of course, the director's job is to ensure that such movements are not distracting from the main scene.

After he had met with each member of the cast in this manner, Ockrent called the whole company together, and each one in turn gave a short description of the character based on the meeting. This was stimulating for everyone.

Once individual characterizations are found, it is, of course, important to find the right group relationships. Several improvisations helped the girls at Westover who were playing Tevya, Golda, and the daughters in *Fiddler on the Roof* to be able to behave as one family. In one improv each girl was asked to "model some clothes as Golda approved or criticized their choices or handiwork." In another, the girls "cooked a meal" with their mother. In another, Golda was to "become very ill" and the daughters were to discover their mother's condition and deal with it. In that improv, the two youngest daughters panicked and raced into another part of the rehearsal hall where Tevya was working on a song. They cried out to him to "Come quick!" that they were afraid Golda was dying. The girl playing Tevya ran to the other rehearsal space, where Golda was lying (on three chairs side by side), knelt down beside her in anguish, took her pulse, felt her forehead, started ordering the girls around to get help, boil water, etc. So now the family had a history together.

ADDING SENSORY ELEMENTS

When you can motivate your young actors to make the sensory elements real to themselves, they will be more than ready to move onstage in logical and natural ways. For instance, the pirates sneaking through the dark woods to snare Peter Pan will move on the stage quite differently from the rich people huddling together in the rain hailing a hansom cab in *My Fair Lady*, or the nuns walking in quiet convent halls in *The Sound of Music*. A rolling ship, a lurching train, and an icy path affect the senses and the behavior in different ways.

If a fellow is hot and sweaty and filthy from work, he doesn't throw his arms around his girlfriend as readily as he would at a party. The way a character crosses to a chair and sits can tell us whether she is hurt, angry, exhausted, or happy. How a character enters a room can inform an audience about the weather outside or the person's age, health, strength, and mental state (confused, scared, joyful, curious). Those factors will often determine where the actor goes in the room and where the others in the room go in relation to where he or she is. It's fun for the actors to find all those clues with the director.

Eventually, if your staging will be calling for a whole group to look out into the audience as if (for example) they're watching the clay pigeons that Annie Oakley and Frank Butler shoot, it's necessary for them to begin imagining it early on.

The better everyone understands the words and the story of the play and all its sensory elements, the more fruitful your next important step, blocking, will be. Many directors choose to delay blocking until the actors are champing at the bit to get up on their feet. If their thoughts are beginning to translate into a need to express themselves physically, it's time to get them onto the stage, in the set, and block out their moves. This begins the process of staging the show, the subject of the next chapter.

Sample Audition Cards, Production Outline, and Warm-ups

AUDITIONS

Here are examples of tryout lines to write on your audition cards:

1. For a musical such as *My Fair Lady*:

LONDON URCHIN: Please, sir, have you got a penny? Me mother is sick. She's had to stop workin'. And we ain't got nothin' in the house to eat. Please, sir. We're awful bad off. Me dad's gone off to his great reward. Just a penny—please?

2. For two children in a musical such as *The Sound of Music*:

FIRST CHILD: We started to walk home and suddenly it got all dark, and big black clouds covered up the sun. And then it started to thunder and we saw some lightning. And my little brother started to cry. So we ran back here. I'm scared, too.

SECOND CHILD: Scared?! You think I'm scared? You're off your rocker. You think I'd be scared to go home in a little thunderstorm? That doesn't scare me a bit. I could walk home with my eyes blindfolded. I just came in to see where everybody was, that's all. I just wanted to see what was going on in here. (*Hears a loud thunderclap.*) Heck. I'm not s-s-scared at all.

FIRST CHILD: I don't know what to do. Can we stay here for a while? Can we stay here until the storm's over?

3. For a musical such as *Oliver!*:

YOUNG LONDON HOOD: Come on in, kid. Make yourself at 'ome. Nobody's gonna hurt ya. We're all just down on our luck 'ere. But we stick together and listen to the Boss. He takes care of us s'long as we do what the bloke says—and don't tell nobody. Come on!

SAMPLE OUTLINE FOR A PRODUCTION

When you're doing a large production, an outline of the show is an extremely important aid. It is used by all the actors and crew and all the people who are helping. It's an essential guide before and during the performance. Your outline might break down each scene as shown here:

TITLE OF PLAY

Act I

| *Scene 1* | *Opening number* | *Script Page 1* |

[Here, all the characters in the scene are listed by name and role. For the sake of the sample, there are fourteen. The singing and dancing chorus are not in this scene.]

Names of characters	**Names of actors**
_____	_____
_____	_____
_____	_____
_____	_____
_____	_____
_____	_____
_____	_____
_____	_____
_____	_____
_____	_____
_____	_____
_____	_____
_____	_____
_____	_____

| Scene 2 | Parade is announced | Script Page 3 |

Only the little children are in the scene, as listed above for Scene 1. It is advisable to list these children's names again here, as above.]

| Scene 3 | Parade scene | Script Page 6 |

The fourteen characters in the scene, plus chorus of singers and dancers. [They are listed here by character and actors' names.]

| Scene 4 | The big argument | Script Page 8 |

The fourteen characters from Scene 3, but singers and dancers have exited. [The names need not be listed here again.]

| Scene 5 | Heroine's entrance | Script Page 9 |

The eighteen characters in the scene. [For "heroine" above you will use the character's name. And avoid terms like "leading lady" or "leading man"! Now the fourteen characters are joined by four more. All are listed here.]

| Scene 6 | Hero besieged by fans | Script Page 11 |

The seven characters in the scene. [Here they are listed by name and role.]

| Scene 7 | Crossover in front of curtain, song reprise | Script Page 12 |

The five characters in the scene. [They are listed by name and role.]

…And so on, for every act and individual scene. In one of our productions, there were thirty-six separate scenes, so you can understand how important a guide like this can be. These outlines should be posted everywhere on the set and on all bulletin boards, and copies should be given to every child.

WARM-UP EXERCISES

Exercises preceding the first reading rehearsals, especially if you have not had any previous sessions for preparatory training, are very helpful. They demonstrate flexibility in saying lines depending upon the circumstances of the scenes. You should stress that the kids can use their bodies to emphasize and focus the meaning.

1. Entrances

Line the kids up just off the stage area. Ask each one in turn to ENTER the stage using the verb you give him. For example, bounce on, crawl on, dance on, edge on, fall on, gallop on, hurry on, etc. You can go right through the alphabet: assist, back, cringe, drop, and on to sneak, trounce, unload, voom, etc. Or ask them to choose their own verbs. Hopefully this will let them know there are already many, many ways just to enter a stage to begin with. Of course you'll probably find that a lot of them will want to do cartwheels or twirl onto the stage. That's O.K., too.

2. Truth

Give two children a set of circumstances and ask them to improvise a scene. You can make up the circumstances or try some of these:

> Two kids wait in the principal's office to find out what punishment they will receive after they were caught skipping school and making trouble in the playground.

> Two kids are walking home. One is afraid the other might tell on him or her for cheating on a test.

> Patients wait in a dentist's office. One is in great pain; the other is still numb from anesthetic.

> Dancers or singers warm up for a performance.

> Two soldiers hide from an enemy.

> Two robbers sit in a getaway car watching for their partner to run out of the bank.

> Two people stand on a bridge after they've had a big fight.

The catch is that they can say only things that are *literally* true. For instance, in the principal's office, one kid might get up and pace around, or offer gum to the other, or look out a window, or try to listen at the office door. One might even cry or whistle. But even though the words said are applied to a "pretend" situation, they must be true. If one asks the other what time it is, the other must give him the accurate time at that moment. If one is wearing a blue shirt, the other can say, "That's some blue shirt you've got on." Or another can say, if it's true, "Funny, but I'm feeling great." Or, "I saw Mary yesterday" (if he or she really did). Or, "I'm going to tell my Dad about this" (if the actor really intends to tell his or her own father about the improv).

They are not allowed to say something like, "I didn't think the principal would catch us," or "What do you think the principal will do to us?" or "We never got caught skipping school before." Since every line has to be literally true at the moment for the two actors, whatever they say may seem innocuous and unrelated to the situation. However, the situation—that they are in trouble—will accent and color their words distinctively. It will, in other words, "show through" if the actors are truthfully playing the scene.

3. ABC game

This popular warm-up game using a change in the relationship between two people is described in Session 3 of the Leader's Guide. We recommend it for early rehearsals.

The way people say things greatly depends on how well they're paying attention to their partners and what attitudes they perceive when their partners are talking and listening.

4. Translator
This is a twist on a gibberish game. Set up an improv situation for two people who speak a different language and cannot understand each other:

> Two diplomats in conference at the United Nations
>
> An employer and potential employee
>
> A lawyer and a client or witness
>
> Two people on a blind date
>
> A dancing teacher and a student

These characters talk gibberish, then are joined by a third actor who serves as the translator. He or she must interpret, in English, what the other two say in gibberish. The first two actors will quickly learn if they have made themselves clear in their gibberish acting.

5. Silent movie
You can also save this exercise for later rehearsals. Let your actors rehearse a scene as if they were in a silent movie, mouthing the words and imagining the music that the movie house organist or pianist might be playing. It helps if someone can play the piano or find appropriate music tapes to play for them.

6. The preceding thought
This exercise is described in Session 6 of the Leader's Guide. We recommended it to demonstrate how differently lines can be said, depending on the circumstances. For example, you might say "I beg your pardon" one way if your preceding thought was "Oh, no! I shouldn't have done that!" and quite another way if your preceding thought was "What an insulting thing to say to me!!"

Chapter Six
Staging and Blocking

ONCE YOUR YOUNG ACTORS' ideas begin to translate into a need to express themselves physically, it's time to get them onto the stage, and block out their moves. That is, you will now assign them certain positions onstage and give them other positions and moves as the scenes dictate. That's why the job is called directing, and it implies that you must be in charge.

It has been said that directors in theater, stage, and television are supreme, that they must be the ultimate authority, a dictator. Otherwise, there can be chaos. Perhaps that's the reason a few of them become pompous, authoritarian, and overly impressed with their own position. Those few forget they can be hired and fired at will by those who hold the purse strings: the corporate CEO, the executive producer, or the school principal. In our own world, away from klieg lights and show-biz pressures, we find there is some justification for this concept of director as ultimate ruler. Someone has to create the conditions, decide on procedures, and be the final arbiter in all disagreements.

We remember when, early in rehearsals of a large production, two or three different interpretations of a scene were being debated by about thirty children. Control disappeared rapidly as everyone talked and shouted louder and louder about the process. Finally our director walked over to the edge of the stage, slammed her hand down, and shouted, *"Quiet!"* There was a stunned silence. They weren't fully acquainted yet with the actress who had taken on this responsibility. She said, firmly but quietly, "There is only one director of this show, and I am it. I welcome your suggestions when you offer them quietly and courteously, and I will listen to them and then make a decision."

After another moment of silence, they all applauded and listened carefully. We were pleased they had quieted down, but were more pleased at their approval. In general, everything was now under control, which actually made them very happy. It remained that way during this and other productions.

CHARACTERISTICS OF A GOOD DIRECTOR

Because the director is the link between the performance and the audience, he or she keeps in mind the varied audience that will see the production. They will be parents and grandparents, neighborhood friends, church groups, small children, and others. If you are using a school facility, there will be a special performance for all the students. In other words, there will be the very young and the very old. Clarity of speech and simplicity of plot should be kept in mind. Bolder emphasis on some characters or story elements to underline certain scenes may be necessary.

It won't necessarily be a sophisticated New York City audience, so be sensitive to local values when editing dialogue and scenes if you are doing a show that originated on Broadway. Censorship? Sure! Those are kids onstage and in the audience.

The director also has responsibility to the play and, especially when working with children, to the actors. This includes enlightening them not only about the world of the play (the London of *My Fair Lady*, for example, or the seventeenth-century Salem witch trials of Arthur Miller's *The Crucible*) but about working together as a team, explaining things they need to know about the process of putting on a show, and shepherding them through it.

All young members of a cast require individual handling, which will allow them to grow. Therefore you must know what you're going to do and what you want from the actor. As the director you will tell the actor what that is, but you must tell him or her not by giving an order but by *explaining* what the circumstances require. To elicit the best line readings from the kids, try asking them questions about how the character feels, suggesting what the characters' motives are, or giving them an "as if" from their own lives. It's best to avoid showing how to read a line or make a movement, but you may occasionally have to do that for the youngest. Sometimes just laughing and showing them a big exaggeration of how you'd like it to be done will give shy children a green light to break loose. But if you always seem to just want the kids to imitate you, their own creativity will be sadly dampened.

A good director will encourage the actors to bring their own creative ideas to the blocking rehearsals. When we were doing *South Pacific*, we had about thirty boys playing sailors. We were starting to block the "Nothing Like a Dame" number, so we asked the boys to name some of the things the sailors might carry around with them. They suggested snapshots of their families and girlfriends, address books, magic tricks, jingling coins, small Bibles, pocketknives, souvenirs, cards, dice, and even Japanese-English pocket dictionaries. We asked them to bring in as many of these items as they could find. One boy who was vain brought in a comb and used it constantly. Others gathered to play cards, roll dice, or show one another snapshots. They provided countless ideas for staging that easily led into the song and helped fill out the behavior in the early parts of the number.

PREPARING TO STAGE THE SHOW

A primary task of the director is to ensure that rehearsal schedules are maintained. Thus, thorough preparation well ahead of time is essential, to avoid crippling delays later.

Before the reading rehearsals begin, you should go through the entire script, noting all the givens—entrances, exits, crossings from one side of the stage to another, the moment a character pulls up a chair to sit, hangs up a coat, falls down, and so on. Then jot down in the page margins any business you believe is motivated by the dialogue and characters. *Business* is a term that refers to physical movements and other actions that help to make a point in a scene, bring out a facet of a character, or add a moment of laughter in comedy and farce.

If you are doing a production of a previously produced play or musical, chances are that movements and other directions, including the use of props, are already indicated in the script. Use them if they fit into the space you have. They were planned by the original director of the professional production and therefore should be beneficial. But you can always change anything to suit your needs, and even your youngest actors will occasionally have a better idea than you or the professionals had. (Just swallow your pride and go with it!)

Richard Carter, who directed many Shakespeare plays with children, used actors to create not just characters but effects. In *The Tempest* the young actors created the storm, vocally and visually; in *Twelfth Night*, they linked hands in the shape of a boat, surrounding the characters within; in *A Christmas Carol* they threw snowflakes. Incidentally, an audience member told Mr. Carter that he was "painlessly teaching Shakespeare."

When the reading rehearsals are completed, the first day of "being on their feet" arrives, and everyone begins to move, including you. As director, you have a fundamental obligation to the audience as well as to the children, and during rehearsals you must become the eyes and ears of the audience. The actor is encouraged in his or her creative imagination, but the director is responsible for the final product and has the final word on how it all looks from the house.

During early rehearsals, you want to resist the temptation to jump in and solve problems for young actors. Be a benevolent dictator. Give them a chance to solve problems as they emerge; you can always fix things later if they still need fixing.

A few years ago we were directing a group of short one-act plays for our Young Angels Theatre Company. Four of the plays were written by young members of the 52nd Street Project in New York City. Each had only two to five characters. After casting them, first we read through each play a couple of times and talked about the sensory elements in each one and the five Ws. Second, we set up the necessary stage pieces like markings for doors and windows, furniture, and essential props. Then we asked the young actors to improvise each play using only gibberish, numbers, or letters of the alphabet instead of the real lines. The *plays almost staged themselves.* The youngsters had to think about what their characters were trying to accomplish in that situation and use their bodies instead of words to make the story clear. It's a neat shortcut that we highly recommend.

Those of you who have experience in theater or have directed productions in a school with even a limited amount of equipment will already know some or much of what follows. Skim through it, if you like, and consider any parts that will help you.

STAGE MOVEMENT BASICS

Any profession as old as the theater will collect arcane language and customs over time. On all the world's stages, stage directions are defined from the point of view of the actor as he or she faces the audience. Thus, stage right means to the actor's right. Two terms stem from long ago when most stage floors were *raked*, or slanted down, toward the audience (some still are for certain productions). Moving *downstage* thus means moving toward the audience, and *upstage* toward the rear wall.

As the director gives the actors directions about where and how to move on the stage, they will find it helpful to jot down arrows and other symbols in the script. Here's a list of common ones:

SR & SL: Stage Right & Stage Left

UR & UL: Upstage Right & Upstage Left

CR & CL: Center Right & Center Left

DR & DL: Downstage Right & Downstage Left

UC & DC: Upstage Center & Downstage Center

C: Center

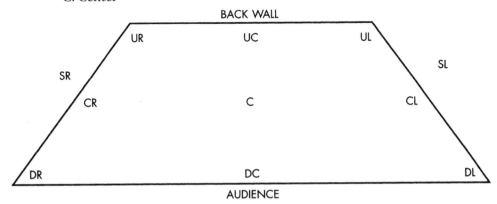

Combinations of these can indicate diagonal movements. Actors will develop their own shorthand, and there may be some who can remember most of the movements without marking the script, as many dancers can. Directors and many actors commonly use the picture notations shown on page 130.

ACTOR STANDING   ACTOR SITTING   ACTOR RECLINING

ACTOR RISING OR SITTING DOWN

TABLE

CHAIRS

WINDOW

DOOR

MOVEMENT AND DIRECTION ARROWS

ACTOR MOVES UL,
SITS IN CHAIR

ACTOR RISES,
MOVES DL,
LIES ON BED

There are two ways for actors to acquire and understand moves onstage that fit the character and the action. In one, the actors determine their own movements by groping their way through, trying this and then that, and eventually coming up with an insight into the stage "picture" in relation to themselves and the other actors. This may work well in a theater where experienced actors, writers, dancers, musicians, and one director all work together over a period of time in various productions—in a repertory company, for instance.

In another approach, among professionals who haven't worked together and especially with younger amateurs, the director determines the movements, at least in a general way beforehand, then gives the actors their blocking—that is, tells them when to move, sit, lie down, go up the stairs or onto another level, move the lamp, or pick up the sword. Actors will often realize or figure out later why the move was made, if it's not obvious immediately.

At other times actors may ask the reason for a move or piece of business and be told by the director that *they* must determine the reason and method of getting there because that's where the director needs them. It's always helpful, if you have the time, to give the child actor a motive for the move yourself, unless your actors are already able to justify directions on their own, as we discussed in Chapter 3.

GUIDING THE AUDIENCE'S EYES

Did you know that some places on the stage are more interesting than others? The eyes of the audience (at least, those of an American audience) move more naturally from left to right; they are accustomed to seeing more important things there such as the lead story on the front page of a newspaper or a stop sign on the corner. Therefore, being downstage left (DL) will hold the attention of the audience better than being downstage center (DC).

The following are other practical guidelines for guiding audience attention:

> Moving downstage from upstage center (UC) is a powerful movement or entrance, but remaining downstage center (DC) can be dull.

> Downstage left (DL) is the most interesting position. (Remember: DL is to the audience's right.) DR is the only other position that is normally advantageous.

> The best entrances besides UC entrances are DL. But an entrance made near the actors onstage will be the most important.

> DR is best for an exit.

Melt a Witch? Ask a Kid.

It was a nine-year-old who found the way to melt the Wicked Witch in our production of *The Wizard of Oz*. She and Dorothy were playing a scene standing just in front of a curtain that was raised three inches above the floor and was almost touching the Witch's back. When Dorothy threw the bucket of water (aluminum foil scraps) on the Witch, the Witch writhed and screamed, "No, you mustn't throw water on me, you wicked girl!" Then she moved her arms up under her wide, full-length cape, undid a hook at the throat, and, as she twisted down to her knees and then to her stomach, she gradually lifted the neck of the cape up to the brim of the hat, making sure her entire body remained covered by the cape. She shoved her feet and legs behind her, under the curtain, where a fourth grader was ready to pull her back and out of sight. The Witch's hat gradually settled down onto the crumpled cape on the floor, and that was all that was left of the Witch. Dorothy swept the hat and cape off the stage, and the entire audience rose to give the kids a big hand.

Once, in a frantic summer-theater dress rehearsal, an actress we know was supposed to enter in a heavy winter coat. But she barely made her costume change and accidentally entered the stage through the closet door. When an entrance or an exit happens, it is usually the most important thing happening onstage. So entrances and exits must not only be from the correct place, but must always be motivated, well-timed, and in character. Characters don't just wander in and out or across the set.

Entrances are often "built up" by the playwright. For example, a mother is talking about her son, then he makes his entrance. As director, you can point up such moments with offstage effects like a doorbell, the sound of a car pulling up, or a crowd murmuring. (If you create crowd effects offstage, have a mixture of people randomly speak the words "Murmur, murmur…Walla, walla…Tennessee, Tennessee." It will really sound like a crowd.)

Delayed entrances, where everybody is staring at the door, can be effective if well timed. And unusual entrances can be very arresting—by way of trap doors, swinging on a rope, even tripping on a rug—but be careful: they must make sense and have a real point.

Most exit lines are split lines: "I'll come later—if I feel like it." The first words are delivered on the move toward the door, the last words as the actor passes through the door.

EXPRESSING RELATIONSHIPS

The key to directing the blocking and all the movements onstage is to express people's relationships so that the audience picks up on them visually. Put them in physical terms and they will be "read" immediately. Exploring and using the Who questions, especially in terms of relationships, is a big help in doing this. For example, when "lovers" is the answer to Who, you know that, generally, the characters will stay fairly close together, make gestures of support to each other, and echo each other's movements.

When the question Who is answered "families" or "roommates," you know you are talking about people who are generally comfortable being around one another. Sometimes a family member can nudge another out of a comfortable seat—whereas a nonmember, such as a guest, will wait to be offered a chair.

A protective older brother consistently keeps his younger sibling beside or behind him in situations where they might be vulnerable—at a crowded fairground, for example. And dominating kings and queens will ensure, as did the King of Siam in *The King and I*, that no one's head is elevated above theirs.

In other words, realizing how the characters feel about one another and what they mean to one another will often dictate how they move and position themselves onstage.

That said, also keep in mind the guiding principle that all the actors must be seen, not hidden behind other actors.

Some Common Rules

The attention of the audience can also be drawn by such devices as having an actor turn toward another, drop a prop, or rise from a chair suddenly. However, the director or the actor must always justify these movements if they are not inherent in the script. Here are some other useful points to use in blocking:

Generally, downstage is better than upstage for most scenes. A scene played in the far upstage right corner of the stage might give the impression that what's going on back there can't be very important.

That which is new in a scene draws more attention than that which has been there; this includes the actors.

An audience generally looks where the actors look; if the actor stares at a desk, the audience probably will, too.

An actor framed in a doorway is generally more attention-getting than one out in the open.

The character who is speaking gets more attention than those who are silent.

A moving person gets more attention than one who is static, unless others are also moving.

A full-face stance is stronger than a profile.

An individual is more arresting than a group.

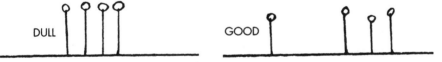

STAGE COMPOSITION AND GROUPING

In the visual-arts world, composition has been defined as "an arrangement of artistic parts to form a unified whole." This applies primarily to paintings, photographs, and displays of some sort, designed to produce a pleasing balance in the distribution of people and things. On the stage we go further than that, because we also deal with movement and story.

A simple rule to remember is that characters are usually more effective visually when put into groups that bring a visual balance to the stage and reflect the conflict in the scene. Arrangement of actors onstage should mirror a cause-and-effect relationship inherent in the scene, and should not be the result of haphazardly scattering them about or lining them up with no justification or purpose. The position of the actors and the physical relationships between them should help the audience understand the answers to the five Ws.

One aspect of stage composition is to *focus* the eyes of the audience on a certain point. Compose the stage so as to create a center of attention. We all do that when we snap pictures with our cameras, placing the important subjects in the center of the picture or having them visually offset by objects in the landscape.

Some Staging Don'ts

There will naturally be exceptions in certain circumstances to the principles we list below. For instance, in farce and in some comedy there is often much "sneaking around." But the person doing the sneaking is more often than not the most important person onstage at that moment, so you want the audience to watch him or her, no matter what anyone else is doing or saying.

Generally, the following rules are sound and workable, but your own judgment will prevail and, as with anything else, it must all adapt to the kids' abilities.

When one actor speaks or moves, then nobody else should, unless there is a good reason and the movement is justified. In farce, however, this rule is often ignored.

Actors should not make distracting upstage crosses behind other actors. Avoid sneaking around or moving opposite to the flow and action of the scene.

The speaking actor normally crosses in front of other actors rather than behind them, especially if approaching an exit, but there may be valid exceptions to this.

Actors should not always stop moving exactly at the end of their line; it can become monotonous after a while.

Avoid giving business to one actor that cuts into or distracts from another's lines.

Upstaging is a no-no. The term traditionally refers to the upstage movement of an actor who forces an actor speaking to him or her to turn away from the audience and become less audible. Meanwhile, the upstage actor faces the audience. Unless the director needs that movement for a reason, upstaging is a bad way for an actor to gain the audience's attention.

We have all seen the example in professional theater when actors turn toward the door upstage and observe the star's entrance. She swishes past them from upstage center to downstage left, martini in hand, and demonstrates poise at the fireplace mantel, where she pauses as thunderous applause greets her. Grouping actors can focus the audience's interest on an entrance, an exit, or a key character or action in a scene. In the example above there was no question in the minds of the audience which character was to be the key person in resolving the conflict in the plot—anymore than when Peter Pan flew through the bedroom window into a bright spotlight.

Usually the center of the stage will serve as a kind of fulcrum, but this can vary with lighting and visibility for the audience. Note in the diagram below that the single actor on the left assumes importance as he or she balances two on the right. It's as if he had more weight on a scale, with the fulcrum at center stage. The grouping on the right could be increased significantly, and yet the focus would remain on the actor on the left.

THE FULCRUM

The Basic Triangle

Another basic principle of grouping is forming triangles. This is the best focusing device.

Because the stage is like a vertical picture in front of you, think of the actors' heads as things to be arranged, like apples in a Cézanne painting hanging on a wall. To arrange the heads higher or lower in the picture, you can have your actors kneel, sit, or recline. As you learn to achieve a difference of head levels, begin asking yourself what puts the proper focus on an individual.

As the illustration below suggests, this triangle approach makes good use of levels or platforms, but they are not absolutely necessary. If they are available, you're very lucky, because they can be much more valuable than scenery. Platforms give you more playing space, and with actors moving up and down you can capture an intensity in a scene that you might not otherwise have.

COMPOSE YOUR STAGE PICTURES BY HAVING ACTORS'
HEADS AS THE POINTS OF A TRIANGLE

Grouping Actors in a Triangle

Here's a simple example from a nineteenth-century melodrama of triangular grouping:

THE VILLAIN ENTERS FROM DOWNSTAGE LEFT
AS THE HERO AND HEROINE ARE EMBRACING.
HE ANNOUNCES THAT HE NOW OWNS
THEIR HOUSE. HE TELLS THEM TO GET OUT!

There's a better way to stage this. Put the villain in the middle, up center, and put him on a platform:

THE VILLAIN MAKES HIS EVIL ANNOUNCEMENT FROM UP CENTER. NOW STANDING
MID-STAGE AT THE APEX OF A TRIANGLE, HE DOMINATES THE STAGE.

The difference between the two stagings is that the second has dramatic intensity, and that's the secret heart of the theater.

Visual Lines

The actors' movements are also an effective means of illuminating the five Ws as well as increasing intensity. Etienne De Croux, the French master of mime, teaching at the Actors Studio in New York, pointed out that there are four "visual lines" onstage: the line of threat, the line of retreat, the line of fantasy, and the line of comedy. They have to do primarily with movement and, in other ways, with composition. The first two concern forward and backward movement:

1. A line from *upstage* to *downstage* is a line of threat or intimidation. Something frightening is bearing down upon a character or the audience!

2. Conversely, a line from *downstage* to *upstage* is a line of retreat, abandonment, and desertion.

The effect of those two movements is self-evident. They should be kept in mind by the director at all times.

3. A line that moves in a *diagonal*—from one corner of the stage to the opposite corner, or from somewhere more central to an upstage or downstage corner—is a

fantasy line. It brings a little off-balancing effect to the stage picture, so it's a good movement for something unusual or not wholly earthbound. Ophelia, in *Hamlet*, is often seen taking these routes. This is the line of the dreamer, the mystic, and the magician.

4. A line *directly across* the stage from left to right, parallel to the back wall but far downstage near the apron, is a comedy line. This is more difficult to define, but historically it's probably a legacy of vaudeville, where comics generally performed side by side facing the audience and made their exits right or left with a wisecrack.

Crossovers

The "comedy" visual line is often used in an entr'acte, or, as it's often called, a *crossover*. Used primarily in musicals, the crossover is a short scene played in front of the main curtain during set changes behind the curtain. If the audience only has the curtain to look at as the sets are changed, you'll lose them. So, to ensure that the audience is never abandoned, crossovers with or without small props will keep the show moving. You should create crossovers whenever you think it appropriate. Sometimes all you need is for one or more characters to walk across the stage engaged in some kind of dialogue or activity while the next scene is being set.

The children in our Dramatics Club loved doing these crossovers. Sometimes we'd even bring in the little "mascots," the children in kindergarten and first and second grades who were not actually in the club, but whose mothers were working on the shows. They'd chase each other across in a game of tag (if it was appropriate to the story). In *South Pacific* they came in and sat on the edge of the stage with their legs dangling over it and sang "Dites-Moi."

PSYCHOLOGICAL VALUES

Many good directors plan their blocking and staging with certain sections of the stage "zoned" or reserved for a specific psychological effect—that is, their stage layout might actually set aside certain areas for the emotion of fear, another for joy, another for security, and so on. In our simpler productions with children we can ignore zoning, and if it's a short version of a professionally produced show the script alone might lead us in the right direction. But in a long musical or melodrama this technique can be very useful in your efforts to do a superior production.

Arranging the props and set pieces within zones can create a psychological effect on the audience that may enhance and intensify the drama and tension of the play. This was done, for example, in a very successful Broadway and touring production of Barrie's *Peter Pan*. Mary Martin played Peter Pan and Cyril Ritchard was Captain

Hook. (That same production was also broadcast live—one of television's early hits—using almost identical floor plans and scenery.)

On the floor plans below, the labels indicate the psychological values related to the various areas. These values are for the most part represented by the character or characters that inhabit them and by the dialogue, along with the lights, sets and decor.

The nursery in *Peter Pan*, where Wendy, John, and Michael sleep in the first act, is illustrated in this floor diagram. The other characters in that scene are Father and Mother; Nana, the watchdog; Liza, the nurse; and Peter Pan and Tinkerbell.

Mother's area, where she reads bedtime stories, is labelled "Love and Joy." This is also where Peter Pan teaches the children to fly. At stage right is "Authority." Here, Father's orders and decisions are sternly given. At stage left is "Security," where the children are tucked in at bedtime. Upstage center is "Freedom and Fantasy": the open window through which Peter enters and then flies away with the children and the nurse.

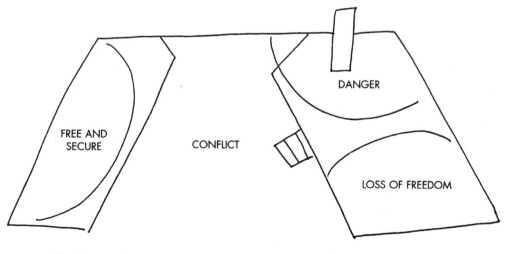

Another scene, in the third act, is on board the ship where Hook ties up the children and battles Peter, who eventually saves them. At stage left is "Loss of Freedom," the hold where the children are imprisoned and threatened with death by walking the plank. At center is "Conflict," the stage area for Hook's defeat by Peter. At stage right is "Free and Secure," where Peter enters to rescue the children.

When blocking the show, the director associated the actors with these various zones. That is, the audience came to associate each area with the psychological values represented by certain characters.

How vital are these psychological factors in relation to your efforts in producing and directing plays with children? That's entirely up to you. If you have the time and the interest, you might find it exciting to experiment with this, in whole or in part. If you are swamped and are too busy with the rest of the production, set it aside and concentrate on other things. You can still design and complete a fine production and have fun doing it.

TIME VALUES

There are three time values in theater work: timing, tempo, and rhythm.

Timing relates to the actor's lines and business. An actor crossing the stage carrying a prop to another actor, speaking all the while, might time the cross by placing the prop in the other person's hand on speaking the final word. Timing also involves silences and pauses appropriately dovetailed with words and business.

Tempo does not necessarily refer to speed. The tempo of a scene is the result of how quickly the actors "pick up their cues." The lines themselves may be delivered slowly, but generally speaking, the actors should deliver them right on the cue from another actor. If your actors are listening carefully, as we discussed in Chapter 2, they will be better able to respond promptly on cue.

Tempos are normally quick. In any case, the right tempo in a scene means that it doesn't drag as the result of time lapses that serve no purpose. Pauses and silences that are needed for emotional effect will not slow the tempo.

Rhythm refers to general patterns of timing and tempo, but also to the speed with which the actors deliver their lines. Actors sometimes "fall in love" with certain lines or speeches and s-t-r-e-t-c-h them out.

If timing and tempo are valid in the separate scenes, the rhythm of entire acts and the play as a whole should be valid. But if the actors stretch out the lines, tell them to pick up the rhythm.

Pauses

A dramatic pause occurs at a point in the action when further speech becomes ineffective. The emotion is so great it can't be expressed audibly, often at the climax of a scene or act, or at the main climax of the play. Though dramatic pauses can be very effective, you should work them in carefully. An old director's precept has been not to hold a dramatic pause for more than the count of six. That's probably still valid. The audience might fall asleep.

LIGHTING, COSTUMES, AND SETS

As we saw in Chapter 5, the lighting, costumes, and sets you have for the staging of your production will depend greatly on the resources available to you in terms of facilities and money, and on the help you receive from other adults. If you have funds for supplies and props, you should be able to make your staging pleasing to the audience and rewarding for the kids.

But lack of these resources does not preempt the joy you and the children can have in doing a show. After all, it's a creative process and a make-believe world. You can find ways to trigger the audience to use its imagination to fill in any gaps in scenery, costumes, and even lighting.

We've seen fine productions on a gymnasium floor with regular lighting, a few set pieces to suggest time and place, and perhaps one old spotlight. We've also seen extravaganzas, overloaded with costly scenery and costumes, which were failures because not enough time was spent with the children in rehearsal and with their work in the individual roles. In Chapter 7, we'll explore some ways you can do just that, spending your time rehearsing your young actors effectively.

In truth, "the play's the thing." And so are those kids.

Additional Exercises, Improvs, and Games

LEARNING BLOCKING DIRECTIONS

As early as you can, ask your actors to walk around the stage as you show them where the stage right, stage left, center, downstage, and upstage positions are. Then, from where the audience sits, call out directions for them to follow, such as: "Cross down left," "Run off, up center," "Meet each other down right," and so on, until they become familiar with the terms and their meanings.

Two high school students working with a group of fourth graders in Waterbury, Connecticut, devised a game of tic-tac-toe to teach blocking terminology. Showing where the front edge of the "stage" would be they then marked a large tic-tac-toe playing field on the floor with tape. Each of the nine squares was marked with its stage position: DSR for downstage right, or C for center, or LC for left center, etc. A leader was chosen for each team of Xs and Os. In turn each leader directed a member of his team where to step. One leader might ask a team member to step into USR, for example. Then the other leader would direct a member of her team to step into C and so on until one team had formed a straight line of three, or until "the cat got it" as we used to say, when no one won.

MAINTAINING TEMPO BY PICKING UP CUES

As is done in the professional theater, ask your cast to do a speed-through line rehearsal sometime during the final rehearsal period, but before dress rehearsals. (Perhaps do this when the technical people are rehearsing cues.)

The actors gather anywhere, not necessarily onstage, and deliver all their lines in order and as rapidly as they possibly can without any pauses. This forces them to listen very hard and to be ready to speak instantly on cue.

This exercise also reveals where the actors are shaky in their knowledge of the lines. When the tempo is off, everyone will know. It puts the entire cast on its toes and often results in a much better performance.

Chapter Seven
Rehearsals with Heart

WHEN YOU HAVE BLOCKED and staged the show, as we discussed in the last chapter, you have built a skeleton. Now you must, as they say in show-biz parlance, "flesh it out." You and your cast will add the heart (and nerves and muscle). This means going over and over the play, scene by scene. Stop as often as needed to fix, to change, to try different things, to understand better, and keep practicing until you all learn it. Rehearsal means repetition, and repetition guarantees improvement and easier absorption of the lines, movements, and actions. Of course we do not mean repetition to the point of boredom. Keep adding goals to each repetition. You want to build up to doing run-throughs—rehearsals of the whole script without stopping. Partial run-throughs of a few consecutive scenes should be followed by full run-throughs as often as your cast's progress will permit, playing through the entire play.

PROCESS, NOT PERFECTION

Tell everybody you expect them all to make mistakes. That's what rehearsals are for.

Trevor Nunn, the British director, always tries to work out a way in the early rehearsals for the people in the cast to make fools of themselves at least once. When each one has survived that experience easily and found that he or she is not alone, much more imaginative exploration is possible. We're not proposing that you set up specific situations like this for the young people. They won't need any help in making mistakes. They just need help in not fearing the mistakes. We mention it to validate the need for a free, nonjudgmental atmosphere. It is crucial to the creative process, no matter what a person's age or professional status is.

National Public Radio has reported that the people working with teenagers in Chicago's Young Shakespeare Players found that what the young people loved to do most were the drunk scenes. As one fourteen-year-old said, "You get to act goofy and horse around. When you do that in real life, adults tell you to cut it out. But in a Shakespeare play it's all right." Another said, "It's great. You get to be funny and

142

crazy and sort of blissful." Incidentally, the director gave the "drunks" some excellent suggestions. She told them to sway on their feet, and to work hard to enunciate very clearly. That way, they were convincingly drunk without slurring their words and moving toward gibberish.

Of course, there will be very few drunks, if any, in the plays you do. But what those young people said reveals their desire to break free. Cherish and use that desire. It can produce much better acting than the all-too-frequent wooden recitation.

LEARNING LINES

As a rule, children have no problem learning lines and blocking. We have found that most of them learn as we rehearse. The younger the children, the more they want to learn by saying the lines and doing the moves over and over. The older ones learn lines automatically as they make it all logical and real to themselves in the rehearsal process.

But with younger children, during times when they are not involved in the rehearsal, send them off in pairs to "cue each other." Ask the one learning the lines to do some continuous movement as he is being cued, such as pacing, tossing a ball, clapping hands, etc., to keep his body involved. Forgotten lines are usually the result of separating the lines from the body and feelings. If one or a few lines are consistently forgotten, stop, discuss, and change the wording a bit if it's helpful.

After you've had a chance to go over each scene several times, and before you do your first run-through, you should insist that the actors put down their scripts.

They Know the Lines

Don't worry about those young actors learning their parts. They will. When we were doing big musicals at a parochial school, the doors to the auditorium opened onto the playground. They were always open during rehearsals because the children would go outside to wait for their group leaders to call them in for their scenes. Many neighborhood children wandered in to watch rehearsals, and they learned the whole show as they watched! On the nights of technical rehearsals those kids wandered in and begged to go onstage and play the parts so that we could rehearse all the technical cues. They were a great help.

Most of the time they'll know the lines and movements long before the first run-through. But you should set a deadline for having all lines memorized and for working "off book," or without scripts. Otherwise, some might hold onto their scripts as a security blanket, impeding the actors' physical behavior and thus slowing down the rehearsals.

BEING HEARD AND UNDERSTOOD

Hopefully all your vocal exercises and cautious concerns are paying off. But you will probably always have to remind some of your cast to SLOW DOWN and articulate clearly. Tell them to make their mouths, tongues, and teeth work hard. If they are racing too much, they can't be understood easily. Explain to them how badly the audience wants to understand them and that they won't get their laughs if the audience doesn't hear and understand the lines. One very popular TV series lost a lot of its audience because people just couldn't understand what the actors were saying. Therefore they couldn't follow the plots. So—from the beginning also stress enunciation. Make sure they use big voices and lots of careful pronunciation, and bathe in the glory of the moment onstage. Also put a couple of kids in the back as monitors to check volume and clarity during rehearsals.

CHECKING YOUR BLOCKING

Rehearse the play scene by scene, and when something doesn't work, stop to determine why. You may find that some of the blocking isn't working. It may not look right to you, or your actors may feel uncomfortable with it. So change it.

Make sure that movement follows the intention of the character. If, for instance, one of the characters makes an important announcement to the others onstage and you haven't moved him into a position where he can get their attention or haven't moved the others in ways that would help him do so, then fix it. Tell the announcer to stand on a chair, for example, or ask the others to give him more space, to shush the people who are still making noise, to clink a spoon against a glass, sit down, or ask one actor to blink the lights on and off. There are any number of tactics—work it out together with the actors.

As explained in Chapter 6, the blocking should reflect relationships—between characters, even between characters and their surroundings. The spatial relationship between two characters, perhaps a girl and her boyfriend, might be significantly different depending on their being in a scene at the beach or in Aunt Puddy's living room. Should two business rivals still be close together upstage now that the boss of one of them has entered the room? The Who question, as we've seen, becomes an excellent guide for movement and location of the characters around the stage.

In handling large groups, ask yourself how the crowd breaks down. Who sticks together? Who sides with whom in social gatherings? Or political gatherings? Who are the leaders? Who are the outcasts? Or is the important event in the scene a change from the usual lineup of allegiances?

This is the time to look at your blocking critically and make sure that where people stand, move, and sit truly reflects the action and helps to develop the story for the audience. If it's not working right, change the blocking.

The process of checking your initial blocking will continue throughout the rehearsal period as restaging and new ideas affect the actors' positions.

Owning the Space

The stage should never be an intimidating place where an actor will be on display or be judged. Rosemary Foley (whose work with mentally disabled children was described in Chapter 2) first invites her young cast to explore the playing area freely, touch all parts of it, give a shout, see what they can or can't do in it and how it affects the senses, and say aloud how they feel about it. This should give the actor the sense of comfort and familiarity, and help to overcome any self-consciousness.

"Cheating out" and "Countering"

As we said, you, the director must be the audience's eyes. The audience wants to see as many faces as possible and, of course, to hear all the words. Teach your young actors to "cheat out" or "open out" if they're playing to someone who is a bit upstage of them or even in a straight line with them across the stage. That means simply to stand with their bodies angled in such a way that they are "facing front" more than facing the side or back.

And if a character crosses and stands in front of them, ask them to "counter cross": that is, step the other way a bit so that they'll be seen by the audience.

CONCENTRATING ON OTHERS

It's also important to have every child look at the other actors onstage and take in the other players with all their senses. Experienced actors say that a critically important thing an actor must always do is concentrate on the other characters in the play. Not by staring at them all the time, however. We all tend to look mostly at the person to whom we are listening, but certainly not always at the person to whom we are speaking. We often look elsewhere to find the thought or the words as we're saying them. What is important is to be completely sensitive to the other characters, to be affected by them, and to know what is wanted or needed from them. Richard Carter tells his young actors to "say the words as if they just popped into your head" and to "Listen as if this is the first time you ever heard those lines." Ask your young actors to think, as their characters, about how they **feel** about what they are hearing other characters say.

A young singing star was playing opposite a fine experienced actor in a play on Broadway some years ago. She complained to the actor that she felt she was losing her grip on her role. So he invited her to come in early one day and work with him. What he asked her to do then was to play one of the scenes with him but to play his part, while he played hers. It was his way of showing her that she had been concentrating only on herself…that was the trouble. Why not try this with your young actors?

It's time now for your actors, having already concentrated on their own characters, to be fully aware of the others. This is what gives the performance spontaneity and reality.

REVISITING THE FIVE Ws

One of the main things you'll be working on as you begin your stop-and-start rehearsals of each scene or act is making the Who, What, Why, Where, and When of the story clearer and more specific. Actress Glynnis O'Connor, in *South Pacific* when she was in the fifth grade, recalls the sensory elements of the beach scenes (the Where) to this day:

> One of my vivid memories is a flowered towel that was my prop. All the nurses were sitting on the beach singing "I'm Gonna Wash that Man Right Outta My Hair." I would put my towel on the stage floor, and the whole wooden floor became a beach. I could feel sand under my feet, hear the waves, and smell the mussels and salt water. That towel became very special to me. I still have it.

Always make your choices real, interesting, and believable, freely inventing "As ifs"—especially if you feel stuck, don't know how to make a scene work better, or want to help an actor reach the right emotional level in a characterization.

Saying to a young actor who is playing a police officer "It's as if they were all throwing rocks at your little brother" can turn the young "officer" into a "roaring warrior." And before you stop work on a section of the play, ask your actors if they feel okay about the shape it's in. Be sure to go over it again if someone really wants to—unless someone is about to lock up the place. Taking the time then and there to nail things down can save a lot of time later.

SONGS AND DANCES

You want to work on the songs and dances in the same way for their storytelling value. As the kids learn the numbers with you or, if you're lucky, with your music director and choreographer, make sure that what they are doing as they're singing, or dancing, or doing both in the same number, helps to tell clearly what is happening in the story at that point in the show. The late David Craig, the popular expert in performance of songs, gave his workshop members the task, for each song they were rehearsing, of first writing (1) "This is a story about…" etc. This tells the story objectively. And then writing (2) "This is a story about me…" etc. This makes the story personal—subjective. So the song is about the story, not about the singing ability. For example, if a girl playing Eliza in *My Fair Lady* was writing about the song "I Could Have Danced All Night," she would write (1) "This is a story about a poor girl who is ecstatic, having been passed off as a duchess at a ball." And then (2) "This is a story about me and the happiest moment of my life." He also advised people to sing to the "underbelly of the mezzanine" rather than to any part of the audience (or auditioners).

Emphasis on what's happening is one of the strongest elements in the choreography of Susan Stroman, the famous choreographer and director of *The Producers* among other shows. Every number she creates helps to move the story along. In those dances, characters connect with the locale, fall in love, lift their spirits, or establish their needs.

If we can see that the orphans in *Oliver!* singing the song "Food, Glorious Food" are really weak and starving, that their longing for food is making their mouths water, and that their visions of food are real, they will be telling the story. The audience will empathize with them far more thoroughly than if they just stand in rows stepping forward and back, lifting their arms rhythmically as if in a Phys Ed class.

Succeeding with Specifics

We couldn't figure out one time how to do a train scene in *Annie Get Your Gun*, when Annie is traveling with the Indians and all her brothers and sisters. So we threw the problem to the kids. We asked them to improvise it. They brought props like bananas and other food into the train, did laundry, teased the conductor, played games, and generally created havoc. Those kids found many ways to make the scene fun for themselves and interesting to their friends in the audience.

In *The Sound of Music* some fifth-grade girls playing nuns and novices devised a crossover scene in front of the curtain to allow for a set change. In it they composed a beautiful farewell card to Maria and then ran off to find her. This revealed in a nice specific way that Maria was leaving the convent.

When Oliver sings *Where Is Love?* it can be very effective to see him leaning, huddled and frightened, against a wall with a blanket wrapped around his shoulders, sometimes wiping away a tear and gazing out the window. That holds more storytelling punch than his moving to center stage and "delivering" the song.

CHECK WITH YOUR ACTORS

When one of your young actors seems uncomfortable with a move, a piece of business, a line, or a whole scene, stop and examine the problem. Try some changes to see if they make it better. Or just discuss it. Often when a movement looks phony, it's because the actor hasn't discovered Why he or she is doing it. If a child can't seem to remember a line or direction, find out if there's something connected with it that feels wrong.

Using Props

Encourage your actors to rehearse with props as soon as you can. If you haven't got the real props yet, use substitutes.

How actors handle objects tells as much about the characters and the story as the way they handle lines. The way an actor hands a box to another lets us know whether the box is precious to the character or is something to be gotten rid of.

Also, actors need to become familiar with their props; they should not be awkward handling them come opening night. If an actor, as a police officer, has to look down at his gun belt when he's buckling it, the assumption will be he's green, a rookie cop. An actor who can easily balance two plates on his arm and three in his hands will be very convincing as an experienced waiter.

Rumor has it that even the famous director Elia Kazan acquired his nickname, Gadg, because when he was a young actor he was always asking for a gadget to hold and use in scenes he was rehearsing. Indeed, another big advantage of props is that holding and handling them often adds to the actors' ease on stage, especially if they are still worried about what to do with their hands. This is a very common problem and your youngsters will need all the help they can get.

Karen Ziemba, the popular Broadway star, was rehearsing the musical *I Do, I Do* some years ago and was uncomfortable in a rather static scene in which she had to confront her "husband" about his infidelity. The two of them were standing downstage center facing each other and talking. When the director suggested she turn her wedding ring and slide it up and down her finger, she was immediately at ease. Her whole self was then serving the What: deciding whether to stay married.

Whenever you can, give your cast members objects to hold, use, examine, pick up, put down, pass to another, or whatever you can justify in the story. These objects can solve many problems, but it's essential that they be relevant to the action and the character.

And finally, you'll be giving them an incentive to get the scripts out of their hands!

It is important to teach your young company members that responsible care of their costumes and props is a necessity if they want to do it right. You can't stop them from playing games while waiting, but eating spaghetti or kneeling on a cement playground in their costumes should be banned.

A Few Prop Rules

We once had a fine little sixth-grade prop mistress who stood her ground bravely facing a bunch of big mischievous boys. She stomped her foot and yelled at the top of her lungs, *"Nobody touches those props who isn't supposed to!"* She was right. Certain rules are critical:

> Props must be handled *only* by the people who use them
>   in the show or by the crew member assigned to place or
>   remove them.

Props carried offstage at the end of a scene by an actor or stage crew member *must* be put back on the prop table where they belong.

Actors *must* check all their props before the show begins to make sure they are onstage or in the assigned space offstage and in their required working order.

Hilarious and horrible stories abound of scenes that didn't work, even in Broadway shows, because the crucial prop was missing or wouldn't work. It's necessary to teach your company to be better with their props than some of those professionals were.

REHEARSAL COSTUMES

Using costume substitutes in rehearsals can be a big help, too. If girls have to wear long skirts or if boys have to wear capes, pin old beach towels or crib sheets around them for the rehearsals. If boots are required, try to get them early for the kids to work in. Acting in a big hat without enough rehearsal can thoroughly bug a professional. Conversely, rehearsing in a big hat can certainly excite a child, and jewelry can work magic in a little girl.

A member of the audience at our group's *My Fair Lady* production recalled years later that she was thrilled when she saw her little niece, as Eliza Doolittle, entering the big ball scene with a glittering tiara on her hair, glittering earrings on her ears, and glittering braces on her teeth.

Set aside time when you are no more than a third of the way into rehearsals to talk with each cast member about each costume. Whether you and your costume supervisor (if you're lucky enough to have one) are renting, making, or finding costumes in attics, most of the time you'll rely on the cast members and their parents, at least for the basics.

If your children are in the lower grades and there is a huge cast, it's much simpler to ask them to put their basic costumes on at home, wear them during classes, and then to dress rehearsal and performances. There's much less chance of havoc and lost clothing that way. High school students might consider this gauche, or at least not very cool, but there may be more space in their buildings to store the wardrobe safely. Most young kids love to do it ("It makes us feel special," they say), and teachers have never complained. It also helps to advertise the show.

SAFETY

Again, be mindful of safety for your cast and crew as you rehearse. Try to foresee the accidents that can take place in your rehearsal surroundings and eliminate potential hazards. Once we used sawdust on the floor in a rehearsal of a circus show we were doing with a teenage group. The first time an intrepid adolescent ran onto the stage as an acrobat, she slid all the way off the edge of it. Thank God she wasn't hurt, but what a lesson it was—we never used sawdust again.

Mary Procidano, then a sixth grader, is now a professor in the psychology department at Fordham University. She remembers an incident that occurred in another show:

> We were staging the "'I'm in Love with a Wonderful Guy" number in *South Pacific* with half a dozen nurses. We thought it would be great to have Nellie Forbush jump up onto a bench while she was singing and then fall forward into the nurses' arms at the high point of the song. Our Nellie, Cathy Frank, wanted to try it, but the director wouldn't let Cathy do it until she herself had fallen into our arms first. She made sure Cathy wouldn't get hurt and that we all knew how to do it.

PARTIAL RUN-THROUGHS

When you feel that several scenes are really shaping up and that the actors are getting quite secure, start running through the scenes without stopping. It's then that you will grasp how clearly the story is developing and how consistent the actors have become in revealing their characters. You'll see if one event really leads to another. You'll make sure that the focus is where you want it to be. You don't want the audience watching the wrong parts of the stage, or getting ahead of the story.

Strengthening Tempos and Rhythms
In rehearsals you will be working to achieve the right tempos of the scenes. Usually you can just describe to the actors what you want if they are not picking up cues or if they are slowing down their line delivery, or talking too fast to be understood.

"These people are in a big hurry. They never stop what they're doing to listen," or, the opposite, "They're very proper and snobbish and consider it beneath them to rush." Sometimes that's enough. But now and then, especially with the very young, you may need to take more unusual steps. A friend, Georgianne Foley, found it helpful at times to beat out the rhythm of a scene with a little drum or clap her hands as they rehearsed, until they achieved what was needed in their pacing.

Within a scene, individual characters will have their own rhythms: some slow and steady, some strong and deliberate, some hesitant, some alternating, some offbeat.

During the rehearsal of a racetrack scene we asked for volunteers to be horses galloping on the gym floor behind the audience section so that the actors playing the people onstage watching the race could visualize those horses and have a clear idea of how fast their eyes and heads should move, and how quickly. Instantly, everybody wanted to be a horse.

When you are able to start running through scenes without stopping, you'll find out how to vary the rhythms of the scenes to lead logically from one into the next. You will learn whether you're building up the pace enough to lead to the big climax, or slowing down to give breathing space to the events. You'll recognize when you need a breathless, silent moment, or a dramatic pause, or when the lines should roll on top of each other.

Polishing

During rehearsals you may find that an "As if" improv will help bring a scene to life for your actors. Sometimes it's helpful to suggest an idea for an improv on what might have happened to the characters immediately before the scene your actors are now working on: where they came from, what they were doing there. Perhaps after the improv they will better understand the emotional "baggage" each character brings into the scene.

It's generally better to rehearse a scene more often than the actors think necessary. It will pay off in a faster-moving show, quicker timing of cues and entrances, and much freer and more relaxed acting and singing, with no indecisive pauses.

FULL RUN-THROUGHS

Be sure to allow time for plenty of run-throughs of the whole show.

An advantage of frequent run-throughs is that they help you identify any holes in the flow of the show—parts that have too slow or too fast a pace, or when nothing really seems to be happening. Seeing fairly clearly which parts of the show need the most work, you can concentrate on those parts separately before your next run-through.

In the run-throughs you can occasionally recognize a break in the show when there is not enough time for an actor or group of actors to get from one side of the stage where they've exited, to the other, where they have to reenter. Sometimes they have to go down to the basement and come up on the other side of the stage. Or, you might discover during a run-through that you haven't allowed time for a costume or set change. Or, if you and your kids created the play yourselves, you may discover you forgot to allow for a passage of time within one scene or one act. These are times when the old crossover device that we described in the last chapter can solve many problems.

One of our most popular crossovers was in *South Pacific*, after Lieutenant Cable had done his solo number downstage left. A squad of Japanese soldiers sneaked up the aisle from the back of the auditorium, leaped onto the stage, and attacked the Lieutenant. Some of the American officers ran onstage to help their comrade, and the whole group engaged in a spectacular jiujitsu fight. One of the boys who knew jiujitsu staged the fight. They loved doing it so much that whenever they were tired of working on some other scene we told them if they did the scene one more time they could also do the fight again.

If, wisely, you have been calling to rehearsals only those who will really be needed, so they aren't just sitting around, many of the kids won't have a sense of the whole show. They won't be clear about what follows what, and how quickly, until they experience these full run-throughs without stopping.

During each run-through, you should sit in the back of the auditorium taking notes on what doesn't work. After the run-through, gather everyone around for the "notes session" and discuss your comments with all the people involved. Watching a run-through, a director tends to write terse notes in a sort of shorthand as reminders of what needs fixing. They might read "First scene too slow" or "What's bugging Marian?" or "M's entrance no good" or "'Maids' song not working." Later, when you give the notes to the actors, deliver these criticisms in more constructive and tactful terms.

We usually kept a young assistant nearby to help with whatever was needed at the time. It was a highly sought-after job. But one time, without telling the director, our aide took it upon herself to go around to the cast and read them the notes to save time. The director's heart stopped when she saw all those long faces afterward! Always make an effort in the notes session to avoid being only negative. Tell your youngsters how to improve without giving orders, and sprinkle in plenty of praise.

Consider a Parade

Parades, like crossovers, are great ways to give your crew a chance to reset the stage behind the curtain. If you and your colleagues have the time and energy to create one, a parade gives a show pizzazz and uses everyone in it and everyone who ever wanted to be in the show. We staged a grand parade in one show, all around the sides and back of the auditorium, up the aisles, onto and across the stage.

There are advantages to having a parade or similar activity near the beginning of your show. A chase, a fashion show, a quick preview, a newsreel, a rally, a pageant—whatever you and your young actors can devise—allows your young company to get right out there, let off steam, and perform where their families can see them at the very beginning. It helps them avoid excess nervousness or stage fright. It reduces the impatience of those who would otherwise have to wait a long time to get onstage. You also know they will all be ready on time. Just make sure that these activities are justified by the story.

TECHNICAL REHEARSALS

Unless your production is relatively simple and short, or you are just doing a scene or two, you're soon going to have to face at least one technical rehearsal. Technical ("tech," for short) rehearsals can be long, hard, tedious, and frustrating. But they happen at an exciting time, when you're all getting close to the show date. During technical rehearsals, tell your actors to stay home and rest and study their parts, while your "techies" learn their own jobs.

In tech rehearsals, your stage manager, sound crew, lighting crew, prop crew, and backstage crew are given a chance to rehearse all their own work by themselves. Every member of the stage crew wants to be involved, and they need time to go over all their chores in the show. They need to make lists of their cues to focus and switch lights on and off, turn on and off tape-recorded sounds and music, and create other sound effects at the right times. They have to practice the placement and timing—where and when to move props and sections of scenery and other set pieces. The exact placement of the furniture must be rehearsed for each scene. When to pull that final curtain, if you have one, must be practiced a number of times to get it right.

The stage manager must be prepared to make sure the actors are in place at the right time. He or she must follow the script during the entire performance and be prepared to prompt any actor during performances. Also, the stage manager must know and practice all the cues for each activity. The stage manager's script should have all cues carefully marked; these cues are generally the last line said by an actor just before a spotlight goes on, a set piece is moved, a sound effect is heard, or a curtain is raised or lowered.

The crew members must understand and learn how to follow the stage manager's directions. Tech rehearsals will be the time that misunderstandings come to light and can be corrected.

After you have completed your technical rehearsal with the various crew members, it's a good idea, especially on a sizable production, to hold one or even two technical rehearsals with the entire cast and crew. This gives the crew extra rehearsal, allows the actors to orient themselves to the completed sets and props, and makes your next step, the dress rehearsal, work more smoothly.

Since the crew has already rehearsed, these extra sessions should go relatively fast because all the songs and/or scenes can be greatly abbreviated. The actors don't have to go through an entire scene just to make sure they know the sets and props and learn when they have to get out of the way of a scene change.

Try to gain access to your rehearsal space far ahead of time so that you can set up prop tables on each side of the stage with all the props listed and placed in order. Tape your prop lists on the wall above the tables and copies at other places where the kids can see them. If you can manage a whole prop room, all the better.

Prepare the same kind of lists for the technical cues with which everyone should be familiar. List all the information for set changes, light and sound cues, and curtains. These are taken from the stage manager's script, which should have all the cues carefully listed. Tape those sheets on the walls where they can be easily checked by the crew members and are available for anyone else in case of an emergency. Make sure that the necessary people have copies. Samples of prop lists and technical cue sheets are on pages 156–158.

Maintaining Order

Be sure your sets and furniture are placed where they can be moved on and off in the right order. It's a good idea to put multicolored pieces of tape on the floor of the playing area to remind the crew where the different set and furniture pieces are to be placed for each scene. An esoteric term for this in the professional theater is "spiking."

Also, don't forget to put glow-in-the-dark tape at the edges of steps or posts or anything that must be seen in a blackout between scenes to keep people from falling or bumping into things.

Clair Reilly Walcovy, production manager through most of our shows, recalled:

> We made sure that the latest, revised outlines listing the order of scenes and all the people in them were taped to the walls back-stage. As their scenes were coming up we'd send runners down to tell the group leaders to bring their people up and get set for their next scene. The kids could not wait to get onstage.

Depending on an intercom backstage is not always a good idea...with younger kids, anyway. Intercoms certainly save time. But you still must be sure directions and prompts have been heard by excited youngsters.

To put makeup on the kids, help with costume changes, deal with crises, and mostly to keep order commandeer any volunteers you can get (mothers, fathers, and big sisters and brothers, perhaps).

Maintaining quiet backstage can be a losing battle even in professional productions. Kids between the ages of six and seventy-six have a difficult time keeping their mouths shut when they are not onstage emoting. Children have a hard time resisting the temptation to act silly, tease one another, or show off. Teachers and mothers know all about these antics. In the theater they are most common backstage during final rehearsals with the numerous stops and starts. Your entire cast will be involved in the dress rehearsals, when things can go wrong, so there can be many kids who have to do a lot of waiting. Doris Fugazy, a mother who helped backstage, said:

> While they were waiting down there for the runners to warn them, the kids stayed in the big all-purpose room of the school. We mothers called it "the holding pen." The hardest thing was to keep them down there because they all wanted to crowd backstage to watch the show.

Joking around is an actor's way of staying loose, avoiding boredom and anxiety. You can't let things go too far, but a little fun on the side can keep things light. When we put on *Oliver!*, about seven of the members of Fagin's gang did a crossover looking for Oliver after he had run away. In the dress rehearsal they broke us up while crossing in single file as directed, looking all around, and calling out in their cockney accents, "Oleevuh! Oleevuh!" But then they began looking for him in their pockets, under their caps, in the trouser cuffs, and under one another's sleeves.

DRESS REHEARSAL

It's a good idea to schedule more than one dress rehearsal if you can, since it's often necessary to redo a scenery change or try an entrance or a light cue again. The second dress rehearsal will be closer to the real thing.

Before the first dress rehearsal, as soon as everything is ready to go, gather everyone together in one place and do a group relaxation exercise, to settle the nerves and slow the heartbeats. Just shaking every part of the body and taking a few deep, slow, easy breaths can help everyone calm down.

Use this moment also to remind the whole group of their goals and obligations to the show and the other actors.

Assure them all that you trust them and are looking forward to seeing a fine production. (We usually started each rehearsal with a little prayer, but that is up to you and the children, the PTA, your local politicians and school board, Congress, and the Supreme Court.) Tell all the children to gather together in the same spot when the rehearsal is over; at that time you will have your notes session and they can tell you what problems they had so that you can solve them together.

It's a good idea to teach the youngsters how a professional show is "called" and what is expected of them. There is a formula for this which is the bible of all skilled theater people. On the days of dress rehearsals and performances, actors must be in the auditorium or theater at least thirty minutes before the show is scheduled to begin (actually, your kids will probably be there two hours early). That's when the stage manager calls over the intercom, or goes to each dressing room or classroom, knocks on the door, and says, "Half-hour, please." Fifteen minutes later the stage manager calls, "Fifteen minutes, please."

The next call, "Five minutes, please," is the command for all performers to move to the area where they are supposed to be at the "top" or beginning of the show. Then, in five minutes, the stage manager calls, "Places, please." This signals that the beginning of the show is imminent and the first cue is about to be given. All are to be in their exact opening spots onstage, and all chatter must cease. Here again, the group leaders can help, especially with the younger cast members.

Curtain Calls
Your last task at the dress rehearsal is to stage the curtain calls for the end of the show.

We never had individual curtain calls. The feeling of a big accomplishment by the whole team was more important to us than any sort of hierarchy. The "star system" was irrelevant to our goals of kids' self-respect, mutual respect, and equally shared joy. Of course, you can set up the curtain calls as you choose.

We arranged for the children to come on with their own groups (nurses, sailors, principals, maids), and when everybody was onstage, all bowed together. Sometimes flowers were brought to the stage. In much smaller productions all came on at the same time, formed a single line, and bowed two or three times. The customary way to do this is for the person in the middle of the front row to bow and everyone follows, bowing at the same time.

Let them keep bowing until the applause begins to die down. You'll probably have to pull the curtain, dim the lights, or just shoo them off the stage. A good solution is to make arrangements with one of the responsible group leaders to lead the exodus from the stage to the backstage area and then into the arms of their happy friends and families.

Our producer, Louise DiGeorgi, mother of four cast members, recalls:

> What everyone involved with the shows loved most were the curtain calls. The kids could hardly wait to get on. They entered in groups, filling up the stage, row upon row, all the principals, all the overture singers, all the crew. One hundred and fifty kids bowing and grinning. It was awesome.

Don't even think of attempting anything like this unless you have a team of fierce mothers and fathers to help you!

If your rehearsal runs long and it's late, especially for the younger members, you should postpone your notes session and send the children home. In that case, call everyone together before the beginning of the final dress rehearsal, or try to get around to the ones who were excused early before they get ready for the rehearsal or the show. Some of your group leaders can help you with this.

It's a good idea to announce at the beginning of your dress rehearsal, when you have everyone present, that you will have a party after the last show and a meeting a day or two after it's over to talk about what you have all learned.

After your young company has giggled its way through the curtain call rehearsal and you've sent them home for a good night's sleep, prepare the environment, as Maria Montessori taught, for the kids to do their best in the performance to come. Be forewarned, though: You may spend half the night putting things back in order.

SAMPLE PRODUCTION PREPARATIONS

To provide you with a brief guide, here are lists of props and technical needs and a rehearsal schedule for a production of the scene "Spark of Liberty," at the end of Chapter 4. The lists are fairly complete, but remember, you can use pantomime for many items and set pieces.

This is a short scene—probably about five minutes long, depending on how elaborate the production is. Presumably, you will have only one or two hours each day for the rehearsals, it will be performed on some kind of stage (although it will even work in a classroom), and you will have a few of the props and some of the furniture mentioned here.

The schedule presumes you will take advantage of many of the suggestions in the book and use exercises and improvs to give the kids experience in the best methods of rehearsing a scene or play.

Prop and furniture list

Two muskets, or equivalent (perhaps broom handles)
Table with dishes, food, mugs, silverware, pitcher
Bottle of "rum" (water colored with a bit of a cola drink)
Chairs, footstools
Table
Four filled suitcases and one canvas bag
Fireplace or stove
Three coats or capes on hooks
Candles in candlesticks
Two oil lamps

Technical list

Actually, the scene will work without any set pieces, but try to find:

Set piece with a working door, if possible
Set piece with windows, if possible
Sound-effects tape with horse noises: Horses galloping and then stopping, horse walking. The tapes may be made by you and the kids on your tape machine, if you have one. The galloping and walking can be faked with two halves of a coconut husk or equivalent, clapped rhythmically onto a flat surface. And try out imitation horse neighing or whinnying with some of the kids. Or, if you have access to horses, all the better. Tapes can also be rented from professionals. You can find them on the Internet or in the yellow pages of your phone book.

Ten-day rehearsal schedule

First day: Begin with an exercise. Then read the scene and discuss historical background.

Second day: Read the scene with a concentration on the characters and how they differ. Discuss the five Ws and the five senses. Do some improvs.

Third day: Stage and block the entire scene.

Fourth day: Rehearse the blocking and try a run-through with actors holding their scripts.

Fifth day: Rehearse and make any necessary changes.

Sixth day: Do another reading—an opportunity to let the kids relax, read the script again, discuss the characters, and report on anything else about the story they may have learned. Then, improvs and exercises—without scripts if the kids are ready. If you have time, do another run-through.

Seventh day: Two full rehearsals without scripts.

Eighth day: Technical rehearsal. Make sure all the props are available. All furniture and set pieces are in place. Actors familiarize themselves with any new props. Lights and sound effects are ready. (You may not even need this rehearsal day if you have only a few props.)

Ninth day: Two dress rehearsals.

Tenth day: Performance.

Chapter Eight
On with the Show!

FINALLY THE BIG DAY arrives. Everybody's excited. Phone calls, well-wishers, flowers, hugs, happiness, thrills, and colds. You may be feeling as if you can't move fast enough to get off the tracks before the train bears down upon you.

As mentioned before, the producer could be you, but on a large production you need another person. The producer will take care of:

> Security: Appointing two or three older brothers or sisters to stand at the doors and keep order if there is any disturbance on performance day. Depending on the situation and surroundings, you might think about police presence.

> Ushers: An easy job. Get relatives or others who can help people move in and out of the seating areas. Rope off the VIP section.

> Tickets: Most of the time, productions like yours will be open to the public and, of course, donations will be gladly accepted (by the ushers). If you are using an already published script, you have already arranged for permissions and royalty payments. (See Chapter 4, p. 89) If you sell tickets, get parents or relatives to lend a hand once the kids have distributed flyers about their show.

> Preparation of the auditorium: On performance day, supervise the placement of seats if you use an empty hall (like a gym). Check out the lights, air conditioning, spotlights, and audio gear, and deal with any last-minute problems that arise.

The producer will also be responsible for the programs. With a computer, laser printer, and copy machine, one person at home or at a school can create a very classy program, listing the cast and crew along with credits for others who worked on the show, acknowledgments, some information about the story and the playwright, and perhaps even a few advertisements. On the other hand, a simple typewritten sheet may be all you need.

If you have an intermission, selling refreshments is not a bad idea. You can make some money for expenses. But then you'll need still more volunteers.

And don't forget reserved seats for VIPs. Make sure the maintenance people know just what you're doing and are prepared for it. The last thing you need is to be running around looking for someone to unlock a door.

If you don't have that wonderful producer and a team of angelic volunteers, all is not lost. Conscript a spouse and a high-school or college student to stand at the door to welcome the people and direct them to their chairs. These ushers can then tell you when it seems that all or most of the audience has arrived, and you can tell the stage manager when to call "Places, please" and give the cue to turn off the house lights and start the show.

All the rules and suggestions for dress rehearsals apply as well to performances, with the exception of one. After the performance there is no notes session, only praise and congratulations and a wonderful, satisfying feeling of accomplishment.

If more than one performance is scheduled, then you will meet with those actors and crew members involved in scenes where mistakes were made or something just didn't work right. But, generally, there are no other efforts to improve the show or make a scene just a little bit better. You want to let the actors enjoy their accomplishments and relish the thought of doing it again.

We've always believed that a single performance is in some ways unfair to the kids. They should be given the opportunity to repeat it once or twice, to enjoy all those feelings once more. Most of our large shows with elementary school children were done four times: two matinees for the students in the school and two evening performances for families and friends. So try for two or three performances. If that's not possible, just settle for one.

PRESHOW CONCERNS

Most performers on opening night in a Broadway show, trying to deal with butterflies in the stomach, will think, "Oh, why am I doing this? I could be home cleaning the carpets." The children will get nervous, too, but they often change fear into excitement. Most of the time they're exhilarated and eager beyond measure. Sometimes one or two of them will suddenly come alive in a performance though they had not before in rehearsals.

One boy playing a sailor was given the task of doing a crossover in front of the curtain while whistling one of the songs from the show and mopping the "deck." He had been fine in rehearsals but not great. When he went out there and experienced the audience's pleasure, he became so excited we thought we'd never get him off the stage. In each performance, he stretched it more. He mopped, he scrubbed, he danced with the mop and caressed it, he tried it on his head, he skipped around it, he polished his shoes with it, and he scraped gum off the deck. He was cheered by his buddies as well as the audience.

Last Advice and Reminders

It's a good idea, these days, to make a short welcoming speech before the show pointing out exits, length of intermission (if there is one), and requesting audience members to turn off cell phones. Charlotte Moore, director of the Irish Repertory Company, ended her welcoming talk by holding up a piece of paper (actually it was blank) and saying, "And if your cell phone rings during the performance, I have in my hand a document which gives me permission to kill you!"

The children will require some counseling about what happens when there is an audience out there. They have to be warned about pausing for laughter and applause, which may come at very unexpected places in the show. There will be rustling of programs, coughing, late arrivals, and other departures from decorum that will distract the actors. Then there's the little sister in the audience shouting out "Hi, Patty" to her big sister who is playing a serious scene at that moment. Just be sure to discuss these things with the actors and encourage them to ignore them as much as possible.

By the same token, remind your actors not to "count the house," trying to see how many people are out there or spot Grandma. Their only task is to concentrate on the scene. Tell them that if any one of them is looking out into the audience instead of paying attention to what's happening onstage, the audience will be distracted by their actions. This could hurt the show as the audience finds it more difficult to follow the story.

It always helps to gather your cast together at the half-hour call, take a head count and do a final check of the costumes. When you're all together, do some relaxation exercises as you did before the dress rehearsals. This is done by professionals. When the play *Quilters* was performed on Broadway, the whole cast gathered at the fifteen-minute call to form a circle, hold hands, and focus on helping one another to do the best show they could so that the audience would leave the theater, as the actress playing Sarah McKenzie Bonham put it, "with a greater zest for living than they had when they came."

MAKING IT ALL WORK

Somehow our kids' shows always came off even better than we expected. That's one of the perks of doing shows with kids. You always have a house full of supportive people who want with all their hearts for everything to go well. No one ever failed to appear or to do the job in any performance we can remember.

More often than not, when things went wrong it was the young people who saved the day. During a performance of *Oliver!*, our little troubleshooter, Kate, ran to us with pigtails flying to warn that the red transparent gel that colored the light in the fireplace was falling off and very soon we would have a white fire there. Billy, on the spotlight, heard her and handed the spot over to the director. He ran backstage, grabbing two other boys on the way. They somehow got the gel back on the light, saving our red fire, without being seen by the audience. As he commanded the spot again, Billy beamed, "Have we got a crew or have we got a crew?"

Baseball has been the only extracurricular activity that was disruptive to our efforts, and we tolerated it because it was beneficial to the boys (it was not open to girls in those days). On one performance day, we released some of our crew members for a Little League game, and some mothers tried to substitute for the boys without the greatest success. It started to rain shortly after the show began, and within minutes five boys in wet baseball uniforms dashed into the hall and resumed their jobs backstage.

Things can and will go wrong—they always do. After all, this is live theater. It's the thrill of the risk. Theater people will try anything to ensure success: a rabbit's foot, prayer, meditation, sayings scrawled on mirrors, a lucky pair of socks. But when you've done the best you can, and the kids have done their best, too, it's the concentration and the love for one another that helps make it work.

Part III
Extending the Work

Chapter Nine
Working with Older Kids

THE SAME BASIC PRINCIPLES we discussed in all the previous chapters apply to working with people from about thirteen to twenty years old. They still need to know you respect them, will listen to them, and are eager for them to solve problems with you. You have to urge them to concentrate, trust one another and their own imaginations, dig deeper for specific answers to the five Ws, and make the sensory elements of the story real.

But they are older, stronger, more experienced in life, more skilled in many ways, and more complicated. Younger children are concerned with finding out what the world is about. Teenagers are very concerned with finding out what they, themselves, are about. This is one reason why, for example, teenagers are more likely to connect to Shakesepare than younger children might. The author of a recent study of Shakespeare noted that the way to look at Shakespeare is in the numbers one and two. He said that Shakespeare's characters usually have two opposing qualities and their intentions are often at war with each other. This is a challenge teens—whose lives are often filled with a growing sense of complexity—might relish, but younger children would probably find confusing.

Teenagers' sense of themselves is more often determined by what they perceive outsiders, particularly their peers, think of them. Expect a lot from them and they'll match it. Encourage them to take risks, but make sure there is some wisdom in the risks.

As actors, teenagers can deal passionately with ideas more subtle than those they experienced as younger children. They're often much more sensitive than they'll ever reveal. They will understand when you tell them to start with something that's really true to human behavior. For instance, in farce, human behavior is exaggerated, but the teen actor will understand how to stretch a scene for laughs without making it dishonest.

Later in this chapter, we describe a number of more difficult acting exercises and warm-up theater games to stretch the skills of your young adults. Actually they're even fun for forty- and seventy-year-olds.

Working with a group of teenagers in New Rochelle, New York, we initiated the Westchester Young Actors' Theater (WYAT). This eclectic group of about eighty teenagers came from a wide variety of racial, social, religious, and economic backgrounds. We found a workplace for them in the assembly hall at the local Presbyterian church. We developed shows such as *In White America* and a series of short sketches that we performed in camps, nursing homes, and other community centers. A number of former members of WYAT, on looking back, have said that the group was important to them because of its cultural and racial diversity. They said anything not multiracial seemed strange after the experience of those years.

A former Dramatics Club member voiced the general feelings most of the kids had as members:

> I saw a lot of people come out of their shells. It also gave us something to do every week. It gave us a social thing. It enabled us to get along with a lot of different kinds of people. For the boys and girls to get along without this artificial dating situation. I wish everybody had a chance to have what I had. I feel so lucky.

A few months ago about seventy former WYAT members had a reunion in Pelham, New York. They came from Texas, Scarsdale, Arizona, Pennsylvania, Maryland, Massachusetts, and even Kyrgystan. Most of them hadn't seen one another for thirty-five years. Eileen, now a mother of two teenagers, said that night:

> I had never been exposed to people who were from different racial or economic backgrounds. I was also painfully shy and was afraid to let people get to know me. I cannot imagine what my life would have been like without WYAT.… You showed us that it was okay to make ourselves vulnerable, because our trust and vulnerability were respected and even treasured. We learned to accept each other and ourselves for who we really were. The more we risked, the more we gained.… We were a team where everyone gained and everyone was valued.… As we got to know and love people different from ourselves, we wondered why the rest of the world found that so difficult to accept.… Tolerance was a powerful message that has colored everything in my life. It seems especially relevant today.

STAGING *THE LOTTERY*

There are many interesting and different ways you and your teenage group can put shows together. One of our projects at WYAT was a production based on Shirley Jackson's harrowing short story *The Lottery*. We describe what we did in some detail here; you may want to model a project of your own on our experience.

After reading the story we talked about its meaning and importance. It's a fantasy about a small rural community and their secret annual event, the Lottery. The secret about this lottery is that whoever draws the "winning" card with the black circle on it is the person who will be stoned by all the villagers at the end of that day.

The WYAT members understood it to be a sad, tragic, and angry picture of the human need to belong. It exposed the way many people set aside their values and principles and do what they know is morally evil out of fear of being cast out of the group to which they belong. They do what all the others are doing. It's a bizarre parable about how conformity can lead to totally irrational behavior, and the ominous point was not lost on the young people. Author Jackson skillfully gave it all a grotesque sanity.

We created all new characters, ensuring there were enough parts for all our actors. We wrote a script together, read it through several times, and followed it with the Gossip Game (see page 117). That helped the members to develop their own characters, relationships, and standing in the town.

The next step was to create a real sense of community. We drew maps of an imaginary town, and decided what kinds of houses, farms, or businesses populated it. We worked on the sensory elements of the place: dust on the items in the front window of the general store, the high curb up to the main sidewalk, the smell of burning leaves that autumn day, and so on.

We spent one meeting exploring the idea of community rituals. All through the meetings and rehearsals the members spoke as their characters and addressed one another by their characters' names. They organized fictional 4-H clubs, quilting bees, and Kiwanis clubs to help understand the bonding in this community. They did improvs in which one person was in trouble and some of the others helped him out— pushing his car out of the mud, putting out a barn fire, bringing food to a sick person. They began to find special relationships and special resentments. One girl decided that her husband had been killed in a previous Lottery. She couldn't look at the woman whose husband always managed to break his leg at the time of the Lottery and so wasn't allowed to come.

We also set up two or three other lotteries with milder consequences as a game, not necessarily for rehearsal purposes but rather to introduce the sense of trepidation or concern in the story. In one of them the punishment for "winning" the lottery was eating a whole onion. The boy who won actually ate it, and nobody went near him for the rest of the session. Of course, we never allowed anyone to be hurt.

After all the preparation, we staged the show in just one afternoon. It practically blocked itself, we just had to move people around occasionally so that a tall person wouldn't be hiding a shorter person from the audience's view. On the night of the performance, we decided to precede it with a real "community fair" of contests, square dancing, games, and a cake auction. One of the fathers even came with his tape recorder and interviewed all the "townsfolk."

We never charged admission, but we did ask the audience members to draw lots as they came into the assembly room where it all took place (there was no black circle). The show was very successful. At the time, "The Lottery" was a very well-known story, but some people hadn't read it and were shocked at the end of the evening.

About twenty-five years later, our Young Angels Theater Company, in Connecticut, did its own version of "The Lottery." The actors were distressed by the "down" ending, so they created a whole new Act II, which brought that town into the present by adding a town meeting to celebrate the anniversary of the ending of that terrible tradition. They also created a very useful technique to develop their script. Each actor created his or her own character and gave the character a name. Each one then sat up on the edge of the stage in turn while the others interviewed him, asking where he lived, what he did, what was important to him, what his goals were, how he felt about the Lottery, the town, and others in the town. We taped the interviews and, using those different characters, added the other Ws and started improvs that turned into their script.

STAGING *THE WHITE CLOWN*

When he was seventeen, our son, Brian O'Connor, created a production inspired by Federico Fellini's film *The White Clown*. In Italy clowns in white costumes and facial makeup are the classic circus performers. He first discussed the film and all he had learned from it about clowns and circuses with WYAT members. Then he cast as the central character one member who was a fine acrobat and mime. He cast another member as the bandleader and split all the other teenagers and children into groups: clowns, roustabouts, hawkers, animal trainers, ringmasters, and so on.

Using the whole stage and the central part of the assembly-room floor, he split the show into three parts. The first was the preparation for the circus, establishing the characters, place, and atmosphere. The second was the circus itself, with parades, music, acrobatics, and many wonderful clown acts. At the end of the circus the white clown has a mental breakdown. The third part of the show was a repeat of the whole circus but as seen through the nightmarish distortion of the white clown's mind.

We invited a friend, Jay Devlin, an actor who had been a clown, to come teach us some clown routines, techniques, and makeup designs. We had to have an unusually large prop crew to make or find things like rubber chickens, horns, huge shoes, unicycles, big toy cars, juggling pins, and strings of rubber sausages. Exaggerated versions of some props were needed for the third part.

Then it was time to stage the frightening climax in which the white clown becomes the delirious master puppeteer manipulating all the circus members with imaginary strings. Crazed by jealousy, he pantomimes cutting the bandleader's strings. The bandleader and everyone else in the circus collapse, the music suddenly stops, strobe lights flash, and the white clown becomes master of the circus. Following a blackout, the lights go on again and everyone takes a bow.

Brian gathered the whole group together, spelled out each thing that needed to happen, and said, "Now let's try it." The kids did everything exactly as he had described it to them. It suddenly went perfectly. At the end, when the lights came back up, everyone stood up and cheered.

AN ELABORATE MACHINE

One of the most successful shows we created with teenagers was based on the warm-up improv The Machine (see Session 4 of the Leader's Guide). Here, the kids create mechanically rhythmic movements with their arms, legs, and heads, each one building on what the previous one had created. The movements are accompanied by all kinds of machine noises they make with their voices. We began to elaborate on this by giving the machine different characteristics.

For example, a different Who each time. Sometimes the person who started it would be a vigorous, aggressive type. Sometimes a suspicious, reluctant one. Sometimes a ditzy one. All the other actors adapted their movements to fit the personality of the machine established by the first actor. Then, once everyone had joined the machine, the initiator, simply going on instinct, began to accelerate the movement up to a certain pitch, and then to decelerate, until eventually the entire machine ceased all movement.

In response to various requests for one-act performances by our group, Rosemary Foley had the idea of turning the machine game into a metaphor for the birth, growth, and final resolution of human life. They all jumped on the idea and soon developed it into an unusual, adaptable forty-five-minute theater piece.

When it began, all the cast members were crouched under and hidden by an enormous pink drape donated by one of the parents (the size of your cloth, should you choose to perform this piece, will depend on the number of actors; the show can be adapted to almost any number of youngsters). The audiotape began then with the deep, sonorous voice of one of our eighteen-year-olds reading Carl Sandburg's poem "The Machine," accompanied by the rising and falling of the cloth. The tape continued with a series of breathing sounds, followed by popping noises (which we had made with our fingers and our cheeks) and finally a shredding sound.

We had cut slits in the large drape and positioned the kids under them so that at each popping sound something suddenly appeared and disappeared: a foot, an elbow, a grinning head, someone's backside, and so on. After some shaking and rumbling and a long humming sound, the actors threw the whole cloth over their heads toward the back wall, and three of them emerged and moved tentatively downstage as newborns. They began with fetal positions, opening their eyes, discovering hands and feet, rolling over, wobbling, flopping, bumping into one another, and starting to rise in different ways—some buttocks first, some with heads up but grabbing another for support.

They then made the transition into the "baby machine," transforming human infant movements into machine movements.

Gradually the movements became more secure and childlike. Three of them spun out to the front of the stage, the machine behind them froze, and they did a short scene as children playing in a sandbox. At this moment, two actors as Mother and Father called them in to dinner. They ran back to their original positions in the machine group and another child spun out of it. With her back to the audience she started a game of Simon Says, which gained momentum until they transformed into an older machine.

When that reached adolescence, rock music played and the machine turned into a group dancing. Suddenly the music stopped, and the stage went black. As a spotlight picked out different cast members one at a time, they quietly voiced their private thoughts in a short monologue.

The lights came back on, the machine "grew up" a bit. The music played, softly and romantically this time, and two young lovers emerged from the machine, as the others froze again. Later, a vignette expressing war broke out. The piece continued in this way, actors going in and out of the machine as it grew older, and scenes depicted middle age, old age, and death. At the end, as each part of the machine "lay dead," the machine noises began again. Slowly all the cast members pushed up daisies, and the lights slowly faded.

Dialogue for this piece is very flexible; you can insert anything you and your group create. We had several different versions of the war scenes—ambassadors spouted platitudes in one version—and of the middle-age scenes, in which typical hurried situations and unrealized dreams beset the actors.

The work we did on the teenage section of *The Machine*, in particular, validated some convictions we've always had about people in that age group: namely, that when teenagers trust you they will come forward with very moving and honest thoughts. They long to be challenged and will not tolerate being patronized. They want to look hard at reality and into their souls.

We started to write and develop the adolescent portion of *The Machine*, in which the actors voiced their private thoughts, by asking everyone to do a long yoga relaxation exercise. Then we asked them all to write about something that they were afraid of, very concerned about, kept thinking about, were ashamed of or embarrassed by, dreamed about, or just wanted to get off their chests—anything they wanted, but there were two ironclad stipulations: They must tell the truth, and they must not sign their papers.

No one was ever to know who wrote what. We said they could disguise their handwriting if they felt anyone would recognize it. And they were not to tell *anyone* what they wrote. We gave them plenty of time and collected the papers without looking at them. Then we told them that some of these might be part of the adolescent section of *The Machine*.

After the meeting, we adults read the papers and tried to determine which ones were written by males or by females so that we could assign an appropriate cast member to say it in the spotlight as his or her turn came up. We typed them, made copies, and passed them out to the cast at the next rehearsal. Perhaps some of them got their own papers back. None of us will ever know. But they learned them, spoke them simply and beautifully, and it was a high point of the show. Here are a few examples:

At night sometimes I just can't sleep. I just think about everything.

What I want most is to be able to trust people and not be afraid to let them know what I'm really like.

I would like to cry for as long as it would take me to get rid of all my guilt and fears. I see people loving and lying, and I want to cry. I see how I cannot help, and I want to cry.

I wish that we could all realize that we're all in this together. That we don't have to be petrified of each other. I wish I could be myself and not be afraid that it's not good enough.

Sometimes I just can't be as happy as I should be for other people. I guess it's because I'm jealous.

I'd love life more if I were free. I mean, if I could do whatever I wanted to do without being afraid of anyone that I don't like. I wish that everyone could say things and no one would laugh or make fun. I wish everyone wouldn't be afraid to say what they feel deep inside.

Of course, not every show WYAT did had frightening qualities. We did *Alice in Wonderland*, *In White America*, and parodies of TV shows. We did a film based on news stories, and a bunch of happy, loopy skits and reviews. An old friend, Paul Newman, came to two of our meetings and performances. He enjoyed the work, gave the young people good criticisms, and even gave the group some financial help from his foundation. His parting comment was, "This country could use thirty thousand more groups like this."

CREATING *GETTING WINGS* FROM SCRATCH

Just a few years ago, Marla Truini, directing our Young Angels Theater Company, suddenly lost her "leading man." Since he was the only member old enough for that part, she decided to develop another show very quickly. She had each member of her cast go down to the prop room, pick out a prop, then come up and do a monologue about it. From those ideas they developed a fine play about people in Grand Central Station on the day Lindbergh flew across the ocean.

USING ACTORS' NIGHTMARES TO ADVANTAGE

Recently Marla Truini developed a hilarious musical with her high-school students using Christopher Durang's play, *An Actor's Nightmare,* as a jumping off point. She chose songs for the cast members to sing individually and in groups. Then by brainstorming and improvising, they created a central character who was having a nightmare typical of actors and performers. They filled the show with marvelously inventive and bizarre situations in which each song was performed.

STAGING *EVERYMAN*

Earlier, we have quoted actor/director James Brennan and his wife Kathel, who have done a great deal of fine work with teenagers in New Jersey. Jim gave us an exhilarating description of doing a production of *Everyman*, a famous moral allegory from the thirteenth century.

> In the course of the play, *Everyman*, the hero, walks along a road and encounters many allegorical people, all of whom have an effect on him. The script has no stage directions. It just says, "Along the road he encountered...." We chose to begin with one character Everyman encountered: Wealth. How will Wealth make her entrance? One girl suggested she be sitting on a mound of money bags, perhaps having jumped onto the bags. So the kids brought in plastic bags painted with dollar signs and we filled them with comforters. The bags were dumped one at a time from a second story, and then Wealth herself jumped into the whole pile. She was frightened of the jump, but the trust exercises had helped her, and the adults and older kids did it first. Once she did it she wanted a second and third entrance, the same way.
>
> The death of Everyman was spectacular. He climbed to the top of a ladder, stood up and rolled forward through a rectangular hole in a huge cloth made of sheets, and into the arms of his colleagues standing under the cloth. Meanwhile Death played a violin in the corner. As Everyman fell through the hole, fishing wires on the corners of the cloth were pulled up, revealing all the actors underneath.

These scenes were conceived or invented by the children and the adults together. And because it was *Everyman*, it gave the children a sense of importance—they were telling a profound story.

WARM-UP EXERCISES FOR TEENS

A few of the improvs and games we've described earlier are too easy for teens, such as the mirror game, the relays with imaginary objects, and the name-writing on imaginary surfaces with parts of their bodies. But they will enjoy and benefit from most of the others. You can demand more from teens with the more difficult exercises throughout the book and from those that follow—just as the shows you do together can be richer and more complex.

Space Rebound

This exercise is one that might be beyond the younger kids because of its complexity.

Briefly, it involves two or more teenagers moving, one at a time with no dialogue, into unusual or possibly grotesque positions, freezing in place, then taking another position after the other actors, in turn, have assumed their postures. On a cue from you, such as a clap of the hands, they all stop in their current positions and begin an improv, creating dialogue and developing normal movements that evolve from those original positions into a short scene. A complete description with examples is found at the end of Session 10 in the Leader's Guide. It's a good challenge that delivers some fascinating results.

One discovery from this exercise is that balancing or "dressing" the stage seems to be a natural inclination when a group is performing. That is, as they are doing Space Rebound, people often seem to move to the best spot on the stage in terms of the stage picture. It's all part of the tendency people have to maintain a distance from others, even when walking along the sidewalk. Onstage, actors will often create their own space, perhaps unconsciously balancing the others—two on one side balancing one on the other, for example.

Here and Now

This helps when your teens are doing a written scene or prepared sketch. Sometimes an actor's work in a scripted show can become vague, uninteresting, and general. As we have seen, an actor may be trying to play the adjective "angry," instead of really "telling somebody off." The Actors Studio Here and Now rehearsal technique, described on page 83, can be very helpful here; if you interrupt and ask what he or she is doing, thinking, and feeling at that moment, between and even during the lines, it will force the actor to realize when his or her thoughts need to be more real and specific. As they give you answers, actors will often be amazed at how many things must be found that they hadn't thought of before. They should then be able to play the same material again with more reality.

If a session or rehearsal seems to be bogging down, ask yourself if the games, exercises, directions, or tasks you've been giving your group are too vague or general. (You, too, can almost never be *too* specific.)

Nonsense Sentences

This is another good exercise to use with teens. An extension of some of the previously described exercises that contained only a few words, a sentence, or numbers, these little scripts for two people can be written by you or by the teenagers; they are not necessarily improvs. There are examples of nonsense sentences in Session 6 of the Leader's Guide.

The value is, as always, to reveal how much words and dialogue can change depending on the specifics of the situation. They should be written so that they can mean almost anything depending on the actors' choices and can be short or long.

Here's a short one:

A: I wasn't expecting that.
B: Time is with us.

A: I thought it was against us.
B: Let's get away from here.
A: Do you really think it will happen?
B: Maybe. Let's go.
A: All right—as soon as I'm finished.
B: I'll wait as long as I can.

We've used this exercise with groups of teenagers we've taken to entertain at community dinners and meetings of the Rotary Club or the city council. We asked members of the audience to call out various lines at random. We wrote them down in order, and then different pairs of kids decided on the five Ws and improvised a scene using those lines.

Vocal Color

It often takes longer for teenagers who haven't done any acting before to loosen up and free themselves from inhibitions. People's self-protective behavior sometimes results in a tendency to flatten out the voice in line readings when they start to act, probably because they don't want to risk "making fools of themselves."

But you can push teenagers harder than younger kids to gain subtler acting skills. Achieving vocal color and variety are major technical goals. Urge your teen actors to listen carefully to people talking and to notice the enormous range and flexibility of pitch, tempo, emphasis, and volume. They'll realize that abundant vocal color and vivid delivery do not necessarily signal overacting, and they will eventually lose their fear of being embarrassed.

The playwright Clifford Odets once tried an experiment in an early Actors Studio session that might be worth duplicating yourself, if you have the time and the resources. Odets brought in the script of a scene with three characters: his aunt and two uncles. The director, Lee Strasberg, gave the scripts to three of the best actors in the Studio and asked them to study it a while and then read it aloud to the others. They did and gave a fine, honest, intelligent reading.

Then Odets played a tape from which the scene had been transcribed. He had hidden his tape recorder under the kitchen table in his aunt's house and taped a conversation between her and her two brothers. The words were the same, but there was a vast difference between the real conversation of people who were unaware that they were being recorded and the excellent reading of the actors. The actors were stunned.

The voices of the aunt and two uncles ranged all over the scale. Sometimes their words tumbled over one another, or were clipped, or were drawn out. At times very loudly and at times with a mumble, they spoke with pointed insistence, and then with laughter. The aunt and uncles were really performing without being aware of it—and responding unconsciously to the sensory elements that were part of the situation. They didn't know what was going to happen at the next moment, and their voices were alive and colorful. And they certainly didn't just drop their voices at the ends of every sentence.

The daunting task of the actor is to re-create that aliveness, and many talented people spend their whole careers trying to learn how to do that. So you can't expect miracles from your teenagers. But you can make them aware of what they hear and help them to overcome their inhibitions.

TEENAGE THEATER GROUPS AROUND THE COUNTRY

Some very interesting work with teenagers has been done in an educational outreach program of the Nebraska Shakespeare Festival, in Omaha. Moira Reilly Mangiameli, the program's coordinator, has written (in *Shakespeare Unbound*) a version of the Shadow Self exercise (see page 59) but with scenes from Shakespeare:

> Assign two students to each role. One set of actors reads the scene as written, the other set stands behind and to the side of them and mimes the character's inner feelings. There are several scenes that work well for this exercise: *Julius Caesar*, Act III, scene i, lines 145–252 and the short scene between Juliet and the Nurse in Romeo and Juliet at the end of Act III, scene v. In *Othello* almost any scene between Othello and Iago will do.

Mangiameli also does an exercise she calls the Two-Minute Shakespeare, in which each group of students must take famous lines and key phrases and present the entire play in two minutes. She encourages them to be as physical as possible. It really works. (This strategy has been employed by professional actors doing *Hamlet* in fifteen minutes, followed by a two-minute encore of the whole play, leaving audiences rolling in the aisles.)

The youth and staff of City at Peace-New York produced their fourth hugely successful off-Broadway original musical in 2005. As the program notes, "An incorrigible group of 70 teenagers from over 40 schools in the city met at least once a week from October to July to learn how to take responsibility for their lives and communities, using the performing arts as a tool to focus on non-violent conflict resolution, leadership, community action, cross-cultural relationship building and much more." No auditions for membership are held. The only requirement is a desire to affect positive change in their communities and the lives of others. They all participate in training workshops for theater skills and in developing community projects to address issues or conflicts that are of concern to them. They meet privately in small groups to discuss their stories and turn them into scenes and musical numbers. But in the final performances they never play themselves. They all play the roles of other cast members whose stories they've heard and helped to develop for the show. Consequently, the shows are inspiring, honest, hard-hitting, moving, funny, frank, joyful, free, and highly energetic. In a word…marvelous. And very successful.

Mrs. Adrienne Lovell, a Latin teacher in Durham, Connecticut, has accomplished the amazing feat of making Latin one of the most popular classes taught in her high school. She and her enthusiastic students create a show each year by translating a well-known story and performing it in Latin. She took one drama course in college long ago, and she and her students have had no theater experience. But everyone loved doing and seeing the shows, and she said the students learned more Latin doing the plays than they did in the classroom.

Leigh Curran, the artistic director of The Virginia Avenue Project, in Los Angeles, described a new technique for teaching communication skills and collaboration to teenage members. The Project brings inner-city children together with professional artists to create theater. They call their approach the Playback Program: Each young participant has already written at least two short plays and performed in two. Each is paired with an adult writer-performer. The young person writes the first half of a one-act play, and the adult writes the second. They then rehearse and perform it together.

The theme of the first series of these Playback plays was Lost and Found. Something must be lost by the characters in the first half of the one-act play and it must be found in the second. As Leigh says:

> What is particularly inspiring about this group of plays is that all the young writers, completely unbeknownst to each other, decided to write about losing qualities instead of things. For example, Ali's play is about a bride who loses her nerve. Elizabeth's play is about a teenager who loses his culture. Ivonne's heroine loses a friendship.

Some of the memorable lines Leigh quoted in her newsletter:

> Ivonne Herrera, age fifteen: I was embarrassed with you—you had a family and I didn't. I felt lonely. I was with that foster family, but I didn't like it there. They would always talk about how I dress, about my friends, and I felt that I was a problem in their lives.
>
> Brisa Perez, age fifteen: Maybe—is it that I wanted something to come to me as soon as I asked for it, but sometimes it doesn't work that way?
>
> Ali Campoverdi, age fifteen: I am nothingness, I am a lonely night, I am a Thanksgiving alone, I am an old lady who dies without a friend. I am nothing and you have called me.

There are more nonprofit organizations like The Virginia Avenue Project, the 52nd Street Project, and City at Peace–New York all around the country. But as Paul Newman said, we wish there were thirty thousand of them. Whatever the makeup of the teenage or younger group you lead or might lead in the future, the skills that the members develop will be useful to any of them in any situation:

> Relaxing and concentrating under pressure
> Finding the best way to say what they want to say
> Increasing their sensitivity
> Focusing their imagination

Creating something alone or with a group
Leading when necessary and following when necessary

And best of all, understanding other people who are very different from themselves.

Pass It On

We long to see as many young actors' theater groups around the country, nay the world, as there are Little League teams. We want people to put scripts into youngsters' hands, not guns! It is our fervent hope that the teens you have been leading will move out into the community and "pass it on."

The PTA After School Alliance reports that 11 million kids have no place to go when school ends. They are urging parental involvement to solve this problem. We propose that teenagers step in to fill the bill. Many high school students around the country are required to do either a Senior Project or a Community Service Project before graduation. Offering to lead an after-school theater group for a few elementary kids is a doable, win/win idea. Let's face it. Little kids would much prefer to have "older kids" rather than adults pay attention to them. Within a week or two the younger kids are like adoring puppies to the teenagers who come to lead them.

One senior girl we knew seemed lost...she wore lots of jewelry and make-up, and had no energy. Her split-up, dysfunctional family left her with no confidence. With our prompting and the guidance of the first edition of this book, she formed an after-school theater group of eighteen fourth and fifth graders at the local school. Within two weeks they were cheering her entrance, hugging her, hanging onto her, and showing off for her. They were even running around the playground during recess writing scripts. At the end of the semester she presented a videotape of their work. She has since graduated *cum laude* from college and gone on to study law.

At the start of a summer studies class in Wolcott, Connecticut, Bobbi Thompson was looking for the best way to help eight of her six- to twenty-year-old special-ed students and twenty-two mainstream third to sixth graders get to know and understand one another. She wanted ways to keep all her kids mentally stimulated. Some of her students had special needs because of neurological impairment. Some were in wheelchairs. Some had impaired vision and/or hearing. Some had Down syndrome. Some were autistic. And, of course, most of them were normal eight- to eleven-year-olds. She wanted to try an integrated class to help them express themselves through theater games, movement and music. She wanted to give her students input in three modalities: visual, auditory, and physical. None of them had ever done any theater before, so it would give them a common starting ground. Her daughter Mandy and three other Young Angels Theatre members stepped up to the plate. Very successfully.

For an hour every day for six weeks they led the class in the high school auditorium. They used the suggestions in our first edition's "Getting Started," "Basic System," and "Skills" chapters. They did warm-ups, relays, and a number of games and exercises, including Chord games, Jack Be Nimble, five senses work, Object Throw Away, Circle Build-Ups, mirroring, walking on different surfaces, imitating and discussing walks and entrances, the musical conductor game, and the students' favorite—Poor Soul (or, as some call it Ruin My Day or Bus Stop). They also did three performances: one demonstration with audience participation and two plays: "Polar Bear, Polar Bear" and "Miranda Finds the Rainbow." Bobbi taught mainstream kids to be peer helpers with the special-ed students. One very shy girl was encouraged by "how the special-ed kids look up to her." They invented a game, The Jungle Walk, in which the students imitated different animals, their sounds and relationships. One girl, who was obsessive-compulsive, did a brilliant imitation of a monkey, picking at her hair and eating flies. One of the young leaders observed, "Sometimes I wonder if we're the impaired ones." Bobbi asked the mainstream students what they noticed about the special-ed students. The answers were not observations of impairments, but rather positive, non-obvious qualities like "he likes lions," "she's very outgoing," and "he loves to make people happy."

The students thought it was "so cool" to be hanging out with teenagers. The teens knew the importance of encouragement, of creating a safe, stable environment that is not frightening, threatening or imposing. They stressed that "no" is a "bad word."

As Mandy put it, "Theater games can get you to the point where you don't need approval, because you tap into your innermost feelings, you become so comfortable with theirs. You trust that who you are is great. Everyone is the same in acting class because you are all going through the same feelings, while you're looking for your character's feelings."

Bobbi was delighted at how quickly all the students got close together, and how much confidence was built. They did indeed learn to trust, to listen, and to understand diversity. One student said, "This class is about teamwork and about helping."

The Young Angels listed some of what they learned: Balance friendliness with firmness and clarity. Don't accept misbehaving. Don't let yourselves down. Don't walk out. Don't get irrational. Don't be judgmental or negative. Always encourage. It's better to choose one show and aim the theater games toward it, after starting with warm-ups. Work on process. Then showcase it, as in sports. And most important, establish a good relationship with the kids so that they don't want to disappoint you. Bobbi listed her most important pieces of advice to teen leaders: 1. Gain mutual respect...learn the kids' names! 2. Point out something special, something positive about the students. 3. Spell out expectations. 4. No one should ever worry about mistakes. 5. There is no wrong game choice.

Additional Exercises, Improvs, and Games

DEEPER LOOK AT WHO

Teens can understand more easily than younger children that how a character feels about himself goes a long way in determining that character's behavior (or his Who). Suggest that your teenager explores how he thinks a character he's playing—in an improv, exercise, of full production—feels about himself. For example, if the character goes through life feeling that he has to correct everyone else's mistakes, or

> should help everyone possible, or
> is no good and must hide from the world, or
> is misunderstood or underestimated, or
> is furious at the world, or
> feels he is too fat, too ugly, too dumb, too nervous, too scared, or
> > just too gorgeous to be believed, or is fated to save the world.

In an exercise, improv, or game, your teen can choose any of these self-images to play. In a production, he can look for the self-images that more closely enrich his character.

LOOKING AT WHAT

Try having a young actor go up and do an activity, such as picking up and putting down a bunch of props. Then suggest a What for that activity—use infinitive verbs (to coax, to resist, to organize, to repair, to win, etc.)—and have her keep doing it over and over, each time adding higher stakes, making the accomplishment of the What more urgent.

DEEPENING THE WHY

Choose an activity, like moving furniture around. Then suggest a What, such as "to find a lost check." Propose that the actor, in the exercise, wants to find the lost check (Why) because he "would like to"; then because he:

> needs to
> has to
> must
> is desperate to
> is determined to
> terrified of failure to

dedicated to

impelled to

Then you can add even more feelings—paralyzing fear, rage, frustration, curiosity, suspicion, etc.

This is what leads to behavior. This is what moves the acting out of just the verbal, mental realm and into the physical. This is what makes acting more understandable and believable, and makes a story clearer.

IMPROVS FROM THEMES

Another way to set up improvs would be to take a theme word and have two characters take opposite sides of the theme—such as compassion, freedom, hostility, democracy, ideal teaching, nature study, self-improvement, dieting, propriety, etc. Then let your young actors choose the other particulars…five Ws, some sensory elements, and an activity. For example:

> Two parents arguing about punishing their child
> Two teachers with different teaching styles
> Two architects drawing different plans for the Freedom Tower
> at the World Trade Center site

ENDOWING PROPS WITH MEANING

Line up a few kids across the stage. Give each one a prop: a toy car, a pitcher, a jewelry box, a book, a bottle of medicine. Ask each one to imagine and then tell the audience what that prop means to her and some of its background. It could be a first possession, belong to a family member who is gone, a gift, an award, a reminder of an illness, or something else.

Or have your members form two lines facing each other. Give those in Line A a prop. One at a time each member in Line A must cross to a member in Line B and give it to him with an "as if" in mind. As if he wants to get rid of it, as if he had taken it away and was sorry, as if it were a reward, a peace offering, an expensive article to auction, a clue to a mystery, etc.

COMMERCIALS

Divide your groups into teams of two to three people. Bring a box filled with disparate objects such as a toy car, a soft drink, a medicine bottle, a prop sword, a scarf, or a flashlight. Ask each team to choose one object and go off together to create a commercial using that "prop."

IMPROVISED DIALOGUE

A busy Hollywood actor who leads an improv group told us this popular exercise: Send two people up to the stage. The first person starts a story or conversation. When he stops, the second person answers, "Yes, and"—and continues the story. Then the first person goes on with, "Yes, and—" going on from where the second one stopped, and so on. (The basic idea, of course, being that to answer "no" is usually the death of any improv.)

NUMBER AND NOUN

Another popular exercise the Hollywood actor suggested is to give a person the number 165 and a noun. The actor's task is to create a short monologue using that number and that noun in the speech.

DRAWING AS IFs

Give one to four people an activity and a What. Have the group members each write a different "as if" on a piece of paper and put them into a hat. Pass the hat and have each member choose one "as if." Each person must perform the activity according to the "as if" they draw, meeting the demand of the What. Remind them that an activity is a piece of stage "business," a physical action, such as entering, leaving, moving objects, putting on clothes, opening windows, etc. A What is a purpose— what the character wants, and/or is trying to accomplish: to escape, to convince, to deny, to amuse, to find, etc.

For example: Tell two actors to move several chairs into a row across the stage to prepare for an important meeting. Actor 1 draws "as if you've just fallen in love with your partner." Actor 2 draws "as if you're so nervous you can hardly breathe." They may choose to tell each other what they drew, or not.

Another example: Tell four actors to form a line to get a movie star's autograph. Actor 1 draws "as if you're old and weak." Actor 2 draws "as if it's pouring rain." Actor 3 draws "as if you can't stand anyone else on the stage." Actor 3 draws "As if you're hiding from the police." Tell them to hop up onto the stage and see what happens.

DIALOGUES WITH ALPHABET LETTERS

Send two people up to have a dialogue. The first person must start the first sentence with a word beginning with "A." The other actor answers with the first word of his sentence beginning with "B," and so on. For example:

Amber: Ask them if we could come a little later.
Jordan: But I thought you were ready.
Amber: Can't you see? I haven't even got my makeup on yet.
Jordan: Don't you remember? I think you look best without makeup.

And so on thru the alphabet.

Another, maybe harder, version is to have each person start her sentence with a word beginning with the last letter of the last word she heard from her partner. For example:

Sophie: Almost time to go, don't you think?
Ian: Kings don't have to worry about time.
Sophie: Every time I ask you to do something you lean on your "royalty" to say no.
Ian: Oh, is that so? Just because you're a queen doesn't give you the right to nag me.

And on until they, or you, feel they've gone far enough.

TRUTH

Give two actors a situation, that is, a set of facts that contains a Who, What, Why, Where, and When. Ask them to start a scene but, every word they say must actually be the truth as it exists for the actors in that moment of real time. So what they say may be about the time, their names, their likes and dislikes, their thoughts, their friends and relatives, their attitudes… but it will be colored by the situation. If your session is at 3:30, for instance, a line they cannot say would be "It's midnight. Let's get out of here."

SILENT MOVIE

Have two or more people do an improv as if it's a silent movie. Then have another team stand on the side and say the lines that seem to correspond to the moves the first group is making.

TRANSLATOR

Ask two people to have a dialogue as if neither spoke the other's language. They must speak in gibberish only. Ask a third person to sit between them and translate their words into English.

SHAKESPEARE'S INSULTS

In a seminar on playing Shakespeare for professional actors, the popular teacher and director Robert Williams passed out this list of insults found in Shakespeare's plays, courtesy of Michael John McGann. To construct a Shakespearean insult, combine one word from each of the three columns and preface it with "Thou."

We've found this is a wonderful way to loosen up teens. It gives them a green light to be as big and colorful as they wish. You can make copies and pass them out to two to four people at a time to use in improvisations. Here is a sampling:

Column 1	Column 2	Column 3
artless	base-court	apple-john
beslubbering	beef-witted	barnacle
bootless	beetle-headed	bladder
churlish	boil-brained	boar-pig
cuttish	crook-pated	clack-dish
droning	doghearted	docpiece
fawning	earth-vexing	dewberry
gorbellied	folly-fallen	giglet
loggerheaded	half-faced	hedge-pig
pribbling	ill-nurtured	maggot-pie
puking	knotty-pated	malt-worm
qualling	motley-minded	measle
rank	onion-eyed	minnow
reeky	plume-plucked	miscreant
saucy	reeling-ripe	nut-hook
spleeny	rough-hewn	pigeon-egg
venomed	wag-bellied	scainsmate
villainous	tardy-gaited	strumpet
wayward	toad-spotted	vassal
weedy	unchin-snouted	whey-face

Chapter Ten

For Teachers:
Using Theater in the Classroom

AS ROBERT COLES SAID in his preface to this book, "Children need to learn their regular lessons, of course, but they also need nourishment for their imaginative life."

Right! Maybe you're a teacher who has already experienced the challenge and rewards of doing shows with your students. Or maybe you're a teacher who is gung-ho to do a show with kids, but you can't because all the arts funding has been eliminated.

So, do it in your classrooms. Use those impulses to help you zap the lessons right into the kids' memories. We know teachers are underappreciated, terribly burdened, and never have enough time. But every once in a while try using the ten elements of acting to build what you're teaching into a skit or an improv for your kids to do in front of their classmates. As one seventh grader said to us recently, "Sometimes our teacher writes little scenes for us to act out, and that's a lot funner!"

A SPOONFUL OF SUGAR

When we see children who never walk when they could run, skip, or jump—who seldom sit straight on a chair when they could squat, perch, or kneel on it—how can we expect them to keep learning when their young bodies are screaming for them to MOVE, to exercise their rapidly growing muscles? Movement anchors thought. To "pin down" a thought, there must be movement. Children laugh about twenty times a day more than adults do. It goes with recognizing what's real and what isn't real.

Most actors are not versed in teaching methods, or pedagogical strategizing. But actors do have to memorize a lot of material. Sometimes they drill lines and "cue each other." Most of the time, however, they learn lines naturally as a part of putting themselves into their character's life situations. As they search, choose, and use the ten elements of acting we've described earlier, the lines automatically fall into place.

By moving, thinking, feeling, and speaking as their characters in that environment, they memorize the lines almost without effort. Funny, isn't it, that actors always refer to "playing" a part, rather than "acting" it.

Perhaps we're all still children at heart. Children's instinctive learning technique is to "pretend like." Through play, kids make sense of their world. Many of you teachers value the use of role-playing because it enables kids to act out any academic situation, to learn it by living it. That's how they get those "wonderful ideas" we all love.

Amanda Smith, an education major at the University of Northern Iowa, said, "I don't want my students to have to worry that they didn't remember the year Napoleon was exiled. I want them to remember what Napoleon was like."

As David Hawkins said in relation to curriculum development, "You don't want to cover a subject. You want to uncover it."

Playing with Perimeters

Recently we observed Pam Luchesi teaching her fourth-grade math class how to find perimeters of different shapes: rectangles, squares, isosceles triangles, octagons, hexagons, and quadrilaterals. She asked for the number of long sides and the number of short sides. She gave a number and asked the lengths of the sides of a rectangle, for instance, that could add up to that number. She gave them shapes to draw and to handle. She defined *rhombus* and *polygon*. She asked for multiples of three. She had them draw shapes from dot to dot adding up to sixteen. She was terrific and the class was attentive.

Afterward we simply suggested that maybe she could have two or three kids take that information and "pretend to be" playground designers with only a certain amount of space to use—walking around the space, drawing shapes on the ground with a stick, planning, arguing, deciding, demonstrating, measuring. What kinds of spaces could they best use for different playground activities? Is a narrow rectangle best for swings? How can you fit a jungle gym into a triangle? Sandboxes should be octagons? What? No room for the basketball hoop? Let one designer be extravagant and excited, proud of his ideas. Another—cautious, afraid of new ideas. Another—wise, experienced, and impatient with the others. They each have an idea they want to sell so that they can get credit. This is a plum job and they want to do it right so that they can be promoted. The class can be critics reviewing the plans.

Most teachers believe that facts are best learned in a practical, life-relevant context. However, that's not always easy. Different children of different ages and backgrounds have different "real life" contexts. But all children—all people—have feelings. If you relate what you want learned to a context that includes feelings and personalities, it will sink into memory more surely than plain unadorned facts. Learning is a need fulfilled. It's a reward, not a punishment. Feelings (Whys) are the quickest route that relates a lesson to what a child already knows. So make use of feelings that kids know. And believe us—kids know them all. Frank McCourt, in his book *Teacher Man*, quotes Lisa, one of his high school students, "Kids have stuff in their heads so dark and deep it's beyond our comprehension." Kids need to explore and use these feelings safely so that they'll be able to control them when they grow up.

Feelings to Answer Why

Fear, surprise, joy, hurt, homesickness, shame, curiosity, pride, happiness, defensiveness, worry, outrage, disbelief, rage, love, jealousy, hunger, desire, exhaustion, wonder, awe, impatience, revulsion, delight, fury, triumph, envy, pain, grief, sorrow, puzzlement. Kids love to pretend to feel too cold, too hot, thirsty, pooped, determined, competitive, cozy, friendly, irritated, anxious, inquisitive, embarrassed, relieved, indignant, humiliated, bored, sorry, thrilled, proud, dangerous, or in danger.

Suppose you're teaching the Women's Suffrage Movement to a middle school Social Studies class. After you've discussed the movement and its development, you could call three girls and three boys up to the front of the room. Put down something to indicate an outdoor speaker's platform and perhaps a fence. Set up your skit or improv something like this:

Who
Emmeline Pankhurst: militant, passionate, brave

Pankhurst's two daughters, who are eager, obedient, observant. They are suffragists, organizers of the Women's Social and Political Union.

A political speaker: urgent, pompous, voluble, dominating

Two policemen: one amused, one resigned but careful

Activity (or "stage business")
Speaker is ranting on. Women are picketing and heckling and threatening to go on a hunger strike. Policemen are moving in, raising their "billy clubs."

What
The suffragists are trying to win women's right to vote.

The political speaker is trying to defend the status quo.

The police are determined to break up the meeting.

Why

The suffragists are passionately determined to win their just rights. They feel humiliated and resentful of being denied the vote. They are zealous to affect change in the voting laws.

The political speaker is outraged and affronted by this unthinkable request to change the law. He is furious at their heckling. He is afraid he will lose his superiority.

The police are worried but feel impelled to do their duty.

Where

The park across from the White House

When

A cold winter afternoon, 1913, when most people thought, "A woman's place is in the home."

Tell them to start the scene and you will stop them when it seems like some good points have been made or if it seems to be bogged down. If they're shy, ask them to do it first not using real words, just gibberish. Then do it again with lines. Have several groups try it.

THE 'PERKS'

Lin Northrup, a holistic educator, M.Ed. in Counseling, has been using our Ten Elements of Acting successfully in classrooms with many kinds and ages of children. She says that incorporating activities from acting and theater games into today's classroom:

> Puts the body back into learning.
> Improves visualization and visual skills.
> Fosters group harmony and connectedness.
> Allows children to express their emotions.
> Links feeling with learning for greater comprehension of
>   material.
> Naturally enhances many of Howard Garner's Multiple
>   Intelligences, along with children's unique learning styles.

There are many other advantages. But our favorite is:

> Expands creativity and joy for learning.

We're not proposing to load every lesson with emotional baggage (content). We're merely suggesting that a teaching choice can often be made to use skits, theater games, and actors' tools to help give kids confidence to work out their own wonderful ideas, to encourage kids to solve problems, to value the unexpected, and to work as a team. And when kids are then each given a different personality to play and the feelings that propel the behavior of their imaginary characters, they are more eager and less inhibited. It relieves them of self-consciousness. The child not only learns to solve problems—he learns to put himself into another's place. He "walks a mile in another's moccasins." It relieves kids of personal responsibility. (Many wonderful actors are really very shy people.)

While the children are acting, although they're using their own feelings (after all, that's all they've got—it's like saying they're using their own feet), they aren't in danger of their own selves being judged. They can be free to go beyond the stiff stance and monotonous reading behind which kids often hide when they're in front of the class.

THE BOTTOM LINE

Many lesson plans are filled with tools that are fun, illuminating, ingenious, and delightful: masks, maps, trips, videos, telescopes, the Internet, overhead projections, crossword puzzles, Power Point presentations, puppets, models, clip art galleries, science fairs, posters that teach helpful and harmful bacteria—all are good and should be used. But engage kids' feelings and you will surely hook their memories. Feelings are what are actable. Feelings are what usually determine our behavior. They don't have to be taught. They go with the territory.

AN ACTOR'S SLANT

Of course there are a lot of theater games we've described earlier in this book that can certainly work well as teaching tools: The Gossip Game, Who am I? Where Am I?, Circle Build Up, Where with Others Joining, Reenacting Current Events, Move and Freeze (with class members calling out elements presently being studied), Stories from Props, etc. But skits are winners.

TRY IT. YOU'LL LIKE IT.

Be brave. Choose an actable situation, like Northerners helping slaves to escape through the Underground Railroad, or scientists in a lab arguing about an experiment. Attach one or two of the above feelings to a standard lesson to be taught, and you're home free. The whole world is your menu. Mix and match them and you'll have a nutritious full-course meal.

You want kids to learn how to make decisions and work as a team? Split them into small groups and assign a skit to be presented at the end of the week using the information they're now studying. Or just set up an impromptu sketch to make a point during the class.

Use the ten elements of acting as a formula. Set up "As Ifs" and "What Ifs."

Give them interesting personalities to play. Kids even love to personify animals, inanimate objects, or even ideas: "freedom," "tyranny," "compromise." And they aren't at all averse to changing genders. Suggest what the imaginary characters are trying to accomplish. Give them good, emotional reasons to want to accomplish it and see what happens.

And if their improv winds up having a beginning, middle, and end, you all get an A +++.

CLASSROOM MANAGEMENT

It's a good idea to "set the stage," that is, set up the spatial limits in your classroom for the skit or the improv. Where's the door, podium, police line, chair, tree, etc.? "Pretend like my desk is the elves' house, and the front window is the magic mirror," etc. (We used to play in the backyard, "Pretend like the sprinkler is the pool and the lawn chair is the lifeguard's seat.") Otherwise the kids all tend to migrate toward one spot so that you can't see their faces.

If you feel your students are a bit nervous or shy about getting in front of the class, start the session with a short relaxation warm-up. We find that usually helps the thinking process. And later, if you, yourself, are willing to be silly, broad, and foolish with them as an example, it always helps to free them.

You can even play a student—perhaps one who can't sit still because he's hot and dying to get out to the playground, or a vain one who needs to show off how smart she is by interrupting all the time. Ask the students to be different kinds of teachers. Let each student, in turn, decide whether to teach the lesson right or teach it wrong, and have the class call out if it's wrong or applaud if it's right.

An Actor Prepares

Robin Ruhf, a teacher at the Glenholme School, uses touch—not threatening, always in groups—to pick up the attention and quality of her workshops. When people are milling about, she has them touch thumbs, or elbows, or lean on each other's backs, or toes if they're seated. She says it always helps them relate to each other and gain confidence. After all, she reminds us, it's akin to monkeys' natural "grooming" behavior.

Above all, please remember what Etienne DeCroux, the master of mime, told the Actors Studio actors. The more specific the limits are that you give a person, the more his or her imagination is ignited.

Frankly, if you put a wig and a costume on a boy and put him into a pageant as George Washington, it's not going to have much of an effect on his sense of history. But put him into a skit with some other kids, tell them it's late, freezing cold, very dark, some of them don't even have any gloves left, they're afraid they're losing to the British, and that General Washington has to keep up the courage of the men whom he's leading as they very quietly get into a boat and start to cross the Potomac…Then watch his sense of history grow.

Here are a few ideas for games, skits or improvs based on various lessons you might be teaching. If you like the idea, you can readily make up your own. Don't give up. Keep trying. It'll work.

You can set them up yourself to begin with, but pretty soon you can just set up a couple of elements and let the actors choose the others, or have the class call out the specifics to the daring brave actors up in the front of the class.

Additional Exercises, Improvs, and Games

HIGH SCHOOL

For English: *Moby Dick* by Herman Melville

Who
Ishmael, a romantic former schoolmaster, turned seaman

Queequeg, a bizarre, hardened South Sea Islander

Captain Ahab, stern, relentless, austere. Has an artificial leg made from the jawbone of a whale. Passionate!! A madman. Eccentric.

Fedallah, Ahab's servant, mystical, a seer

Activity
Trying to site and harpoon the whale. Trying to fight the fire in the masts.

What
Ahab is determined to find and destroy the famed white whale, Moby Dick. The others are following orders and trying to save their own lives.

Why
Ahab believes that Moby Dick is evil incarnate. Others are afraid and want him to stop.

When
Late at night. A terrible storm.

Where
Aboard the Pequod, in the Indian Ocean.

Senses
Rolling of ship, darkness, fire, turbulent sea, fear, smell of salt air.

For History: Reign of Henry II in England

Who
Eleanor of Aquitaine, strong, proud, passionate, wily

Henry II, sensuous, arrogant, high-handed, majestic

What
Henry wants to annul their marriage and have more sons by another woman. Eleanor wants to make one of her sons king. Taunts Henry. Challenges him. Conspires with her sons against him.

Give a student the following lines of Eleanor's from *The Lion in Winter* by James Goldman, and suggest that two students do an improv in which these lines are used:

"I could peel you like a pear and God himself would call it justice."

"What kind of spindly, rickets ridden, milky, semi-witted, wizened, dim-eyed, gammy-handed, limpy line of things would your sons be?"

Why
Henry is disgusted with his sons and afraid of Eleanor's power. Eleanor is enraged.

Where
England. Henry's castle: cold, echo-filled, huge, damp.

When
December 1184

For World History:
Resistance and Rescue: The Fight Against Genocide

Who
Paul Rusesabagina, a thoughtful, caring father and hotel owner, compassionate

Tatiana, his wife, lovely and loving, motherly, capable

Red Cross worker, strong, wise, worldly, brave

A frightened Tutsi family

What
Paul R. wants to hide as many Tutsis from the Hutus as he can in his hotel, but still keep his family safe. His wife begs him to stop. The Red Cross worker is trying to get the Tutsi family to safety by taking them out of his van and hustling them into the hotel. The Tutsi family wants to stay alive. They're scrambling to safety.

Why
Paul R. cannot bear to see the pain and the slaughter. His wife is terrified for her children. The Red Cross worker is determined to help save lives. The Tutsi family members are hungry, thin, sick, and terrified.

Where
Rwanda, the driveway at the entrance to a big hotel.

When
1994

For American History: The End of World War II in Europe

Who
Soldiers, sailors, nurses, WACs (Women's Army Corp), police, USO girls, families, students, waiters, college kids, Broadway performers, children.

What
Rejoicing! Celebrating the announcement that the war in Europe has ended. Germany has surrendered. Waiting for ALL the lights to be turned back on FINALLY after years of darkness and fear—of "blackouts" or "brownouts" to protect us from bombing. Sharing relief, joy, stories, and hopes!

Activities
Waiting and watching, then—as the lights are turned on—cheers, singing, hugging, dancing, crying, embracing, gazing, trading hats and coats. Praying, giving thanks. Drinking. Eating.

Why
Everyone was overjoyed with relief and thankfulness and filled with a swelling of love and wonder. Dazzled by the lights on all the buildings.

Where
NYC. Times Square!

When
V-E Day, May 8, 1945

For Art: Study of Genre Painter, Pieter Brueghel the Elder. An improv based on his painting, *A Country Wedding*

Who
The bride, quiet, contented, stupid grin

Her elderly parents, resigned, not too happy at the cost of it all to them

The Groom, dazed, greedy, gobbling food

A man pouring beer

A helpful guest passing plates of pies or porridge

A pathetic, forlorn hungry musician

A gossipy close friend of the bride's

Other musicians; food servers, lugging an improvised tray

A friar and a magistrate, engrossed in their own conversation

A wild-eyed guest about to spill his drink

A child sitting on the floor, licking the food from his plate, completely absorbed

A crowd trying to get in

What
Country yokels want to be together, to celebrate, to follow tradition, to get drunk and full of food, to talk and laugh together. To gossip. Servers want to get rid of their loads. The bride wants to enjoy her prize. The groom wants to calm himself with food.

Why
To feel good, to feel full or drunk, to overcome weariness and loneliness. Servers feel intent on job. Tired.

Where
A rustic barn, with straw stacked up. Heavy long wooden tables and benches. Empty mugs, hot, noisy, strong food smells, spilled drinks.

When
About 1555

MIDDLE SCHOOL

For Math: Metric Units for Linear Measurements— Area/Mass/Weight and Capacity

Who
A fussy, messed-up American tourist who doesn't know how to use the metric system. Can only speak in terms of feet, yards, and pounds, and doesn't know much French.

An impatient, put-upon French drapery salesperson who only knows how to measure by the metric system…and doesn't know much English.

Activities
Buying and selling

What
American is trying to buy gorgeous material to impress friends at home with expensive drapes. French salesperson wants to close up shop and go home.

Why
American feels inadequate but determined. Salesperson feels tired, hot and sore-footed.

Where
A crowded, musty fabric shop on the West Bank of Paris

When
A hot summer afternoon

Senses
Touch—heat, sore feet, tired muscles, headache. Smell—mustiness, dust. Sight—bare overhead lightbulbs, bright yards of multicolored fabric on stands and counters. Hearing—chatter, cars honking, doors opening and closing, distant sirens, cash registers clicking, phones ringing.

For History and Geography: Ancient Egyptian Farming and Fishing

Who
A young, strong, but careless farmer

An old, wise, but impatient fisherman

Activities
Farmer is clearing the land of stones and dead branches, spreading seed, urging his oxen to trample it. Fisherman is trying to spear a perch or a catfish.

What
They are both trying to get enough food for themselves and their families. Both are trying to get the other person out of the way. They are worried about crocodiles.

They are hungry and irritated with each other.

Where
On the fertile strip of land next to the Nile River

When
November, around 48 B.C.

Senses
Fresh warm air, setting sun, smell of a river water and oxen

For Science: Behavior of Blood Cells

Who
About eight students personifying red blood cells; earnest, protective

Another six personifying an artificial titanium heart valve; earnest, hard-working team

Another four personifying Coumadin, a blood thinning medicine; rescuers, fighters.

Activities
Blood cells move around in a line. Heart valve stays in place pumping. Blood thinner comes to the rescue.

What
Blood is trying to find its way through the body. Stops and gathers together to form a clot when it bumps into the artificial titanium valve, which is working hard. Blood thinner finds the clump and breaks it up. Blood flows freely again.

Why
Because blood cells think they're outside of the body when they sense a foreign

object, so they must coagulate to stop the flow of blood leaking out of the body. Pump obediently keeps working. Thinner feels zealous and protective.

Where
In the hot, airless blood veins near the heart of a human body

When
Anytime

For Math: Algebraic Expressions/Equations

Who
Three students personifying algebraic expressions/numbers. They are CIA agents. One is smart and experienced. One is angry and vengeful. Another is young and impatient.

A student personifying a variable (a letter) in the equation—a spy perhaps, a mysterious person

Activities
Searching through files, taking fingerprints, planning operations, arguing

What
Agents want to find out who the spy is. Is he dangerous? Whom does he represent? Spy, of course, keeps hiding, or masquerading as different numbers.

Why
They will lose their jobs if they don't identify the spy. They are very worried. The spy is tricky.

Where
A dark underground office. Quiet, eerie.

When
Three A.M. Storming outside.

For American History: Columbus' Discovery of The New World

Who
Rodrigo de Triana, eager, excitable young sailor aboard

Christopher Columbus, visionary, determined, ruthless, vain, ambitious

Other sailors, hardy, irritable, hopeful

What

Rodrigo, the first to sight land, wants to shout, to share the ecstatic news with Columbus and all. Columbus wants to see for himself. Others don't believe it, want to go back, or mutiny.

Activity

Standing on a high mast looking through a spyglass

Why

They are all hot, exhausted, anxious, uncertain. Afraid of failure to find the land they sought for so long. Some have scurvy, sunburn, calluses, homesickness.

Where

Aboard the Santa Maria

When

1492

(Teachers: Following the above skit, you could then do a parallel sketch of NASA officers arguing about the observatory on L1 or "Triana.")

For Future World Leaders

A young actress who loves to work with kids urged, "Get them by fourth or fifth grade, before they lose the fire in their bellies to change the world." Give your kids ownership of the books you're reading to them. Give them ways to incorporate the stories into their own bodies, feelings, and experiences.

For Math: Division

Who

Two babysitters. One: zealous, energetic, careful The other: dreamy, vain, selfish. She's often late and doesn't always show up.

The infant's mother, not rich

What

Mother wants them to split the fees between them fairly. Girls argue about what's fair.

Why

Mother likes them both and hates arguments. Girls argue over who deserves the most money in accordance with how much time she spent on the job.

Where

In the front hall. Baby is sleeping.

When

About 11:30 on Friday night

ELEMENTARY SCHOOL

For Language Arts: *The Golden Touch* by Nathaniel Hawthorne

Who

King Midas, passionate, avaricious; thinks his gold is making him happy

Marygold, Midas's daughter, sweet, rosy, affectionate, bright, dimpled, flower-loving

The Stranger, ruddy-faced, cheerful, smiling

What

Midas wants everything he touches to turn to gold. Marygold loves her father and wants to cheer him up when his coffee turned to molten gold. Stranger wants to teach what is truly valuable.

Why

Midas feels happiest in his dungeon counting and weighing his gold. He loves his daughter, but he also loves gold. He is exalted when everything turns to gold. But, when even his daughter turns to gold he is totally miserable and bereft.

Activities

Midas asks stranger for the Touch of Gold. Granted. Midas touches everything and claps his hands in ecstasy when it all turns to gold. He tries to eat, but when even his food and water become gold, Marygold comes in, upset because her flowers have turned to "ugly gold." She goes to comfort Midas about his now inedible food and drink. She hugs him and turns to gold. Stranger enters. Advises Midas to plunge into the river, fill a pitcher of river water, and pour it over everything that he wants to turn back into its natural form. Midas follows the stranger's advice and the spell is broken.

Where
Midas's sumptuous palace; a dark dungeon-like treasure room; the palace break-fast room; a river at the bottom of a garden

When
Once upon a time, long ago.

For Math: Division

Who
Six friends, pleasant, likable, fun-loving. One hostess. One surprise guest.

What
Enjoying a birthday party. Trying to share equally. Only six cupcakes are on the table. Want to figure out how to share them among eight people.

Why
Everybody's hungry.

Where
Hostess's home: balloons, ribbons, ice cream, funny hats

When
Saturday afternoon in spring

For Math:
Fractions—What fraction of the whole team is left after each try?

Who
Fifteen cheerleaders, or whole class full of energetic cheerleaders

What
Learning a school cheer for their football team

Activity
Practicing the cheer for the football team until they get too tired. Some drop out after each try.

Why
They love doing it, but some are not as strong as others.

Where
In the second-grade classroom

When

During a school period.

After each run-through of the cheer suggest that some are too tired and should stop. Ask them, "Now what fraction of the original number of practicing cheerleaders is left?"

(Claire Walcovy did the exercise above with her second-grade pupils. The principal heard all the noise and stopped in to see what on earth was going on. When she saw what they were doing, she said to the kids, "You come with me. I'm taking you up to the eighth grade to show them how to do fractions.")

For Language Arts: Learning Sentence Structure

Who

Kids personify different parts of speech as if they were actors in a play.

An active verb: energetic, pushy, vivacious

A passive verb: laid back, reluctant to make decisions

Infinitive: clingy

Adjective: judgmental and observant

Preposition: thoughtful

Noun: stolid

The director of the play

Activity

Director is lining them up for the curtain call.

What

The director wants them to line up in accordance with the order of a sentence he has in his hand, given to him by the teacher. The actors all want to be in the center of the line for their bows.

Why

The director wants it to look right. He's anxious to get good reviews. The "actors" all are conceited and want the "star" positions.

When

The day before the "opening," when the critics are coming

Where
In a theater, at the front edge of the stage

For Language Arts: Learning Parts of Speech—Verbs

Who
A theater director of a play. The rest of class as actors in that play.

What
Director is "staging" different entrances. Telling his "actors" what to do to enter and cross the stage, or asking them to think up their own ways. Actors are entering the stage from "offstage" in different ways, as different verbs.

Activity
Verbs. Split your class into teams. Send them "offstage" to follow directions, using different verbs to enter and cross the "stage."

Some actors burst on, crash on, circle on, dance on, hop on, hurry on, gallop on, slide on, skate on, or run on.

Some other "actors" do their own entrance ideas. "Director" tells them to "say the verb as you do it." (Of course you'll find several who will want to do a cartwheel onto the stage.)

Why
Director wants his show to look good. Thinks he's brilliant.

Actors love getting onto the stage in different ways. They: 1. Bounce on: happy to tell great news; 2. Back on: to escape, they are feeling scared; 3. Sneak on: to surprise someone, they are feeling excited; 4. March on: to get order, they are feeling angry.

Where
On a "stage" in front of a classroom and across it. Bright lights. Big audience.

When
Now

For Literacy: Sensory Awareness and Imagination

Read a story and have children repeat it to you with details. For example:
"I'm going to tell you a very short story. And will someone tell it back to me but add all the colors and sizes you can? Here's the story: Alexander was a mouse.

He ran into the kitchen, but was pushed away by a broom. He saw another mouse on a pillow. He wanted to be that mouse's friend. But that was a windup mouse. So Alexander found a pebble and the magic lizard turned the windup mouse into a real mouse. And they hid in a hole and played together."

"Now who wants to tell it back to me?" (Ask any child who raises a hand to tell the story back adding colors and sizes.)

For Reading Aloud Skills

Reading lines from books with "as if" situations:
Write some typical lines to read, or copy quotes that the book's characters say. Ask each child to read it once, "cold" as actors call it. Then invent a good strong emotional "As If" for the child to think about as he's reading the sentence again. It works like a charm over and over, with many, many kids. It eliminates the standard trap of "reading the punctuation" and thus losing meaning. And we truly believe it will strongly support any child's silent reading understanding and involvement with what is being read. Invariably the child will read it again with all the color, immediacy, understanding, and richness you would ever want. It never fails. Honestly.

Here are some sample lines from stories, along with "As If" ways for you to suggest the child read the line again the second time.

> The kite went up in the air and crashed down into the grass.
>   (As if that was just awful!)

> "Frog," asked Toad, "was that a true story?"
>   (As if that's hard to believe!)

> "Hey," said a voice, "you're eating my umbrella."
>   (As if you feel that's not right!)

> "I've been waiting for a friend," she said sadly, "but I don't think he'll come."
>   (As if she's about to cry.)

> "Don't you worry," said Mrs. Mallard. "I know all about bringing up children."
>   (As if she's proud of herself and she wants everyone to know it.)

> "Please don't make me go in there."
>   (As if you're really scared.)

> "Where do you think we are?"
>   (As if you're really amazed. It seems magical.)

"Aren't you going to take me with you?"
(As if you're really disappointed.)

"I don't like this at all."
(As if you're really going to get into trouble.)

"Don't be so mean to him."
(As if you're afraid your friend is really hurt.)

"I'm cold. Let's get out of here."
(As if your toes and fingers are getting numb, and you can't stand it anymore.)

"That was really fun!"
(As if you just had a great ride down a roller coaster.)

"Please, can we do it again?"
(As if you're really begging your mom.)

"Get out of my sight!"
(As if you're madder than you've ever been.)

A WORLD OF POSSIBILITIES

So go ahead, give it a try. Maybe you'll be like the recipient of the National Medal of Arts Award, Rafe Esquith, who carefully examined the actions and the feelings of Shakespeare's characters in *Hamlet* with his class of immigrant children from Mexico, China, and Africa. They wound up performing *Hamlet* with such truth and reality the audience was swept up completely.

Or maybe you'll be like Jeff Lantos in California. His students learn history the traditional way four days a week. But on Wednesday mornings they put their books aside and descend upon the school auditorium to take another turn playing out the muggy summer of 1787, rehearsing *Miracle in Philadelphia*, about the Constitutional Convention of 1787, or one of the other historical musical plays cowritten by their teacher. As one student said, "I used to dread Social Studies because it was so boring. But now I look forward to Wednesdays because we get play practice. It's history, only it's twenty thousand times more interesting."

Interesting. A huge part of our lives, including this book, all began when our eighth grade teacher, back in '38, let us create and perform skits for one another in our "auditorium class" once a week. We hope you will take a page from her book. As our grandson, Danny Sven, said when he was six years old, "All kids can act!"

Epilogue
Break a Leg!

THIS FAMOUS AND QUITE curious show-biz phrase became an alternative to wishing actors "good luck." Theater people believe those well-wishing words bring bad luck instead. Hence, the opposite: "Break a leg!"

However, we do hope this book will bring you genuine good luck and affirm your desire to do shows with kids, whether in elementary schools, high schools, camps, community centers, or in your own home or classroom. We believe those efforts will become peak experiences for you as they have been for us. The key to it all is to nurture their creativity. To that end we pass along the following general principles; we have always found that they apply to any group of children or teenagers:

Lead the young people by honest questioning, listening and answering, and genuine caring. Love them. Believe in them. Listen to them. Trust them.

Get them to solve problems. They discuss, choose, then implement, solutions.

Generate energy by being specific with them. Spell out goals and then work together to achieve them.

Give them permission to take risks.

Let the kids share in organizing themselves.

Avoid handing down judgments. Only entertain ideas. Avoid absolute rights and wrongs. Foster a natural discovery of solutions.

Support the youngsters' egos by helping them to demonstrate to themselves the extent of their own courage, imagination, and importance to the whole group.

One of the results of this kind of work with kids, we believe, is to open their eyes,

203

ears, and minds. Their awareness will increase as they learn to look for elements to tuck into their "actors' kits." Just remember that solving problems together is the winning ticket. Ask your cast members stimulating and searching questions. Ask them the five Ws and go deeper and deeper with them into the answers. Ask everyone to answer them as truthfully and fully as possible using the five senses. As you all work on each scene you'll become more and more specific. This will enrich your work and add to the interest and illumination of the scenes and the whole show.

When you direct, consider yourself the eyes and ears of the audience. If your goals for the show are clear, you can determine what needs to be fixed as you go along. You will all find joy in fixing and refining, and then refining some more, as long as you have the time. Build an atmosphere of trust and respect and you can't go wrong.

Some things thrive in one environment, some in another. Plants grow in the warm air and sun. A bottle of milk spoils when left there. Theater can help us see that we are all of value if we can find the places where we rightly belong.

One purpose of theater is entertainment. But it is also recreation, which means *re-creation*. Jacob Lawrence, an artist whose mother enrolled him in a library arts program when he was young so that he wouldn't join a street gang, said, "If we can mold art with our own tools, we can mold our lives." He was talking about painting, but we've seen that the art of theater helps mold children in the same way. We've seen that the theater's environment of creativity and cooperation improves their understanding, confidence, knowledge, and relationships with other human beings.

If we all persevere in the creative process of combining what we can imagine with what we know is real, we can help in the fulfillment of our dreams for our young people.

Addendum A
Leader's Guide

THINK OF THIS as a safety net, a suggested agenda for ten sessions with your young actors, lasting ninety minutes to two hours each. It is for ten- to thirteen-year-olds but the age spread can be larger than that.

These sessions can be scheduled every day for two or three weeks or spread over a period of a few months. Since there will be requests from the kids to repeat many of the exercises, there's probably enough material in this guide for twenty sessions if you have a large and lively group. And, of course, there are more exercises throughout the book that you can use in the sessions or substitute for any of these. Since there may be more listed here than you'll have time to do in any given session, we've marked the most popular ones with a star (*).

After you have completed the ten sessions, you can do a demonstration of skits and exercises for friends and relatives. Then before you begin work on a full show of some kind, do additional sessions using more advanced exercises and games that you invent yourself or select from the book. Use this guide also as a source of activities for periods of preparation and rehearsal of scenes and shows.

SESSION 1

At the beginning of the first meeting, if you are all new to one another, start with a game:

1. Circle of names
Purpose: To develop concentration.

Goal: To learn one anothers' names (at least first names).

Procedure: Everyone sits around in a circle. You start by saying your own first name and then add "and I like...." Fill in whatever you want: pizza, hiking, music.... Go around the circle clockwise. Each person in turn repeats the name of each person who has gone before (starting with you, the leader) and what that person likes. He (or she) then adds his own name and what he likes. The last person has the hardest task, but everyone will be asked to help or correct one another's memories as you go, so it's a challenge for all.

2. Ask everyone to begin thinking about what kind of show to do at the end of the ten weeks or ten meetings.

3. The "business" meeting: deal with any necessary problems, elections, announcements.

4. Establishment of rules: No violence allowed, no hurting one another. Whoever is talking must be heard by all. Therefore, everyone's responsibility is to speak loudly and clearly, and to keep quiet when someone else is speaking. Do not speak for someone else. Each must speak for himself or herself.

5. Relaxation
Purpose: To get rid of tension.

Procedure: Have everyone stand and shake out all parts of their bodies. Then stand very loosely and take a few deep breaths. Now have them stretch out and make themselves as big as they possibly can without touching anyone else. Now ask them to make themselves as small as they possibly can.

6. Many ways to do things
Ask the children to line up and then, one after the other, sit in a chair in the front of the room, each in a different way…backward, squatting, on one leg, etc. This demonstrates how many good ideas they can have.

7. Explanation of the system to the group
Here's a brief version of material covered in Chapter 2. Go over it with the children using any available visual aid.

We learn about the story through the answers to the five Ws: Who, What, Why, Where, and When.

> *How do actors tell the story?* By the words they say and what they do with their voices and bodies, their behavior.

> *What determines that behavior?* Their response in reaction to the sensory and emotional information or stimuli in the story. That is, to what the characters see, hear, smell, feel, and taste, in the story, whether real or not.

When they're not real (not real rain or cold or pain) what makes the
actors respond? They make believe they are real. They relax
their bodies so that they can concentrate. They think hard
about the details of the imaginary stimuli—the rain, the cold,
the injury—and try to see, hear, feel, taste, smell these
imaginary things with their bodies. They let themselves react
in whatever way is natural and believable.

8. Red ants *
Purpose: To demonstrate how we respond physically to imaginary sensations.

Procedure: Ask everyone to stand up and imagine that there is a swarm of red ants
starting to crawl on their feet and legs, biting them. Observe their behavior and point
out that acting without using the whole body is like playing the piano with one
finger.

9. Concentration on a real object
Purpose: To develop sensory awareness.

Goal: To find and describe as many sensory elements in the object as possible.

Procedure: Pass around an apple or give each child a cookie or a small box of raisins.
Call out one of the senses for each to explore in relation to that object—for instance:
"Touch." If it's an apple, the child's responses will likely be, "Hard, round, smooth,
a soft spot near the stem," and so on. Continue going around to each child until you
feel all have exhausted the search or until the time you've allotted has expired.

10. Remembering senses *
Purpose: To develop sensory memory and imagination.

Goal: To remember past sensations.

Procedure: Name the five senses and ask for volunteers to describe something in
terms of each particular sense. For example:

> The sight of colors in a sunset
>
> A sound that's scary—a scream, a shot
>
> A smell they always recognize—garlic, a bakery
>
> A taste they love—fudge, popcorn, the touch of velvet, or warm
>   water, the feeling of being scared or angry

11. Translating a sensation into physical action
Purpose: To respond to sensations physically.

Goal: To move around and relax after sitting.

Procedure: Ask everyone to stand and stretch as if they've been in a cramped box for hours; or they've just awakened; or they're on top of a mountain; or they're blind.

12. Writing names
Purpose: To "physicalize" and focus the imagination.

Goal: To loosen up bodies and sharpen sensory imagination.

Procedure: Ask everyone to move simultaneously to a position where each has enough space. Each person writes his or her name in the air with different parts of the body: elbow, chin, shoulder, toe. Then they all write on various imaginary surfaces such as a steamy window, a dirty car, a recently finished painting. They can use different imaginary tools: a foot in the sand, a pen, or a paintbrush. They can write the name as if they're a teacher using chalk on a blackboard, a president signing an important treaty, a child just learning to write, and so on.

13. Walking on different surfaces
Purpose: To sharpen sensory imagination in the whole body.

Procedure: As in Writing Names above, have everyone give one another enough space. Then they walk around on different imaginary substances, such as snow, hot sand, soft sticky tar, and sharp pebbles.

14. Transforming objects *
Purpose: To stimulate imagination and sensory responses.

Procedure: Pass an object such as a pen or pencil around to each person. Have each one use the object as if it's something else. For instance, a pen could become a baton, a thermometer, a spyglass, umbrella, a microphone, and so on. Keep going until the ideas run out.

15. Break up
Purpose: To strengthen concentration.

Goal: To demonstrate how fully and inventively a person uses his or her whole body to accomplish a clear goal—a What.

Procedure: Select two people and have one keep repeating a poem, quotation, or song without breaking down in laughter. The other must do or say anything to make the first person laugh without ever touching that person. This could be giggling, wiggling, singing, making faces, saying bizarre things—anything. After a minute or two, unless the first person breaks up before then, they trade places. Then go on to other pairs.

SESSION 2

Review the system, and clear up any questions or misunderstandings. In a review of the five senses, ask everyone to examine his or her own hands for sensory details.

1. Relaxation
Tell everybody to relax just the little finger, or just the shoulders. Point out that they can feel the whole body tending to relax in that one effort.

2. Imaginary object
Purpose: To strengthen sensory awareness.

Procedure: Everyone does this at the same time, still sitting. Name for each person an imaginary object to hold, such as a kitten, an ice cream cone, a cup of hot chocolate, a sharp knife, a warm washcloth. Ask questions as they are holding them, such as: How heavy is it? What color is it? Does it feel soft? What is its temperature? How does it smell? Any taste? Can you hear it? Can you make any sound by tapping on it? Without answering aloud, all concentrate on answering the questions to themselves in their own sensory imaginations. Then have them put the imaginary object down or hand it to another person.

3. Homework
Purpose: To demonstrate the value of practice.

Procedure: Ask the kids to practice brushing their teeth for a week with the "other" hand—the one they do not normally use. Plan to discuss the results after a week.

4. Relays with imaginary objects
Purpose: To strengthen imagination and sensory awareness.

Goal: To physicalize imaginary objects.

Procedure: Ask ten kids to face one another in parallel lines of five each. They should line up in such a way that no one's back is to anyone watching. The first person in Line A pantomimes carrying an imaginary object directly across to the partner on the opposite line. After handing it to that partner, he or she takes the partner's place in Line B. The partner, pantomiming the same object, carries it back to first person's place in Line A. The second person in Line A does the same thing with the partner in Line B, pantomiming a different object, and so on. If a partner can't guess what imaginary object is being pantomimed, he or she can ask before carrying it back. Next, let the kids in Line B originate the imaginary objects to carry and proceed as before (see page 13.).

5. Many ways to open a door *
Purpose: To spark the kids' imaginations and sensory awareness.

Goal: To find as many ways as possible to open an imaginary door.

Procedure: Line up everyone across the stage. Ask each in turn to pantomime opening a door. Challenge each to do it in a way that is distinctly different from any of the others. Continue until your time or their ideas are exhausted. A good variation of this exercise is to ask them all to find different ways to sit in a chair.

6. Slow motion *
Purpose: To strengthen observation and concentration.

Goal: To imitate a physical action perfectly in slow motion.

Procedure: Call three people to the stage. Ask one to do something fairly simple, such as pick up a book, leaf through it, put it down, and walk away. Ask the other two, in turn, to do exactly the same thing but in slow motion. Then have the rest of the group discuss what was accurately done and what was not. Next, with different actions, rotate the tasks among the three. Continue with several more groups of three. Encourage the kids to suggest other physical actions.

7. Mirror *
Purpose: To improve concentration and attention.

Goal: To keep the audience from knowing which person is the mirror and which is the one looking into the mirror.

Procedure: Send half the group onstage. Ask them to pair off and secretly decide which one should be the mirror. Then they line up facing each other and move together exactly, so that no one watching can tell who is leading and who following. This means the person "looking into the mirror" must move slowly and carefully enough that the partner can imitate the movements at the same moment they are being done and thus "be the mirror." After the paired actors have been moving together a while, stop them and see if the group watching could tell who was the mirror. Then bring the watching group on to try it. You can extend the exercise by calling out "Switch" several times while the pairs are moving, meaning that they must switch roles without stopping. Sometimes you can call out "Switch" somewhat rapidly and often, so that they lose track of who was who and begin identifying with each other totally.

8. Physical Attitude *
Purpose: To demonstrate the many ways the whole body and voice can be used to find different Whos.

Goal: To say meaningless words but with a clear physical characterization.

Procedure: Ask one person at a time to say a common nursery rhyme like "Jack Be Nimble" as if she is "this kind of person." Then, to demonstrate, you simply take on a strong physical attitude, such as vehemently shaking your finger at someone, or slapping your forehead in anguish, or being in a prayerful attitude, or doubling over with laughter.

(This is one of the most popular exercises we've used.)

9. Where *
Purpose: To activate sensory awareness of place and environment.

Goal: To imagine as many sensory details of a particular place as possible.

Procedure: Ask someone to name a place. Ask different people to call out whatever element of that place pertains to the particular sense you name. For example, the place called out is the beach. You say "smell," and someone in the group says "salty air." Then you say "hearing," and someone says "waves breaking." Continue until their ideas fade.

10. Acting in a Where *
Purpose: Increasing awareness of physical surroundings.

Goal: To make the kids' location clear by their behavior in an imaginary place.

Procedure: Send one person onstage to choose a Where and whisper the choice to you. Without telling anyone else or using any words or real props, he or she begins to behave as if he or she were in that place. As the others figure out where the person is, they each whisper their guess to you to verify. If they are right, they come up and join in the activity in that place—not necessarily doing the same thing, but anything they might be doing in that same place. For example, tell one girl secretly to be a cheerleader on a football field. She starts leading cheers (but without words), and the others join her and follow the cheers, or run onto the field as players, or sell hot dogs, and so on. Continue until everyone has joined in onstage after solving the Where.

SESSION 3

1. Relaxation *
Purpose: To relax the whole body.

Procedure: Ask all to stand. Talk them through tightening all the muscles, beginning with the toes and working up to the tops of their heads. Then they reverse direction and start letting go, relaxing the tension in each part of the body starting with the scalp and moving down to the toes. They take deep breaths, bend over slightly, and shake out the body.

2. Who am I, Where am I? *
This very popular exercise is fully described on page 29. Each actor chooses a specific answer to the question Who, What, Why, Where, or When, and describes its sensory details without naming it; the others guess the answer.

3. Homework
To sharpen your actors' observation of people, ask them to watch people's walks before the next session and bring in an imitation of one of them then. They should watch what people do when they're just standing and talking, and be prepared to do it and discuss it.

4. Picking up an object *
Purpose: Using the senses to stretch the imagination.

Goal: To find as many ways as possible to pick up an object.

Procedure: Place an object—a book, a glove, a ruler—in the center of the stage. Have the group line up on one side of the stage and walk across it one at a time, pick up the object in the center, put it down or carry it, and walk offstage. (They put the object back for the next person's turn, of course.) Trying especially to use the different senses, they must find different ways to handle the object, as if…

> it's beautiful. (Sight)
>
> there's a knocking inside of it. (Hearing)
>
> it smells weird. (Scent)
>
> it's mouth-watering. (Taste)
>
> it's sticky, burning hot, or delicate. (Touch)

For instance, some of the ideas kids have generated with a scarf include wiping up a spot, shining shoes, shielding themselves from the rain, and waving for help. One used it as a shawl, another as a picnic cloth, and one decided it was filthy and threw it down again.

5. Where directions from the group
Purpose: To get practice in giving and following directions.

Goal: To explore a Where possibility fully with a partner.

Procedure: Select a pair of kids and suggest to everyone Where they are. Ask the others to give the pair specific directions as to what they see, feel, hear, and smell in the location you've suggested. Without using any words, the two respond as fully as they can to the directions, moving around trying to sense and act out whatever the others call out. Do this with other pairs of kids. Stop them after a short time, unless they're begging to continue.

6. Circle: 1 to 50 *
Purpose: To promote ensemble skills.

Goal: To build from one extreme to another gradually.

Procedure: Have the group stand in a circle. Going around one person at a time, count from 1 to 50: The first person whispering "1" as quietly as possible, the next person saying "2" a little louder, the next speaking louder still, and so on up to 50, the loudest. Each one must be careful not to make such a big jump in volume that the group reaches the extreme of loudness before the number 50 is spoken. But also take care not to do the opposite, making each increase so tiny that the last numbers to be said require large jumps in volume. The group can repeat the same exercise but with different extremes: from loudest to softest; from Mona Lisa smile to falling on the floor laughing; from slightly concerned to terrified; and so on. The kids should justify to themselves silently the reason for the amusement, terror, or rage, as they're doing it. Or give them a justification to keep in mind as they say the numbers.

7. ABC game *
Purpose: To explore how people respond to each other, and to begin working on the Who.

Goal: To learn how to pick up another person's tone or attitude.

Procedure: Ask two people to sit or stand facing each other and begin saying the alphabet together, alternating the letters as if they're having a conversation (that is, one person says, "A," the other says, "B," and so on.) The first person at the start chooses an attitude, for example: "Can't wait to tell this funny story," or "You told a lie about me that makes me furious." The second person must pick up that same attitude while saying the next letter. Gradually, starting with the letter M, the first person must change to the opposite attitude and, as the second person says the letter N, must reflect this change in attitude. They continue until they've said the whole alphabet. It's as if they are having an entire conversation, changing their minds in the middle of it. Next, let the couples trade places, and then give others who want to play a chance. This exercise may seem difficult, but kids like it and find it easy.

8. Who—exercises
Purpose: To learn more about characterization.

Goal: To explore different behaviors according to what kind of person a character is.

Procedure: Have the whole group line up on one side of the stage. You or the kids in the group give each person in line a different Who. Ask each one to walk across the stage, stop in the center, and then continue across as if he or she is that character: an old person, a sales clerk, a cop, a lost child, an athlete, a thief, and so on. Continue until everyone has done it.

9. Who—exercise in pairs
Purpose: To develop characters by how they relate to each other.

Goal: To explore how different people behave with someone like themselves.

Procedure: Assign Whos to two actors. Ask them to walk across the stage from opposite corners, meet in the middle, and shake hands saying only each other's names. By their behavior they create the characters you assigned. Then they walk on to the opposite corners. Use some Whos from this list or your own:

buddies	enemies	politicians
rock stars	suspects	drunks
soldiers	cops	spies

Next, repeat with the group calling out the Whos.

10. You are what you do
Purpose: To find a character's behavior by what that person does.

Goal: Build characters not from adjectives (characteristics), but from verbs (actions).

Procedure: Teach your young actors that they can't truly act an adjective, but they can act verbs: what that person does. Ask them to write on slips of paper the kind of person they like most, according to what that person does. On other slips they write the kind of person they dislike the most, according to what that person does. For example: "I like the kind of person who helps when you're in need." "I dislike the kind of person who won't share anything." Tell them not to sign the slips—no one should know what anyone else wrote. Next, send about four or five onstage to do an improv. Give them a situation—for instance, one is a clerk in a music store and the rest are all trying to buy the last two copies of a hot new CD. Or you can ask the others to give the group a situation to play—that is, a Where and a What. Now have each person draw one of the slips of paper out of a hat and make his or her actions fit the kind of character described on the slip. After a few minutes, stop them and ask the viewers if they can tell what each actor's slip of paper said. Have other groups of four or five draw other slips and do other improvs suggested by you or the group.

11. Homework
Remind the kids that they should have been brushing their teeth each day with the "other hand," and that the group will discuss that in another session.

SESSION 4

1. Relaxation
Ask everyone to make themselves as loose as cooked spaghetti or wet laundry. Then they imagine they are lying in the most restful space they can imagine, such as:

in a hammock	on a waterbed
in a pile of leaves	in tall grass
on a lawn chair	on a cloud

2. Homework
Tell the kids to review in their imaginations every night before falling asleep a strong sensory event from that day—a clap of thunder, the pain of a fall, a surprising taste. Give them an example of your own, recounting all the sensory details as specifically as you can. Tell them you will discuss them in the next session.

3. Observation of people
Ask your young actors to do the walks they've observed (as previously assigned as Homework in Session 3) and discuss them. Examine the specifics, asking what kind of person might walk like that. Next, ask them to show you what they've observed about what people do with their bodies when they're just standing and talking to one another. Discuss this, and ask them what people do, especially with their hands. Look for the Ws that explain or cause the observed behavior.

4. Different "As Ifs" with one spoken line
Purpose: To learn that there are as many ways to say the same thing as there are to do the same thing.

Goal: To endow the same spoken words with different meanings, depending on the situation and five Ws.

Procedure: Ask the kids to say, "It's raining," and to imagine an "As If" that you give them—that is, have them imagine the sensory elements of the given "As If" while saying the line. For example, as if the person...

> wants to go on a picnic.
> is a farmer who has been suffering through a drought.
> is running into the room soaking wet.
> is a TV weather forecaster whose prediction was wrong.
> is homeless.

Let them take turns, and keep it up as long as it's working. You can change the given sentence and have the kids choose the circumstances. Another "As If" could be imagined as they say "hello" into an imaginary phone and then repeat it. By the way they say the second "hello," let others know who is calling: a best friend, a doctor with bad news, a teacher, a pesky kid brother, a sales person, someone they thought was dead, and so on.

5. The Machine *
Purpose: To strengthen ensemble skills.

Goal: Find imaginative yet logical ways to fit bodies and sounds together to create one large "machine."

Procedure: This theater game is described at length in Chapter 9 (page 168). Ask one child to begin making a repetitive sound, like "beep-beep," while doing some repetitive movement, such as moving an elbow up and down, as if a part of some machine. Then ask the others to join in with other mechanical sounds and movements that will go with the first child's. They need not be a specific machine—just an all-purpose contraption with gears, wheels, pistons, and so on, along with noises. As others join in, the first person should intensify his or her sound and movement. The others follow suit until they are all at fever pitch. The first actor then leads them all to gradually wind down and bring the machine to a halt.

SESSION 5

1. Relaxation
Concentrate on relaxing the jaws, shoulders, hands, temples, and small of the back.

2. Discuss questions, assignments, and the sensory event you asked them about in Session 4.

3. Building up the five Ws *

Purpose: To learn how to find and follow the essential elements of a story.

Goal: To fill a simple activity with behavior that reveals a story, using the five senses.

Procedure: Send six people to one side of the space, and put a chair in the middle of it. Ask them each to enter in turn and move the chair without using any words. Each does it in a different way, revealing different answers to the questions Who, What, Why, Where, or When, and using as many sensory elements as will fit. For example:

> One actor simply moves the chair.
> A second moves the chair showing Who he or she is—an elderly
>   person, perhaps.
> A third moves it showing What he's doing—maybe reaching a
>   socket to change a bulb.
> A fourth moves it showing Why he's doing it—perhaps feeling
>   anxious in trying to please a customer.
> A fifth moves it showing Where—perhaps at a table in a
>   restaurant.
> The sixth moves it showing When—maybe at the end of a very
>   hard day.

Next, select five people to move the chair. The first one moves the chair showing Who the person is. The next uses the Who and adds the What. The other three continue to build on the action, adding another W, until the fifth person combines them all. For instance:

> Who: An old person with an injured leg.
> What: She or he stumbles on the chair and thrusts it aside in an
>   effort to get out.
> Why: She feels she must reach her grandchild before flames do.
>   She is very frightened.
> Where: In a burning building.
> When: A very dark night.

Another exercise is to have five other kids move the chair, this time each making a different choice and doing all five Ws at once. As these are done, you and the group can comment and discuss.

4. Entrances *

Have the kids line up and give each a different verb to do as they enter: i.e. amble on, back on, charge on, drop on, ease on, flee on, etc. Then ask each to make an entrance onstage in a different way, using the five Ws and senses, as above. This time they needn't follow any order. Just let them keep coming on, one after the other, as long as their ideas flow. Give them some time beforehand to think about and plan what they intend to do.

5. Saying their own names
Purpose: To introduce vocal color.

Goal: To put meaning into the way things are said.

Procedure: Everyone sits and relaxes for this "As If" exercise. Ask each, in turn, to say his or her name as if…

correcting someone.	sick with a sore throat.
being arrested by the police.	afraid people will laugh.
meeting someone.	reading it in Braille.
volunteering for a dangerous job.	

Let the kids invent other "As If"s to try.

6. Two people saying each other's name
Purpose: To introduce dialogue.

Goal: To convey meanings and relationships by the way even simple things are said.

Procedure: Up to this point we have seldom allowed dialogue because young actors tend to use just words instead of behavior to tell a story. Have two kids go onstage, enter from opposite sides, meet in the middle, greet each other, and say each other's name as if…

warning of danger.
one is almost deaf.
reading a newspaper announcement of an award.
believing the other had died.

The group can continue to provide other ideas for the actors. Next, ask pairs of actors to meet and greet each other saying each other's name. Their voices and behavior should tell as much as possible about their relationship. Suggest that they are…

conspirators	business wheeler-dealers
competitors	victorious
teammates	best friends
employer and employee	consoling each other after a disaster

Continue working in pairs as long as they choose or time permits.

7. Who—focusing on body parts
Purpose: To free the body and imagination while exploring a Who.

Goal: To create a characterization based on a common description using the name of a part of the body.

Procedure: Get four or five kids on their feet and give each one a description to use as a basic characterization. They will play someone who...

> sticks his nose into everything.
> leads with her chin.
> is all thumbs—or all ears.
> elbows her way into a crowd.
> is stiff-necked—or keeps a stiff upper lip.
> carries the world on his shoulders.
> is weak-kneed or strong-arms everybody.

Then to help them improvise, ask the group to give them a situation suggested by What, Where, When, Why—for example, watching the Olympics (What), in a garden (Where), on a cold day (When), or in a hurry (Why). Stop them after a few minutes and let another group try it with another situation.

SESSION 6

1. Relaxation
Have everyone lie on the floor, totally relaxed with their heads resting on a rolled-up jacket or pillow for protection. Walk around checking at random, lifting an arm here or a leg there to make sure it's limp and loose.

2. Homework
Discuss the brushing of their teeth with the "other hand," which they should have been doing since Session 2, and also their observations of walks and groups standing (from Session 3). Point out the value of practice and observation. An actor, like a good reporter, should be curious about people and things. Discuss those sensory memories you asked them to think about before going to sleep each night (Session 4).

3. Assigning of skits *
Ask your young actors to start planning and rehearsing short skits together outside of the sessions. They will start performing them for the group after a couple of sessions. If there's time at the end of a session, let them go off in small groups into separate areas to rehearse their skits. Let them choose their own "skit-mates" or

assign skits to different groups, or let some do monologues. You can suggest one-word themes for their skits, such as:

celebration	friendship
fear	respect
teachers	parents
snow	hospitals

4. Nursery rhymes with different Whats *
Purpose: To let a situation inform the way something is said.

Goal: To make action or a situation clear through physical behavior and delivery of lines.

Procedure: Ask each member in turn to say a nursery rhyme, such as "Jack Be Nimble" or "Hickory, Dickory, Dock" and show what they're doing as they're saying it. Some say the rhymes as if they were barking phone orders in an office, or trying to understand a recipe while cooking, or trying to win a race, or stealing secret papers from a safe, and so on. Get them started and they'll find plenty of ideas of their own. Let them continue until their ideas run out or the time is up.

5. Thoughts while speaking and thoughts while listening
Purpose: To learn to think as the character while talking.

Goal: To give different meanings to a simple phrase.

Procedure A: Ask each child to say "I'm coming" while thinking a different thought. One might be thinking, "Don't leave without me." Another might think, "For the tenth time." And another, "I'll never be ready on time." And another, "I hate to do this." You can give them the different thoughts, or let them supply their own. If they supply their own, make sure you know what the thought is, so you can tell whether they're doing it right. When actors are really thinking their character's thoughts, they're always more believable. Don't overwork this. Move on after you've made your point.

Procedure B: Ask a child to say a line to another in different ways, and ask the other to describe what the child feels as he or she hears it.

6. The preceding thought
Purpose: To learn how to find the best ways to say the lines.

Goal: To make line readings more real and truthful.

Procedure: While they're all seated and relaxed, ask all the kids, in turn, to speak a line, such as "Where is everybody?" or "This is incredible." But before each one says the line, give an example of a thought or situation to consider that will affect how the actor speaks the line—for example:

They're all a bunch of morons.	Something's wrong here.
I'm trapped! Help!	Deserted!
Is this a surprise party? Great!	Finally, I'm home.

You can keep changing the line and the previous thought, perhaps after every five people have tried it.

7. Freeze! *

Purpose: To stimulate a rapid imaginative process.

Goal: To create and tell a situation quickly that fits the position in which the actors find themselves.

Procedure: Send four or five actors onstage. Ask each one to move at random in any bizarre, silly way possible and to keep doing that until you call out "Freeze!" At that word the actors must stop in exactly the position they were in when you called it out. Then, when called on by you, each must (without moving) answer the five Ws—who he is, what she is doing, and so on. For instance, if one stops when he's down on his knees, he might say, "I'm a student looking for my assignment paper under my bed, and I'm late for school, and I might get kicked out because the teacher hates me anyway." The kids move freely and think quickly when "Freeze" is called. This is fun, but not too easy. Don't push anyone to do it who isn't ready.

8. Nonsense sentences

Purpose: To learn how to make dialogue fit any situation.

Goal: To give as much meaning as possible to meaningless sentences by applying the five Ws.

Procedure: Give two people each a card with the same set of nonsense sentences written as a dialogue between characters "A" and "B." The sentences could mean practically anything, depending on the situation. Ask the actors to go off together to make up a situation and then come back and act the scene for the group using the nonsense sentences only. Here are two sample dialogues:

SAMPLE 1

A: Here, let me.
B: I'm O.K.
A: But I want to.

B: No, really.
A: But why?
B: You don't have to.
A: I know that, but…
B: Stop worrying.
A: I don't feel right.

SAMPLE 2

A: You go first.
B: Oh, no, you go.
A: I really can't.
B: Sure you can.
A: Why don't you.
B: I don't feel like it.
A: Please!
B: Why is it important?
A: It just is!

Some situation choices could include the following:

> Lifting and trying to move a heavy object.
> A parent trying to help a child with homework.
> Fighting over the TV remote control.
> Trying to bandage a bad cut.
> Firefighters placing a ladder.

There are more examples of nonsense sentences and choices on pages 71 and 72. Explore as many of the five Ws and use as many sensory elements as possible in the playing of the scenes. Have a number of dialogue cards ready. They will all want different dialogues, and they might want to make a choice. Keep going as long as you have time. Some sentences can be just numbers, and the actors doing them could be drawing lots for doing a dangerous deed, playing Bingo, or trying to open a bank vault—and so on.

SESSION 7

1. Relaxation and trust *
Purpose: To develop trust among a group of actors so that staying relaxed is possible.

Goal: To fall relaxed, knowing that the others are trustworthy and will catch the falling actor. Also, to be a dependable catcher.

Procedure: Teach the kids that trust is necessary for actors to work together. For an exercise that develops a strong sense of ensemble, separate people into groups of six or so. Ask them to form a tight circle and put a seventh person in the center of the circle. Person 7 must turn around and around, reciting something from memory, such as a poem or a song. Then he (or she) simply falls backward, sideways, or forward, with eyes closed, whenever he wishes to. The people in the circle must be ready, willing, and able to catch the center person and never let him fall completely or be hurt. The person in the center must simply fall in any direction, keeping his feet in the same place, trusting that someone will be there to catch him. You must take great care to ensure that the circle is small and tight with no empty spaces. Floor padding is very strongly advised, just in case.

2. Group counting *
Purpose: To get in tune with one another.

Goal: To count—one person saying one number at a time—as high as the kids can go without duplicating any numbers.

Procedure: Everyone stands together in a circle. If there are more than ten kids, divide them into two circles. One person, unassigned, starts counting with the number 1. Another, anywhere in the circle, says "2," another, "3," and so on. No one knows who is going to say the next number. But if two or more people say the next number at the same time, the whole group must go back to the beginning and start again at 1. The kids must try to sense when someone else is or is not going to say the next number, and when to go ahead and say it. Continue as long as there is time and the group is having fun.

3. Listening *
Purpose: To learn that listening is an important What—a strong action.

Goal: To listen actively, to make use of what was heard and to base choices on a perception of it.

Procedure: Ask someone to tell the group something she (or he) did at the beginning of the day, or within the last day or two, that involved the handling of objects—any objects. The others in the group must listen carefully while supplying in their minds the colors of the objects that are mentioned. Call upon one of the kids listening to tell the story back to the group supplying the imaginary colors of the objects mentioned. For example, a child says, "I got up, went into the bathroom, and picked up my toothbrush." The person called upon will say something like, "I got up, went into the pink bathroom, and picked up my yellow toothbrush." Call on different people to take turns talking and listening. You can also ask listeners to relate the shapes of objects. A popular variant is to have the speaker tell of an incident, true or not true, and ask the listeners to say whether they think it was true or not, and why. Then ask the speaker to tell the group which it was.

4. What—standing still *

Purpose: To demonstrate that strong actions, or Whats, can be done in the actor's head without indicating to the audience what the action is. Indicating is fake acting: it's when actors cop out on use of the five Ws and the senses and just move the head, eyes, and body in some way to make the audience think they're really seeing, hearing, thinking, feeling without really doing so. In a way, it's lying to the audience.

Goal: To fulfill a mental action strongly while standing still, not making any movements.

Procedure: Only small instinctive movements that may arise spontaneously as a result of doing the mental task are allowed in this exercise. This way, an audience's trust and belief in the actor as the real character are built. Ask one of the kids to stand still, relaxed and not rigid. With the group listening, give your actor something to keep doing mentally while just standing there, such as:

> Hearing a bizarre sound and trying to figure out where it's
> coming from.
> Smelling smoke and trying to decide if it is dangerous.
> Planning what to say to someone who hurt you yesterday.
> Waiting to hear the outcome of surgery on a loved one.
> Trying to make up an excuse for being late.

Ask the actor to keep doing that until it's clear and believable to the rest of the group. Ask the rest of the group to watch carefully and raise their hands as soon as they believe the actor is really doing what you asked. Next, ask for volunteers to come up, one at a time, to do the exercise. This is an illuminating exercise in which all the kids become quiet, focused, and involved. The reality they discover is often very moving.

5. Adjectives and verbs

Discuss adjectives in relation to developing a Who. Point out that adjectives can't be acted; they must always be turned into active verbs. Otherwise, the acting gets phony. For example, if a girl tries to act "shy," she becomes general and unreal. She must try to do whatever a shy person does in order to:

> keep from being noticed.
> avoid looking people in the eyes.
> remain as quiet and unobtrusive as possible.
> calm her nervous twitch.

Name some other adjectives and discuss with the group what that kind of person does.

6. Do skits for one another as time permits.

SESSION 8

I. Relaxation
Everyone takes deep breaths and loosens all muscles. All check their own muscles for tension.

2. Group mirror
Purpose: To improve ensemble work.

Goal: To stay absolutely together as all move slowly.

Procedure: Everyone stands in a large circle and does a large group "mirror." Let one person begin the movement with everyone mirroring him or her. Keep changing the leader. Ultimately, tell everyone to stay together without an assigned leader. The kids must concentrate on one another, stay together, relax, and "go with the flow" of the whole group. Do not continue this for too long, only until you feel the whole group is relaxed and focused.

3. Strong sensation *
Purpose: To concentrate and believe.

Procedure: While all the kids stand in a circle, ask them to think of a strong sensation and concentrate on it until they believe they:

> hear a piece of music.
> smell ammonia.
> feel hot water.
> taste a lemon.
> see oil reflecting colors in a puddle.
> taste buttered toast.

Continue only for a few minutes.

4. Improvs *
Purpose: To train the imagination, develop concentration and spontaneity.

Procedure: Ask people to form groups of about three to do improvs based on Who, What, and Where, which others in the group suggest. You add a Why and When to the suggestions. Prepare a list ahead of time on a card. (You can take ideas from historical events if your group is up to that: signing a peace treaty, marching for civil rights, dumping tea off British ships, and so on.)

5. Auditions—Part I *
Purpose: To strengthen reading aloud skills for younger children.

Goal: To bring color and meaning to words read aloud.

Procedure: Hand out sheets filled with numbered lines taken from stories or books. Ask a young actor to read one of the lines, and then ask him to read it again with an "As If" which you give him. For example: "Just then Pretzel's face appeared over the edge of the hole." After he has read it once, ask him to read it again as if it feels like a miracle, because it's such a wonderful relief. You will find a list of these lines and As Ifs in Chapter 10.

Auditions—Part II *
Purpose: To strengthen dialogue-reading skills (for older students).

Goal: To make the five Ws believable and interesting while reading dialogue.

Procedure: Bring several prepared cards with speeches from plays on them. Pass them out for the kids to read, think about for a while, and act out for the group, one at a time. (Some examples can be found on page 121.) Each actor must read a card, determine the five Ws of the situation, and decide what the Who (the character) is thinking and means by the speech. Then everyone reads his or her lines aloud to the group as genuinely and fully as possible, using the body in any way to assist in the reading. Give each actor some direction—perhaps a limitation that fits the situation to make the audition more specific and real. For example: "Play it as if she's in a big hurry," or "Now as if you are telling them the best news you've ever heard." Then ask the actor to do it once more, following your directions.

6. Perform skits for each other. See the suggested themes and topics on page 15.

SESSION 9

1. Relaxation *
All lie on the floor and hold each arm and leg in the air as long as possible, then drop it to floor. Take a deep breath.

2. Review of senses *
Ask one person to remember an incident and to describe only the emotional feeling that resulted (fear, anger, joy, jealousy) in physical, sensory terms, but not necessarily the incident that caused the feeling. Suggest that the rest of the group

empathize with the feelings being described. Talk the person through the process by asking questions: "What happened to your breathing?" "Did your mouth get dry?" "What did your hands want to do?" The group can also ask questions or add specifics.

3. More improvs
Purpose: To strengthen imagination, responses, and spontaneity.

Goal: To increase the urgency in a situation.

Procedure: Select two people for an improv. You and the group decide on a Who, What, and Where to give them. You or anyone in the group keep adding different Whys and Whens for each pair to play to "raise the stakes" each time they do the improv. In other words, continue to give them more and more urgent reasons why they must do what they're doing. Time periods should represent deadlines to accomplish it: "If you don't find it by tomorrow you'll be expelled," or "You gave it to your friend, but she's on her way out of town," and so on.

4. More nonsense sentences *
Purpose: To prepare for the show they will all do for their parents and friends.

Procedure: Please refer to Session 6, number 8.

5. Ruin my day, or poor soul *
Purpose: To have some fun.

Goal: To tap into the kids' mischief-making creativity.

Procedure: Ask one person to sit on a bench as if he (or she) is waiting for a bus. Then ask another person to enter and do something that spoils the day for the first person and causes him or her to leave the stage. Play a loud radio, sing weirdly, whistle in his ear, burp loudly, push him off—anything except hurt him or her. The second person sits down to wait for the bus and then the third person enters to ruin the second person's day, and so on. Let them each have at least one turn (they'll want more—kids love permission to be gross). Keep it up as long as you have time and patience—this one's popular!

SESSION 10

1. Relaxation *
Lie on the floor and relax thoroughly, as in the previous session.

2. Start to review and decide together what to do in a demonstration show to which parents and friends have been invited.

The demo can consist of examples of the work you have all been doing together: exercises, improvs, games, and skits. It can be held on the day or evening of your last session, or whenever convenient. Next, split up into small groups to plan more skits for a later session. The themes for these skits can be assigned by the leader or decided on by the various groups. The members can rehearse the skits on their own, anytime before the next session.

3. Justifying three moves

Purpose: To learn to think and act quickly and spontaneously, and to follow directions while justifying them.

Goal: To make three arbitrary moves fit logically into a pattern of recognizable behavior.

Procedure: Select one actor at a time to do three unrelated movements: reach an arm up, stomp a foot, turn around—anything. Then ask the actor to repeat the moves but to justify them, or put them into a reasonable context, and to describe them to the others as part of one or several of the five Ws and the senses. For example, doing the above three movements in order, the actor could pretend to be a child trying to be called on by the teacher and angry when overlooked. Other movements can be incorporated, so long as all three moves are done in the same order and are a part of the whole process. This exercise is harder than most, but can be quite rewarding. (If your group seems to you too young and inexperienced, don't try it.) Sometimes actors tend to plan ahead and thus lose spontaneity by preconceiving the moves to fit a justification. If that seems the case, have the group give suggestions to the actor about what moves to do and even about how to justify them. If it goes well, have your group extend the third position of the exercise into an improv, using some of the five Ws and senses.

4. Space rebound

Purpose: To think and act quickly in relation to one another.

Goal: To turn strange positions into a logical sketch or situation.

Procedure: This exercise, an extension of the game Freeze! (Session 6), uses more people and is more complicated. Ask two kids to start moving, alternating but one at a time, into any strange position in relation to the strange position of the partner. They keep up the alternating moves until you stop them with a clap. The players must then improvise based on whatever screwball positions they find themselves in at the moment. The resulting scene need only be a few lines long until they can establish some sort of situation. From one position an actor might start pretending to be a sculptor working on the partner as the statue. Or they might start pretending to be in a gym working out. Whoever gets an idea first, begins. Tell them that turning to the partner and saying "What are you doing?" is not allowed. After they've all had turns, if they want to do more, you can do a group space rebound. Have about five kids move in turn, and when you clap, all start an improv.

5. Repeat

Repeat the most popular games and exercises if you have time to fill. Then plan and rehearse the demonstration, checking on who will do what in what order. Determine who will move what furniture or props; assign the places for waiting, entering the stage, and exiting; and run through the skits and improve them if you can. And wish them a good show!

Addendum B
A Christmas Show for Fourth and Fifth Graders

A FEW YEARS AGO we initiated a project in a tough, crowded, big-city neighborhood elementary school that was a spin-off of BookPALS called StagePALS. We met with a group of about twenty-five fourth- and fifth-grade boys and girls once a week after school. We started with a lot of the theater games we've described earlier in this book. Then in November, out of the various skits and improvs the kids created for one another from their own lives, experiences, and differing talents, we developed the following Christmas show. They performed it after school in a large school assembly hall filled with their family members, schoolmates, and teachers. It was met with resounding joyous cheers and applause at the curtain call. The principal gave a warm speech of appreciation. The cast jumped up and down, hugged one another, gave one another high fives, pounded their backs, and streamed down into the large audience. It was a public school, so we were not allowed to use any religious songs, but the holiday spirit soared.

PEACE ON EARTH

CHARACTERS

Narrator	Mother
Gramma	Grampa
Older Brother	Older Sister
Kid Sister	Kid Brother
Girls' Ringleader	Ringleader's Best Friend
Excited Schoolgirl	Kid Sister's Best Friend
Tough Guy	Gang Leader
Driver	Passenger

Police Officer   Second Police Officer
Hall Nurse   Angry Patient
Doctor   Room Nurse

*At opening entire cast is assembled on DL and DR steps leading to the
stage. The actors stand in the order in which they will appear in the show
so that they can walk directly into the scene. Each one is holding whatever
prop or costume piece he or she will need to bring on to the scene in the
play.* **NARRATOR** *is standing at the microphone at the side of the stage
behind the podium. Front curtain is closed. The first scene is played near
the front edge of the stage in front of the curtain. House lights dim and
stage lights come up.*

ENTIRE CAST: (sings "Deck the Halls")
Deck the halls with boughs of holly. Fa la la la la la la la la.
'Tis the season to be jolly. Fa la la la la la la la la.
Don we now our gay apparel, Fa la la la la la la la la.
Join we now in Yuletide carol. Fa la la la la la la la la.

Scene One

NARRATOR: Ladies and Gentlemen, welcome to our production of "Peace On
Earth." We have almost no props, costumes or scenery. Instead we will
ask you to "see," in your imaginations, the places our actors are in and
the things they will pretend to handle. Our play, "Peace on Earth," takes
place in New York City on the night before Christmas. We take you now
to the apartment of the Rosario family. Mother is making cookies. The
grandparents are trimming the tree. And the four children are supposed
to be helping.

(**MOTHER** *enters wearing an apron. Crosses to DLC.* **GRAMMA**
and **GRAMPA** *enter and cross to DRC.* **GRAMPA** *carries a small
plastic Christmas tree and puts it on the floor.* **GRAMMA** *pantomimes
bringing in a box of ornaments and starting to hang them on the tree. She
hums all the time.*)

GRAMPA: Oh, this is a fine tree. It's going to be a wonderful Christmas. Come
on, we'll get the place all ready. (*Rubs his hands. Looks out "window" DC.*)
Look at that snow. We're going to have a white Christmas, all right.

MOTHER: (*Wiping her forehead with her sleeve.*) Where are all my helpers? I still have
five-dozen cookies to make! Come on, you guys!

OLDER SISTER: (*Calling from offstage.*) Just a minute. I just can't find the stuff I
made for the tree.

GRAMPA: (*to* **GRAMMA**) Don't put those on yet. Put the lights on first. Where are those boys? (*Calling.*) Hey, you boys! Where are my grandsons? Bring the tree lights!

OLDER BROTHER: Coming! Coming! As soon as this creep gives them to me.

MOTHER: (*Calling.*) Now, boys, stop it! It's Christmas Eve.

OLDER SISTER: (*Running on from DR.*) O.K., Mom, I'm all yours. (*Sees the tree.*) Oh, there's the tree. Isn't it nice! Here's the ornament I made. (*Shows it to* **GRAMMA.**)

GRAMMA: Now that's lovely. Come, give Gramma a hug. (*Holds out her arms to* **OLDER SISTER. OLDER SISTER** *hugs* **GRAMMA.**)

KID SISTER: (*Running in to* **GRAMMA** *and* **GRAMPA.**) Can I help? Can I help?

GRAMMA: Of course you can. Give me a big hug first.

(**KID SISTER, GRAMMA,** *and* **GRAMPA** *pantomime putting decorations on the mantle. They can use the curtain.*)

MOTHER: Let's see, here's my recipe, but I have to make five times that much. How am I going to do that? Hmmm. That'll be a pound and a half of butter, three pounds of flour, bottle of vanilla extract, five cups of sugar…

GRAMMA: Good Heavens!

OLDER SISTER: What are you making? Some kind of a monster cake? Can I lick the bowl?

OLDER BROTHER: (*Chases* **KID BROTHER** *onto stage. Grabs him.*) Mom, make him give me those lights.

GRAMPA: Now, you be careful. Don't break those ornaments. They've been in the family for years.

OLDER BROTHER: (*Pointing to one* **OLDER SISTER** *gave* **GRAMMA.**) Not that one. I bet she made that. That's stupid.

OLDER SISTER: It is not!

KID SISTER: It is not!

OLDER BROTHER: Mom! You said I could do the lights this year. He got to do them last year.

KID BROTHER: I did not. I started to, but then he grabbed them. Besides, he got to put the star up on top.

MOTHER: Will you kids never stop fighting?! Chris, go down to the store and get me five more pounds of sugar. Ask Gramma for the money. She keeps it in a special hiding place.

KID BROTHER: Can I go, too? I want to get out in the snow.

KID SISTER: Can I, too? Can I, please! Please!

MOTHER: All right. But dress warm, now. It's cold out there. And hurry back.

GRAMPA: BE CAREFUL!! It's been snowing all day. The streets haven't all been plowed. It's very slippery. Be careful of the cars.

(**GRAMMA** *hands them their scarves and some money she takes out of her sleeve or her shoe. They run out DR After a moment, as the music comes on,* **GRAMPA** *exits with tree.* **GRAMMA, MOTHER,** *and* **OLDER SISTER** *exit DL*

Music, "Let It Snow, Let It Snow" starts playing. Then fades down under narration.)

NARRATOR: We take you now to the street around the corner from the family's apartment. The snow is piled high in big drifts and is still coming down hard. Most of the storekeepers still haven't shoveled their walks. Some of the girls are building a snowman on the sidewalk in front of the bakery.

Scene Two

(*Curtain opens. Music fades up again.* **GIRLS** *enter the scene, start to giggle, build a snowman, brush snow off one another's hair and shoulders, look up into the sky, hug one another, twirl around, exchange gifts [all in pantomime].*)

GIRLS' RINGLEADER: Look at the snow! Isn't this great!?! Come on, you guys. This is really awesome.
RINGLEADER'S BEST FRIEND: Cool! I love it! I wanna make an angel. (*Lays down and starts to make an "angel" in the snow.*)
RINGLEADER: Let's make a snowman. Let's put him in front of the store like he's a customer or something.

(*They start to roll up the snow for a snowman.*)

EXCITED SCHOOLGIRL: Let's make a whole snow family.
KID SISTER'S BEST FRIEND: Great idea! There's enough snow.
RINGLEADER: What'll we use for his eyes?
RINGLEADER'S BEST FRIEND: (*Reaching down, brushing away some snow.*) Here's a couple of bottle caps.
EXCITED SCHOOLGIRL: Cool. I wish we could find an old carrot for his nose.
KID SISTER'S BEST FRIEND: I could run home and get an old hat for him.
RINGLEADER: No, then your mother would make you stay in.

(*They roll snow and build for a while…maybe even starting to sing "Jingle Bells."*)

RINGLEADER: Do any of you know what you're getting for Christmas?

RINGLEADER'S BEST FRIEND: No, we don't open gifts until tomorrow.

> (**OLDER BROTHER, KID BROTHER,** and **KID SISTER** enter.
> They see the girls and the snowman.)

KID SISTER: (to **KID SISTER'S BEST FRIEND.**) Hi, Denise. Merry Christmas. (They hug.) Building a snowman? That's cool.

> (**KID BROTHER** picks up some snow and tries to put it down the back of **RINGLEADER'S** neck.)

RINGLEADER: Stop that! That's cold.

RINGLEADER'S BEST FRIEND: Quit it, stupid. Here, how'd you like this?

OLDER BROTHER: Yo, Dude. Mom wants us to get some sugar.

KID BROTHER: Wait a minute. This is fun. (They all start to chase one another, laughing and rub snow in one another's faces, etc. In the midst of this **TWO BULLIES** enter.)

TOUGH GUY: (Entering with a swagger.) Aw! Look at the little snowman. (To **KID BROTHER.**) Did you make that, Dude? (He shakes his head, "No.")

GANG LEADER: (Moving up next to **TOUGH GUY.**) I think it's really stupid. I'll show you a real man. Let's knock him over.

OLDER BROTHER: Hey. Cut that out! Why're you messin' with us?

TOUGH GUY: Get out of my face, stupid! (Turns his back to **OLDER BROTHER.**)

GANG LEADER: Yeah. Why're you hangin' around with these losers? Let's trash this place. (They start to kick at the snowman.)

> (**OLDER BROTHER** bends down. Makes a tight snowball and throws it at **TOUGH GUY'S** neck. **TOUGH GUY** grabs his neck and brushes off the snow.)

TOUGH GUY: Who did that!?

OLDER BROTHER: I did. Why don't you two get out of here?

> (**OLDER SISTER** runs in. **TOUGH GUY** and **GANG LEADER** start to make snowballs.)

OLDER SISTER: (Yelling to her brothers.) Hey you guys. Mom's waiting for you. She needs that sugar. She's really mad. Come on!

OLDER BROTHER: Watch out, Stephanie. Get out of the way.

> (A big snowball fight starts among all the boys and girls except **OLDER SISTER** who keeps trying to pull her brothers away and get them to come home. At two different times we hear a car horn and the kids who

are closest to the street (the downstage edge) jump out of the way. In the course of the snowball fight **GANG LEADER** *shoves* **OLDER SISTER** *toward the "street" DC. She slips and falls and starts to get up. We hear a car horn and a screech of brakes. Suddenly everyone on stage freezes in horror. For a moment. Then the girls rush toward* **OLDER SISTER** *and kneel down toward her.*)

DRIVER: (*Steps in from SR toward* **OLDER SISTER**. *He is frightened and shocked.*) I—I didn't see her!!!
OLDER BROTHER: (*Furious. Goes to the driver.*) What's the matter with you? Why didn't you look where you're going? I'd like to kill you!!

(**KID BROTHER** *grabs* **OLDER BROTHER** *and tries to hold him back.*)

DRIVER: I swear. I didn't see her. The car slid! I didn't see her. She fell right in front of me. I couldn't stop. She's not dead is she?
PASSENGER: (*Who has followed the driver on from SR.*) That's right. We didn't see her. He wasn't speeding.
POLICE OFFICER: (*Entering from L with* **SECOND POLICE OFFICER**. *Blows whistle.*) All right. Stand back. Stand back, everyone! Clear the way. (*Goes to* **OLDER SISTER**, *kneels down, checks her breathing and heart. Pulls out his cell phone.*) Car 42. We've got a ten fifty-three at corner of 169th and Broadway. One injured. Send an ambulance. (*To crowd.*) Don't anyone move her till the ambulance comes. Now, what happened here? Who saw the accident?
SECOND POLICE OFFICER: Anyone here related to the girl?
KID SISTER: Yes.
KID BROTHER: We know her.
OLDER BROTHER: She's our sister.
POLICE OFFICER: Go tell your mother we're taking her to Columbia Hospital.

(**KID BROTHER** *and* **KID SISTER** *run off. Sound of an ambulance siren. Curtain closes.*)

Scene Three

(**OLDER BROTHER, RING LEADER, RING LEADER'S BEST FRIEND, KID SISTER'S BEST FRIEND, EXCITED SCHOOLGIRL, TOUGH GUY, GANG LEADER, POLICE OFFICER, DRIVER,** *and* **PASSENGER** *enter in front of the curtain from DSL.*)

NARRATOR: We are now in the hospital waiting room. All the young people are waiting to hear the doctor's report.

(*They are all standing or sitting on the floor, quietly. Some are fidgeting, some sniffling, a couple pacing.* **RINGLEADER** *has her arm around* **RINGLEADER'S BEST FRIEND.**)

TOUGH GUY: (*To* **OLDER BROTHER**.) Listen, man, I'm really sorry. You know. I really am.

GANG LEADER: (*Also to* **OLDER BROTHER**.) Yeah. This is really a bummer. We didn't mean for anybody to get hurt.

OLDER BROTHER: Yeah.

(**HALL NURSE** *enters from DR, starts to walk across stage.*)

RING LEADER, OLDER BROTHER, RING LEADER'S BEST FRIEND: (*To* **NURSE**.) How is she?

HALL NURSE: I'm sorry. You'll have to wait for the doctor to tell you. She's alive and gaining consciousness. She's a brave girl.

ANGRY PATIENT: (*Walking in on crutches or a cane.*) Are you all here to see that little girl that was just hit by a car? Huh! Nobody here to see me. What's the matter with everybody? Well, stupid drivers. Nobody ought to be out driving on a night like this anyway. Is she going to be all right? (*No one answers.*) Is her mother here?

OLDER BROTHER: She's coming.

DOCTOR: (*Enters with clipboard.*) Are you all here to see Stephanie Rosario?

RINGLEADER: How is she, Doctor?

DOCTOR: She's going to pull through. She has a dislocated elbow, severe cuts on her head, and a lot of bruises. But we're not sure if she can still walk. (**ALL** *gasp.*) We're going to have to keep her here for at least two weeks.

GANG LEADER: Two weeks!!

TOUGH GUY: Two weeks. That's tough.

DOCTOR: I'll let you know when you can come in and see her. (*Exits.*)

HALL NURSE: (*To* **ANGRY PATIENT**.) Come on. I'll take you back to your room now.

PATIENT: Naw! I want to stay here. I want to see what happens to that little kid.

RINGLEADER: This is awful! Poor Stephanie. We ought to do something.

DRIVER: Oh, if only this hadn't happened! If only I hadn't gone out in the car tonight.

OLDER BROTHER: If only we hadn't been fighting.

PATIENT: I'll tell you what you ought to do. You ought to give her something. Some gifts. Some flowers. Make her feel better.

KID SISTER'S BEST FRIEND: But what can we give her?

OLDER BROTHER: We haven't got any money.

RINGLEADER: We already spent it all on Christmas.

GANG LEADER: Yeah. We're flat broke. (*Pulls out his empty pockets.*)

TOUGH GUY: We haven't got money. We need money.

DRIVER: Maybe we could at least make her laugh. I can wiggle my ears. See? (*He does that trick with his ears.*)

OLDER BROTHER: Hey. That's right. Maybe we could give her a laugh. At least maybe we could make her smile. We could entertain her. Give her a good time for a while.

ALL: (*Ad-lib.*): Good idea. Let's try it. How about…etc. (*They get into a huddle to plan it.*)

DOCTOR: You can come in and see her now. But be very quiet and careful.

SCENE FOUR

NARRATOR: And they all go in to see Stephanie.

(*Curtain opens.* **OLDER SISTER** *is on a "bed" made of two chairs, at RC. She has a large bandage around her head and her arm is in a sling. Her* **NURSE** *is taking her pulse and checking the thermometer she takes out of her mouth.* **ALL** *walk quietly into area behind and to SL of* **OLDER SISTER**.)

ALL: (*They all ad-lib.*) "Hi, Steph. How're you doing? I'm so sorry this happened. Are you going to be all right? Etc."

ROOM NURSE: Here, dear, let me put this blanket around your shoulders. Would you like another pillow? How about a drink of water?

OLDER SISTER: No, it hurts to swallow.

ROOM NURSE: Well, look, there are a lot of people here to see you. Won't you just try to smile at least.

OLDER SISTER: I can't. I just want to go home.

GANG LEADER: Look, we're really, really sorry this happened, you know.

TOUGH GUY: Yeah. We really are.

DRIVER: I am MORE than sorry.

(**MOTHER, KID BROTHER,** *and* **KID SISTER** *rush in to the room.* **MOTHER** *goes to* **OLDER SISTER**'s *bed, kneels, and puts her arms around her.*)

OLDER SISTER: Mom, the doctor says I have to stay here for at least two weeks. I'm gonna miss Christmas.

MOTHER: I know, dear. But you won't miss Christmas. We'll bring it to you. (**GRAMPA** *comes in with the Christmas tree.* **GRAMMA** *follows.*) Look, here's Grampa and Gramma.

GRAMPA: Here you are, young lady. Now you're going to have to tell us where to put the rest of the ornaments.

GRAMMA: And, look, I brought the sweet one you made in school. Now let's see a smile.

OLDER SISTER: *(Trying to stop crying.)* I can't, Gramma.

OLDER BROTHER: Well, listen, Stephanie. We've got something to show you and something we want to do.

GRAMPA: Come on. Let's put on a show for her! *(He will introduce the different "acts.")*

*(At this point several of the people onstage will perform for **OLDER SISTER**, depending on what they all can and want to do, such as: dancing, singing, acrobatics. Four or five can do a robotlike "healing machine" in which they have one person lie down on the floor and the others pump him back to health like a complicated machine might. **GRAMPA** and **KID BROTHER** can do the "arms of the person behind seeming to be the arms of the person in front" routine. **RING-LEADER, NURSE, GRAMMA**, and **HALL NURSE** could dance and sing. **DRIVER, TOUGH GUY**, and **OLDER BROTHER** could do their trio. **KID SISTER'S BEST FRIEND** could pantomime jumping rope and pretend to get all tangled up in it. **TOUGH GUY** and **MOTHER** could sing "Jingle Bells" and whole group could then break into "Jingle Bell Rock" dancing. Whatever you all decide.*

*Gradually **OLDER SISTER** gets interested, starts to smile, then laugh, then clap with great pleasure. By this point everyone in the show should be on stage.)*

POLICE OFFICER: *(Entering.)* Well, how's the little girl? Why look at her. She's smiling. She's even laughing. Let that be a lesson to us.

DOCTOR: I think she's going to be all right.

ALL: *(Join hands and sing "Let There Be Peace On Earth")*

NARRATOR: Merry Christmas, everyone!

ALL: *(Step forward in a line, take a bow, and all sing "We Wish You a Merry Christmas.")*
"We wish you a merry Christmas.
We wish you a merry Christmas.
We wish you a merry Christmas
And a Happy New Year!"

CURTAIN

PROPS AND COSTUMES

Scarves for all the children

Christmas tree

Apron for **MOTHER**

Hair whitener and granny glasses for **GRAMPA** and **GRAMMA**

Two police officers' hats

Police cell phone

Two nurses' jackets.

Watch for **ROOM NURSE**

Clipboard for **HALL NURSE**

Crutches or a cane for **ANGRY PATIENT**

Two chairs for **OLDER SISTER**

Microphones

Songs on tape or CD: "Deck the Halls," "Silver Bells," "Jingle Bells," "Let It Snow," "Let It Snow," "I'll Be Home for Christmas," "Have Yourself a Merry Little Christmas," "Let There Be Peace On Earth."

Sound effects: car horn, screech of brakes, crash, hospital corridor sounds, announcements, etc.

Addendum C
An At-A-Glance List of Ideas to Use

DON'T KID YOURSELF. No matter how much you love the kids, no matter how much you care and how much you want the best for them, it's normal to feel scared, anxious, tense, or nervous. There you are, standing in front of a raft of kids who are waiting for you to turn them on. Because if you don't excite, interest, and inspire them, they'll get busy turning one another on and all you'll get is noise. We've been doing workshops for years, with all ages. But we STILL find we must write out our ideas for exercises, games and improvs on a card that we will keep handy. So here's a big backup list from which you can draw ideas when you have no time to think them up yourself.

AS IFs

Speaking as if:
Ask the kids to stand up and one at a time say some letters of the alphabet, or the numbers 1–15, using these As Ifs:
- answering a test question for big money
- covered with mosquito bites— itchy
- defending self
- exhausted
- had an accident
- in a hot desert and thirsty
- in a haunted cemetery
- just bitten on something awful
- just won a prize
- smell smoke
- challenging a rival
- communicating with deaf people
- praying for help
- you're a movie star

Entering the space as if:
- Helping one another across a sticky floor
- barefoot on hot sand
- on sharp pebbles
- in cold water
- just won a big game
- in a quiet church
- you've been chased

As Ifs with props:
Ask a child to give an object, or prop, to a person standing on the other side of the stage, as if:
- it's a big donation
- to award excellence
- to console
- to fix

240

to force another to take it
to hide it
to return a faulty item
to share careful examination for
    clues or appraisal

As Ifs—Line Subtext:
Say the line, in quotes, using one of the
As Ifs below:

Say "I'm coming" As If:
    "Don't leave without me!"
    it's for the tenth time
    "I'll never get ready in time!"

Say "Its raining" As If:
    you wanted to go on a picnic
    you're homeless
    you're a farmer who has been
        suffering through a drought
    your precious paintings have
        been left outside
    you're a TV weatherman whose
        prediction was wrong

As Ifs while listening:
    afraid, worried
    end of a terrible day
    expect to be fired
    freezing
    hate speaker
    love speaker
    looking for clues
    raining
    revolution or rebellion brewing

Picking up objects as if (senses):
    Touch: it's burning, it's sticky
    Smell: weird
    Taste: it would make mouth
        feel dry
    Hear: it's knocking inside
    Sight: it's beautiful

As Ifs—Previous Thought/Phrase

Say, "Where is everybody?" Think:
    deserted
    something's wrong here
    surprise party
    They've got guns!
    Trapped! Help!
    exhausted
    I was right
    I'm sorry
    won big award
    nobody came
    that's hilarious
    "I'll be right there."
    "Wait, wait wait!!"
    I'm afraid to go.
    Great! I can't wait.

Say each other's names as if:
    across a field
    afraid he'll hit you
    beloved boss
    best buddy
    dark cave
    doctor and patient
    echo on a mountain top
    feared teacher
    ghost
    hated boss
    haven't seen each other for
        twenty years
    he fell through ice
    homeless people fighting over a
        spot
    "Hurry up!"
    judge and accused
    just had a bad fall
    meeting in secret to give info
    movie star
    opponent/enemy
    parent and lost child

praise student
principal and rebellious student
to reassure
she's dazzling
sly negotiation
surprised he's here
trying to remember where you
    met
you want him to see something
you're lost

Say your own name as if:
answering phone
answering roll call
arrested and caught
calling for twentieth time
caught cheating and now
    shocked
correcting someone
each time you need to say it you
    have to sneeze
getting autograph from star
giving a ticket
the other person has green and
    purple skin
you have a sore throat
impatient—Is she coming?
in a contest—beauty, spelling
    bee, TV, about to enter, just
    won
introducing self
just had an accident
just ran a big race
leading a march or
    demonstration
meeting the president or a star
old and sick, whispering name
    to doctor or nurse
on a mountain with an echo
reading it on an award or
    diploma
scared of ghosts in a haunted
    house
to a cop after breaking a law

trying to decide whether to tell
    the truth—witness stand
you're freezing

Walk as if on different surfaces:
broken glass
desert
fire
glue or tar
icy cave
mud
rain
slime
snow
top of mountain

Walk as if:
acrobat
blind
high-wire walker
old and arthritic
very proud, a snob

Sit as if:
at a wedding or graduation
on a jury
listening to a boring speaker
taking a test
watching a sad movie

Where and What As Ifs:
All form a straight line across stage or
room. Do a scene as if:
chorus line
construction site
on the edge of a river
on the edge of the Grand
    Canyon
electric fence
holding back crowds
middle of a highway
starting line for a race
waiting turn at bat

Who or What As Ifs—Body Parts:

Act as if you are one who:

always is hot
cracks knuckles
elbows way through
has wandering eyes
is all ears
is nosy
is stiff-necked
is wide-eyed
keeps chin up bravely
plants feet firmly on ground
pounds on furniture
pulls ear
rubs hands
scratches head
shoulders burdens
smooths things out

What As Ifs—Stand still as if:

to figure out a math problem
to figure out where you are
to get up courage
to hear a jury's verdict
to look for a hot air balloon or skydiver
to watch a rescue effort

HOMEWORK IDEAS

Bring in a slow motion description.
Go home and practice brushing teeth with the opposite hand.
Imagine a strong sensory event before falling asleep.
Think up skits using all five Ws.
Watch people's walks and bring one in.

CONFLICT SETUPS FOR IMPROVS

After a car accident. Drivers blaming each other.
Angels in contest. Good vs. Mischievous in a heavenly conference
Animals complaining about their master, and master tries to explain
At a wedding—terrified groom, or bride
Beauty contestants waiting to hear results
Beauty parlor—gossiper and defender
Boy flirting with a girl—girl likes him, but is timid
Builders stopping for a break, hard-driving boss
Child needing a shot—struggles with mom and doctor
Cops grilling prisoner
Couple decorating Christmas tree—1. Thrilled newlyweds 2. Wife wants too much, Husband wants to get back to game
Guru giving advice from a mountain top, windy, freezing
In library. One desperate to study. Other needs to talk—to get answers, to get friend to go to meeting
Judge and accused
Lawyer and witness
Lawyers summing up to jury
Models, hating the designer
Refugees in a strange country
Rescue workers resting, one is hopeless

Salesperson and resistant buyer
Short-order cook in a hurry to
    close the diner
Star or politician being
    interviewed and
    photographed
Two kids accused of cheating
    plead with principal
Two nurses…one is inept
Two thieves…one is inept

    Katherine p. 67; Lavinia
    p. 47; Molly p. 48; Ellie p. 49;
    Cassie p. 68; Betty p. 66)
The Skin of Our Teeth
The Sound of Music
South Pacific
Saint Joan
Summer and Smoke
You're a Good Man, Charlie Brown
The Young and the Fair

SOME PLAYS AS SOURCES OF MONO-LOGUES OR SCENES

A Day in the Life
All the Way Home
Annie
Brighton Beach Memoirs
Broadway Bound
Camp Out
The Children's Hour
The Crucible
Death of a Salesman (Biff and
    Happy monologues)
Ellen Foster
The Grass Harp
Joan of Lorraine
The King and I
Look Homeward Angel
The Lottery
The Man Who Came to Dinner
Me and My Girl
The Member of the Wedding
The Miracle Worker
The Music Man
My Sister Eileen
Oklahoma!
On the Town
Our Town
Picnic
Quilters (Katie pp. 12, 13, 14;

SKITS: OPPOSITES

rich—poor
scared—brave
bullies—helpers
old—young
winners—losers
boss—employee
lawyer—defendant
doctor—patient
immigrants—border patrol
cop—prisoner
wide awake—sleepy
healthy—sick
kind—mean

SKITS: THEMES

frustration
fear
selling
disaster
patriotism
jealousy
happiness
courage

SKIT—THE TWISTER

Write a short skit about a mother, a grandma, a boy, and a girl just before a tornado.

As radio show: Cast: Granny, Mother, Child One, Child Two. Staff-Announcer, Director, Assistant Director, Sound Effects Maker

As silent movie: Cast: Piano Player, Granny, Mother, Child One, Child Two

As movie musical scene: Cast: Granny, Mother, Child One, Child Two

NONSENSE SENTENCES

There are more of these in Chapter 2.

Scene 1
A: You go ahead.
B. No, you go.
A: Not me. I won't.
B: Why?
A: Just do it.
B: Please. I mean it.
A: So do I, really.
B: I don't know.

Scene 2
A: How do you feel about it?
B: That depends.
A. Let's get away from here.
B: That's a good idea. They're all coming.
A: If they come soon you know what will happen.
B: Do you really think it will?
A: Maybe.
B: Let's go.

A: All right—as soon as I'm finished.
B: I'll wait as long as I can.

Scene 3
A: Are you sure?
B: Sure, I'm sure.
A: Well, I wish I had as much confidence as you do.
B: I don't know what you mean.
A: I mean I'm just not as certain.
B: Don't worry. Everything is going to be all right.
A: You first.
B: No, you go ahead.
A: Now?
B: Now.

Scene 4
A: You go first.
B: Oh, no. You go.
A: I really can't.
B: Sure you can.
A: Why can't you?
B: I just don't feel right about it.
A: Please.
B: Why is it so important?
A: It just is!

ACTIVITIES

Each activitiy can become the basis for an improv.

- Arranging flowers
- Boring a hole in a piece of wood
- Carrying flowers
- Cleaning your room
- Closing a window
- Combing your hair
- Exercising
- Gardening
- Hiding in a closet
- Knocking on a wall
- Not answering the phone

Painting a fence
Pouring water in a pot
Sitting alone on a bench
Sitting on a table
Standing on one leg
Taking a photograph
Trying on clothes

WHO, WHAT, WHY, WHERE, WHEN

Choose from these lists and combine with an activity as the basis for an improv.

Who

Athlete
Beggar
Cardshark
Cheerleader
Cop
Doctor
Homeless person
Jogger
Judge
Lawyer
Lost child
Nurse
Old person
Pilot
President or politician
Rebellious kid
Religious person
Salesperson
Sick patient
Teacher
Toddler
Victim of crash or earthquake

What

To control a situation
To figure out a problem
To finish labors
To get warm
To impress an audience
To prove one's worth
To rescue as many people as
    possible
To win an election
To antagonize
To learn secrets
To protect
To blame
To defend

Why

Adore partner, in love
Afraid of being killed
Can't let people die
Dedicated self to others' welfare
Need to know
Need to prove your courage or
    invulnerability
Overwhelmed by work
Curious
Defensive
Confused
Trying to understand
Want to get crowds' approval
Worn out
Hot
Freezing
Enraged
Relaxed
Irritated
Excited
Proud
Furious
Confused
Confident
Compassionate

Where

Airport
Bakery
Big hotel kitchen
Car repair
Cemetery
Church
Circus
Cornfield
Desert
Dump
Farm
Football game
Forest
Haunted house
Hospital
Locker room
Lunch counter
Museum
Parking garage
Photography studio
Picket line
Planetarium
Playing in a band
Scene of accident
Sculpture class
Subway
Supermarket
Train
TV studio

When

1860 or 1740 or 1492
About to go onstage
About to make big speech
After an accident
After dust- or rainstorm
Before getting married
Before making a sad
    announcement
Fall
Just been chased by a mugger
Just had an accident
Just heard a terrible secret
    about other person
Just woke up
Just won a prize
Just won the game
Late for deadline
Shipwrecked for three days
Summer
Winter

Bibliography

SOURCES OF PLAYS AND SCRIPTS

The following catalogues list and often describe plays, including plays for children. Most require royalty payments.

Theatrical Catalogues and Organizations

Samuel French, Inc., 45 W. 25th St., New York, NY 10010-2751; (212) 208-8990. Musical Department: (212) 206-8125; fax (212) 206-1429.

Dramatists Play Service, Inc., 440 Park Ave. So., New York, NY 10016; (212) 683-8960; fax (212) 213-1539.

52nd Street Project, New York City, 500 W. 52nd St., #28, New York, NY 10019. Plays are developed by young writers along with mentoring actors.

The Virginia Avenue Project, 1653 18th St., #2, Santa Monica, CA 90404. A West Coast version of the 52nd Street Project. Scripts written by the young members are available.

Stage Kids, The Edutainment Co., 1178A King St. W., Suite 111 Toronto, Ontario, M6K3C5; (416) 538-0299/(888) 537-8243; fax (416) 538-3609. Plays and musicals developed for young audiences and for young performers.

Young Playwrights Publishing, 431 Fifth Ave., 6th Floor, New York, NY 10016. (212) 594-5440; (fax) 212-684-4902. Plays written by writers aged eighteen or younger, produced Off-Broadway in the Young Playwrights Festival.

Other Publications Containing Plays

Some of the publications listed here contain plays that are free of royalties and do not require permission for performance; others require royalties and/or permission. Always check with the publisher, since requirements can change. We have starred the entries below to indicate the following:

*All the plays in this publication require permission for production; some require royalties also.

**Some, but not all, of the plays in this publication require permission or royalties.

***None of the plays requires permission or royalties, provided that the productions are not-for-profit. Reproducing of some scripts may be prohibited, so you must buy extra copies of the publication.

Boiko, Claire. *Children's Plays for Creative Actors*. Boston: Plays, Inc., 1981. (See below). ***

Burdett, Lois. *Shakespeare Can Be Fun* (series). Buffalo: Firefly, 1995–2002.

Carter, Richard. Original one-act 80–90 minute long adaptations of Shakespeare's *The Comedy of Errors* and *Taming of the Shrew*, suitable for middle and some primary school students. And abridged, two-hour versions of *As You Like It*, *All's Well That Ends Well*, and *Love's Labor's Lost*, suitable for high school students (and some middle schoolers). To order, e-mail rjcarter@rockisland.com or go to www.communityshakespeare.org

Kamerman, Sylvia E. *The Big Book of Christmas Plays*. Boston: Plays, Inc., 1988. *

Kamerman, Sylvia E. *Holiday Plays 'Round the Year*. Boston: Plays, Inc., 1983. *

Murray, John. *Mystery Plays for Young Actors*. Boston: Plays, Inc., 1984.

Plays, the Drama Magazine for Young People. The monthly periodical of plays for children (October through May). P.O. Box 600160, Newton, MA 02460. (617) 630-9100/ (800) 630-5755, fax (617) 630-9101 ***

Rockwell, Thomas. *How to Eat Fried Worms and Other Plays*. New York: Books for Young Readers/Henry Holt, 1953. *

HELPFUL THEATER PUBLICATIONS

Asher, Jane. *Jane Asher's Costume Book*. Menlo Park, CA: Open Chain Publishing, 1991.

Brady Johnson, Maureen. *Middle Mania: Imaginative Theater Projects for Middle School Actors*. Lyme, NH: Smith and Kraus, 2002.

Bray, Errol. *PIaybuilding*. Portsmouth, NH: Heinemann, 1994.

Cahill, Elizabeth Kirkland, and Joseph Papp. *Shakespeare Alive!* New York: Bantam Books, 1988.

Carter, Jenna. *What Are the Educational Impacts for the Participants of Community Shakespeare Company?* Research Paper for Prescott College, April 30, 2004.

Catron, Louis E. *Overcoming Directorial Mental Blocks About Blocking*. Samuel French, Inc. (See above). An excellent pamphlet.

Greenhowe, Jean. *Stage Costumes for Girls*. Boston: Plays, Inc., 1975. Good, with fourteen period and ethnic costumes.

Ionazzi, Daniel A. *The Stagecraft Handbook*. Cincinnati: Betterway Books/F&W Publications, 1996.

Lewis, Robert. *Advice to the Players*. New York: Theatre Communications Group, 1989.

Lord, William H. *Stagecraft One: A Complete Guide to Backstage Work*. Colorado Springs: Meriwether Publishing, Ltd., 1991.

Polsky, Milton E. *Let's Improvise: Becoming Creative, Expressive and Spontaneous Through Drama*. Englewood Cliffs, NJ: Prentice-Hall, 1980.

Raoul, Bill. *Stock Scenery Construction Handbook*. Louisville; KY: Broadway Press, 1991. This book is popular in high schools.

Scher, Anna, and Charles Verrall. *200 + Ideas for Drama*. Portsmouth, NH: Heinemann Educational Books, Inc., 1992.

Schwartz, Dorothy, and Dorothy Aldrich (editors). *Give Them Roots—Give Them Wings*. New Orleans: Anchorage Press, 1985.

Sklar, Daniel Judah. *Playmaking: Children Writing and Performing Their Own Plays*. New York: Teachers and Writers Collaborative, 1990.

Spolin, Viola. *Theatre Games for Rehearsal*. Evanston, IL: Northwestern University Press, 1985.

Spolin, Viola. *Theatre Games for the Classroom*. Evanston, IL: Northwestern University Press, 1986.

OTHER HELPFUL PUBLICATIONS

Basset, Carol. *Walk Like a Bear, Stand Like a Tree, Run Like the Wind: Cool Yoga, Stretching, and Aerobic Activities for Cool Kids*. Berkeley: Nubod Concepts, 2003.

Coles, Robert. *The Moral Intelligence of Children*. New York: Random House, 1996.

Csikszentmihalyi, Mihaly. *The Evolving Self*. New York: Harper Collins, 1993.

Hannahord, Carla. *Smart Moves: Why Learning Is Not All in Your Head*. Kansas City: Midpoint Trade Books, Inc., 2005.

Lark, Liz. *Yoga for Kids*. Buffalo: Firefly Books Inc., 2003.

LeDoux, Joseph. *A Celebration of Neurons: An Educator's Guide to the Human Brain*. Association for Supervision and Curriculum, 1995.

Walton, Stuart. *A Natural History of Human Emotions*. New York: Grove, 2004.

Wolfe, Patricia. *Brain Matters: Translating Research into Classroom Practice*. Association for Supervision & Curriculum, 2001.

Index

About the Authors

LENKA PETERSON, often with her husband, Dan, has been happily producing and directing plays and leading youngsters' theater groups for forty years. Early productions included their own children, and they have since gone on to work with hundreds of other young people, whenever their professional obligations afforded them time. Lenka's professional acting career began with a USO play touring the South Pacific at the end of WWII. Since then she has been featured in fourteen Broadway plays, many Off-Broadway, regional theater, and summer theater productions, two national tours of musicals, six feature films and has made over one thousand television appearances. She earned Tony award and Helen Hayes award nominations for her work as Sarah in *Quilters*. Her proudest moment, however, was a surprise birthday party when about one hundred alumna of a teen theater group she founded reunited from all over the country after thirty-five years to tell her how much that theater group had meant to them.

DAN O'CONNOR was with NBC-TV news for thirty-four years, most of that time producing, directing and writing documentaries and special programs, several of them winners of the Overseas Press Club Award including one for his three hour documentary *New World—Hard Choices*. Prior to that, following his service in World War II, he earned a master's degree in theater, taught English and theater at Creighton University and St. Louis University, and managed a classical music radio station. During this time he met his future wife, Lenka Peterson, at the local community theater in Omaha, Nebraska. That combination brought five children into the world: two lawyers, Kevin and Darren; one professional actress, Glynnis; one film graphic artist, Sean; and one theatrical director, Brian, who also created all the illustrations for this book.